Marginalization

The *Society and Church* series addresses the question of the future of British society. Such an issue is not simply one for those who live in Britain, for this country was the first industrialized nation and it has in recent years been transformed into a multicultural, pluralist society. It is a society in which, for instance, employment in traditional manufacturing has little place, and yet it is also a society in which traditional institutions such as the monarchy still survive. Britain is a fascinating example of how a society can adapt in the twenty-first century, and can be profitably studied across the globe.

There is one topic which is especially pertinent. Britain now appears to be a highly secular nation and the contribution of the churches to political life is very different from 50 years ago. This series is not a historical one. It takes that change for granted and instead asks the question, 'What contribution can the churches, or the Christian faith, make in such diverse areas as the possibility of a war in the Middle East, or the environment, or the search for well-being in mental health?' Such a question is to be answered not simply from the perspective of those people who still believe and perhaps attend church, but from the viewpoint of everyone. Have Christianity and the churches anything relevant to say to our society as it wrestles with these issues?

The series believes that the answer is yes, but that the way in which this contribution is made will be diverse. There will not necessarily be agreement between the different authors as to their responses. Some will still seek to work within established political and social institutions while others will reject these for a very different approach. That is to be welcomed, for the debate in the twenty-first century will be about the very survival of the churches' contribution to the apparently secular society that is Britain today.

Alistair McFadyen and Peter Sedgwick
Series Editors

SOCIETY AND CHURCH

Series Editors: Alistair McFadyen and Peter Sedgwick

BOOKS IN THE SERIES:

Wellbeing, Alison Webster
Identity, Vernon White
Marginalization, John Atherton

FORTHCOMING:

War, Charles Reed
Crime, Tim J. Gorringe
Globalization, Peter Sedgwick
Race, Kenneth Leech

Marginalization

John Atherton

scm press

To
Carl-Henric Grenholm, University of
Uppsala, Sweden.
Ronald Preston (1913–2001), Manchester.

British Library Cataloguing in Publication data

A catalogue record for this book is available
from the British Library

0 334 02919 8

First published in 2003 by SCM Press
9-17 St Albans Place, London N1 0NX

www.scm-canterburypress.co.uk

SCM Press is a division of
SCM-Canterbury Press Ltd

Printed and bound in Great Britain by
Biddles Ltd, www.biddles.co.uk

CONTENTS

Preface   vii

Acknowledgements   How a Project is Formed   xi

Introduction   How I Changed My Mind:
  Problematics and Processes   1

PART 1   ON CHANGE: THE FIRST ESSAY

1   Unresolved Dilemmas: Challenging Global Change   9
2   Death or Mutation: Changing Christianity   31

PART 2   ON MARGINALIZATION: THE SECOND
          ESSAY

3   Marginalization: Why Some are Rich and
      More are Poor   53
4   The Great Double Whammy: A Case Study of
      Marginalization and Religion   93

PART 3   RECONNECTING CHRISTIANITY AND
          SOCIETY: THE THIRD ESSAY

5   Performative Christianity: Demarginalizing
      Theology and Church: Reflections on
      Religious Theory and Organization   105

6 Engaging Marginalization by Reconnecting
Economics, Ethics and Religion: Reflections
for a Reformulated Tradition of Christian
Political Economy   142

Notes   Including book references   180
Select Bibliography   196
Index   202

PREFACE

Society and Church

Why is there any need to commission books on society and Church? Is there anything really to discuss? That suspicious question may be asked from at least two quite diverse perspectives. On the one hand, most people in our highly secularized society will regard Church as, at most, an institution of voluntary association (like the Royal Society for the Protection of Birds or a Cycling association), attracting like-minded people. It may (or may not) be thought a good thing (for other people, who are into that sort of thing). Church is unlikely, however, to be considered essential to the fabric or self-understanding of society as a whole, even by those who admit Christianity's historically significant role in the self-understanding and development of our society and polity. Entirely marginal to society, like the RSPB and cycling groups, it may allowably engage with wider society in order to pursue its special interest agenda (protection of birds, provision of cycle lanes). But it would have to do so by arguing and campaigning on commonly agreed ground, not by appealing to some special sense of society and social good.

On the other hand, those within churches might feel there is little point in asking whether and how Church relates to society, since it is manifestly obvious that, empirically, it just does. Simply as a social institution existing within society, the Church is necessarily and unavoidably actively engaged in it theologically, spiritually, educationally, whilst, as institution, it has had to respond to its changing context. At one level, this is an empirical statement, yet it is one that will often receive a theological expression and interpretation. Social engagement is often seen, not as incidental, accidental or peripheral matters – what the Church *does* – but aspects of its central self-definition – what the Church *is*. The

Church's institutional engagement in education, welfare, government, and so on, may be seen in terms of the Church's self-defining mission, or as part of its self-understanding. The ways in which Church is engaged in society reflects a long history in which, at its best, the Church has held a dynamic and historical vision of its task and existence, grounded in the mystery of the Trinitarian God. (In the last century the Church has abandoned a static view of ministry, and no longer sees itself as given its final form by Christ at its origin. Theologians and church members respond in many changing ways to the world around it.) The Church as an institution adapts to its changing circumstances, whilst also pronouncing on matters of societal concern within those areas historically within its remit.

Yet such a confident note belies the crisis which afflicts the very existence of the Church in British society. In the last fifty years culture has become almost completely secularized in its public sphere. The language of God, once quite common in public life in the first half of the twentieth century, and for centuries before that, is now muted, if not almost silent. The occasional politician refers to God in a half-embarrassed way, or religion is seen as dangerous, irrational and the cause of wars and terrorism. The Church and God-talk are marginalized. Moreover, where the Church does engage with society, on issues of social and political concern, it finds difficulty in seeing the possibility and significance of God-talk too. The Church tends to adopt secular modes of discernment and secular criteria in its reports and contributions to debate. In this situation it is far from clear how the rapid changes inside the churches in the last fifty years relate at all to the indifference of the world. How may the churches make any contribution to British society?

Asking this question is the task of this series. The purpose of *Society and Church* is to ask how the churches may claim public space, as *Christian* churches, in a legitimate and effective way in a society that has become as secular as British society now is. The question will be answered in a way that engages with three overlapping, but distinct audiences. First, there will be church people who care about the future of the Church and of society. Second, there are those who might be called the half-believer. They will read religious articles in the press, or will listen to religious programmes on radio and television, but are unlikely to enter a church building except occasionally: they believe and doubt (or believe but fail to find the relevance and significance of God – or at least Church) at the same time. Third, there are those suspicious of the Church, or not terribly interested in religion, but who are committed to the topic and will read the book for the sake of the subject.

The series will address the central issue of the marginalization of the Church by commissioning books on specific topics, in a concrete way that avoids abstraction. On this issue is there anything which is illuminated by referring to a theological standpoint, within the specific historical, cultural, political and ecclesiastical dynamics of the situation? The purpose of this approach is to see how the distinctiveness of what is modelled in one work may illuminate another quite different situation. 'I had not thought that you could look at it in this way.' The series will not share one particular way of reading the situation, nor hold a particular theological or political viewpoint. We shall commission from left and right (whatever those terms might mean in our postmodern world), but we will always emphasize that the relationship of Church and society has changed so much in the new millennium that conventional religious and theological strategies are no longer appropriate.

It is clear that this analysis is not shared widely inside the churches. There is rather a sense of complacency about the present and future status and contribution of the Church to national life in Britain. Equally there is no clear understanding among the churches either of what their relationship to society might be, or how it might be effectively defended. Theologically there is grave doubt as to whether public theology is possible any more. A public theology has theological integrity in addressing society, while being responsible to the issues in society. In Church terms, it means that the idea of being 'a Church for society' is deeply problematic.

Those who write in this series are those who take this crisis with the utmost seriousness. They believe that the Church still has something to offer society, and believe that it is part of its very rationale that it should do so, but who understand all too well the difficulties of the present time. The series will take into account the massive changes that have occurred in British society and politics since 1945, and authors will refer to these developments in their particular work. But the series is not an exercise in contemporary history. The aim of the series is to initiate a conversation as to whether public theology is any longer possible. Have the churches anything to say which it is worth the world listening to? That is the stark question addressed by this series.

John Atherton writes at a time when issues of marginalization are high on the political agenda. Marginalization is both a domestic and an international issue, and it encompasses poverty, powerlessness and a deep feeling of being ignored. There have been many studies of this issue in the last few years, but what is unique in this book is the way in which he pulls together not only the social and economic agenda, but also the future of the churches in the great industrial cities of Western Europe. Manchester is a splendid example of this and the situation is described in graphic detail in this book. This need not surprise us for the author has not only written about poverty and Christian political economy throughout his life, but has also been engaged deeply in the struggle to create a more just and humane city. This is a book in which the experience of the author illuminates the discussions of political economy, the future of the churches and the ability of our political institutions to respond to the marginalization of those trapped in poverty and powerlessness. It is a manifesto for change, and makes a very powerful contribution to the series *Society and Church*.

Alistair McFadyen and Peter Sedgwick
Series Editors

ACKNOWLEDGEMENTS
HOW A PROJECT
IS FORMED

An invitation to be Visiting Professor in the Faculty of Theology at the University of Uppsala, Sweden, in 2001 provided inspiration and opportunity to test the arguments of this book. I am deeply grateful to the Faculty for the space, support and friendships they generated. International relationships is a central theme of this project, and the global community of scholarship bears witness to its reality and possibilities. The visit particularly allowed me to develop the three essays which constitute this book through lectures, seminars and consultations. These three essays form Parts 1, 2 and 3 of the book. The doctoral research seminars in ethics at Uppsala were an important arena for sharing ideas and experiences, including my introduction to feminist justice theories and economics. Uppsala's leadership in the interdisciplinary research project on Ethical Reflection in Economic Theory and Practice, funded by the Bank of Sweden Tercentenary Foundation, is an outstanding example of theological engagement with the heart of globalization processes. Its publications, and the opportunity to make a presentation to one of its consultations, were therefore particularly useful. Behind all this activity is Professor Carl-Henric Grenholm. His invitation to Uppsala, friendship and intellectual stimulus lie at the centre of this endeavour. I will always be thankful for that, and for the opportunity to visit and teach in the new University of Linköping. Its work in applied ethics, under the leadership of Professor Göran Collste, embodies the emerging importance of interdisciplinary work on practical problematics, ethics and the Christian contribution to that, a basic thesis of this book. These more structured opportunities for the exchange of thinking are the bread and butter of world academic communities. But the possibilities these interchanges offer are so often and richly complemented by chance meetings of ordinary human intercourse. In a church hall in Uppsala I met Mehari Gebre-Medhin, Professor of International Child Health at Uppsala. For hours we talked about famines, Ethiopia, women and children, and Amartya Sen. The books he lent me that day, and the encouragement he provided, particularly to develop the Christian contribution to these debates, came at an important time during my stay in Sweden. All of this links to my ongoing work in Manchester.

The Department of Religions and Theology, my academic teaching home since 1975, continues to provide the stimulus of colleagues, and the regular teaching and supervision which are such an indispensable arena for testing and sharing ideas. For example, my yearly course in Christian social ethics is where work on economic-theological heresies (the heteroclitical tradition) is emerging. Sharing intellectual journeys with research students is also always rewarding. Here I acknowledge the recent stimulus provided by Dr Chris Baker and Dr Rod Garner, and their work on urban life and ministry. Linking research supervision with Uppsala is Dr Normunds Kamergrauzis. I was one of the examiners of his doctoral presentation in Sweden, and over the years he has become a good friend and colleague. His thesis on Ronald Preston and theological realism provides an important connection between Sweden, Britain and the USA.

Central to all my work has been my awareness of standing in a great tradition of Christian social thought and practice. Ronald Preston was its leading exponent for 50 years. Based in Manchester, supervisor of my research degrees, then colleague in the Department of Religions and Theology, he provided friendship and support for many in Britain and beyond. My interest in Christian political economy, central to this book, is due to him. Sadly, he died in December 2001. May he rest in peace. And he will because, led by Elaine Graham, Ronald's successor but one, as Samuel Ferguson Professor of Social and Pastoral Theology, Manchester is set to become, once again, the leading academy in Britain in Christian social thought and practice.

Manchester is more than my academic home. It is the location of the origin of modernization processes which shape the world and

this book. It is in my bones. An indispensable part of my enmesh-
ing with urban realities are three institutions embodying crucial
aspects of this book. First, the William Temple Foundation, which
I joined as a member of staff in 1974 with David Jenkins, and continue to serve as Council member and company secretary, reinforces the importance of theological reflection on the practices of
marginalization and regeneration processes in the North West of
England and beyond. Commitment to practical problematics as
the primary theological task is developed through this book. The
Foundation's new programme precisely addresses these matters.

Second, the Anglican Diocese of Manchester, and its new Board
for Ministry in Society, has inspired and resourced my work on
the double whammy of marginalized churches in marginalized
communities. As its vice chair, and member of its Urban Regeneration Think Tank, led by Bishop Stephen Lowe, I have been privi-
leged to collaborate with Alison Peacock, research officer for the
Board. Her information on local churches and communities
provides the basis for Chapter 4. The search for answers to the
seminal question 'can the urban church survive?' arose out of
papers I gave to a Think Tank seminar and to the Anglican
Association of Social Responsibility Officers' National Conference
in Liverpool in 2000.

Third, the Anglican Cathedral Church of St Mary, St George and
St Denys, Manchester, has been my spiritual and practical home
since 1984. It roots me in the daily worship and service of a community at the heart of Manchester. I am grateful to colleagues on
the Cathedral Chapter for their agreement to release me to
Uppsala, and for their continued support in my theological tasks,
and particularly to Canon Paul Denby for reading the manuscript.
Not least, I am grateful to our office staff, Lyndsey Feilman and
Joanne Hooper, for providing secretarial support. They illustrate
the multifaceted nature of such a project as this book. Although
written by one person it is dependent on a series of rich collabora-
tions. That is how it should be, and for that I am thankful.

John Atherton
Feast of the Venerable Bede, 25 May 2002
Manchester

INTRODUCTION
HOW I CHANGED
MY MIND
Problematics and Processes

Can the urban church survive? That is the question this journey
began to address. Why the Church appears to be in terminal
decline has been much debated, particularly by sociology of
religion and secularization theories. Is there something about
modern urban-industrial processes which spells the end of organized Christianity in Britain and Europe? For those who live in
Manchester, that question is a matter of life and death. On current
trends, many local churches will cease to exist in the coming
decades. Facing an imminent end should clear the mind. Yet the
death of Christian Britain,[1] as one commentator has described it, is
a problem not just for the churches. For people, communities and
governments concerned to regenerate deprived localities and
overcome the damaging consequences of increasing social disease,
the decline of the churches should also be a matter of great concern.
For churches have traditionally been centres of voluntary activity
and volunteering, indispensable in rebuilding changed lives and
neighbourhoods.[2] The likely demise of that contribution to civic
society should set alarm bells ringing in all public corridors. As
important, the increasingly intrusive questions we face as global
citizens, from environment to population movements, and from
new technologies to global economies, all raise fundamentally
moral concerns as well as complex technical issues. The with-
drawal of the Christian contribution from such emerging life-
threatening debates should be a matter of profound concern for all

sensible people and institutions, despite the sometimes wilful deafness and blindness of liberal elites and establishments in church, politics, academia and media.

My original question, can the urban church survive?, is therefore of momentous importance for society as well as Church. Yet the golden rule of research is never prejudge outcomes. So the more I pursued the question the more I came to see that the Church's problem was connected to much wider societal problems. For example, in Manchester, we discovered that churches facing most difficulties were disproportionately located in those urban communities facing most difficulties. That therefore drove me to broaden my enquiry into examining marginalization processes themselves. It took me into the great historic problematic of why some are rich and more are poor. It led me into exploring the growing marginalization of peoples within and between nations, between peoples and their environment, and the growing marginalization of Christianity from all that. Maybe then I could shed greater light on the question, can the urban church survive? And maybe that could be of benefit to all who seek to face up to marginalization processes in our society, church and world.[3]

Addressing that great marginalization problematic has therefore been a great personal learning process. For example, immersion in human and environmental global crises has given me new respect for liberationist traditions, and particularly feminist political philosophy and economics. Serious engagement with such awesome and awful crises will not be achieved by traditional Western dominated politics, economics and theologies alone. They will certainly not be overcome by the US-led war against terrorism following the dreadful events of 11 September 2001. I know that, because on that same day when 3,000 people died in the terrorist attacks, 40,000 children died unnecessarily and unheralded in the world, and we lost one species for ever. The critical difference is that the mortality figures for children and species will occur every day and not just on 11 September. I have also learned that if we are to be interdisciplinary in our approach to understanding and responding to such problematics, and I am convinced that must be the case now and for the future, then dialogue with mainstream economics, politics and theology has to be taken equally seriously. There is no radical starting again. There is no avoidance of insights and convictions of traditional disciplines and practices. My task has therefore been to explore ways of connecting such liberationist and mainstream traditions and experiences, tested by their ability to reduce the damaging consequences of marginalization processes. Reconnecting Christianity and churches to the lives of people and the public domain is an integral part of that wider task.

I can best describe this research journey in terms of the importance of problematics and processes as a metaphor for the task of living constructively in today's global context.

Take *problematics*. This is recognition of the significance of focusing on practical problems generally acknowledged to be of central importance for human living in local, national, international and environmental contexts. Such prioritizing of human effort has wide support across traditions. In political economy, from Adam Smith to Alfred Marshall and J. M. Keynes, focusing on practical economic problems brought together the 'abstract and concrete in the same flight of thought'.[4] Similarly, contemporary liberation theology begins the theological task with practical problems rather than intellectual assertion. Both are therefore centred on the human and its struggles for human fulfilment and against those obstacles which prevent it. They therefore emphasize the centrality of taking our context seriously but through one of its main concerns.

Marginalization processes are demonstrably one such problematic, straddling local, national and international contexts, and engaging the formative influence of economics and politics in contemporary life, including their increasing interaction with the environment. In other words, marginalization is a question affecting our lives and the life of creation. And that is of profound importance for all human beings, and therefore Christian discipleship. For at the heart of Christian belief are questions of what it now means to be human, of what is our understanding of social flourishing, of what is the right and wrong way of promoting human living in and through its environments. The commitment to human flourishing in all its fullness is both a human and divine imperative inspired and informed by the Christ-like God who 'came that they may have life and have it more abundantly' (John 10.10). It is acknowledgement that 'Christians have every reason to suppose that God wishes human life to flourish, and has put us in this world in the first place not as Christians but as human beings'.[5] And that therefore connects the Christian task to wider contemporary concerns and debates in philosophy, economics and politics, with their increasing interest in human flourishing. It is that recognition of the role of Christian insights which can be fruitfully seen as 'a series of illuminating fragments that sustain the life of the community of faith which nurtures them and claim also to be in some sense "public truth" '.[6] In other words, we address such a problematic as marginalization as Christians and human beings, thereby connecting to wider morally concerned people and debates. As faith is a fundamental part of that engagement with the Other as people and problematic, so engaging with marginalized church and faith is also fundamentally part of engaging that wider marginalization problematic. The task of this book is to interact faith and problematic for their mutual advantage. So the problematic both sets this agenda and is set by it. It is both required and informed by this agenda, and in turn requires and informs it.

Finally, take the Christian and human task as *process*. The organization of this book illustrates the important part played by methodology alongside problematic. In an increasingly plural context, shaped by forces of post-industrialization and post-modernity, addressing such highly complex matters as marginalization cannot be dealt with adequately by traditional systematic expositions. There is now an incredulity towards metanarratives, a profound suspicion of grand narratives in politics, economics and theology which claim to explain everything, and patently don't. I have therefore chosen to write the three essays contained in this book on the changing context, marginalization, and reconnecting faith to both.[7] Each generates particular perspectives on the central problematic of marginalization, and the promotion of human flourishing. Together they project a series of overlapping consensuses on what we understand by human fulfilment, what are the obstacles to it, how they can be addressed, and what is the contribution of Christianity and church to these processes and to that end.

Connected to the decision to produce three essays are a number of related convictions.

First, the complexity of contemporary contexts and their daunting problematics require such plural treatment because no one discipline or experience can explain and deal with such intransigences and complexities. The commitment to interdisciplinary endeavours becomes totally essential. And that makes fundamental demands on all disciplines, including economics and theology, as we shall see. But that engagement with the Other, as an essential part of constructing all our identities, goes even further. For Christianity in general, and Christian social ethics in particular, it will mean increasingly entering into interfaith explorations and endeavours. Again, at certain parts in the book that is identified as a key development.

Second, this leads to the acknowledgement that the format of the three essays illustrates the episodic and unfinished nature of this and all such projects. There is no one answer to these problematics. There is no arrival point. They will always be about ongoing business, always unfinished. Much in the essays is therefore about preliminary enquiries, a quarry of ideas to be tested further. In the economist Marshall's words, they are essays which suggest a 'mine rather than a railway'.[8]

Third, a series of perspectives on a central problematic cannot but become aware of recurring themes which reflect different contributions and how they frequently overlap. One such theme, central to understanding and engaging marginalization, is the requirement to hold together inclusivity and difference in a profoundly testing but equally creative relationship. We will see how this will inform our understanding of what it means to promote human flourishing, democratic governance, economics, church and theology.

The three essays are developed in the following way. The first (Part 1), on the changing context, is recognition that whatever we think and do needs to take account of the contemporary nature of global change. Chapter 1 explores that nature of change, the characteristics which need to inform our interpretations and responses to great problematics, and the consequences of such change for marginalization processes. Chapter 2 reflects on connections between such change and the changing nature of Christianity in the West in terms of church decline and religious mutation.

The second essay (Part 2) examines the nature of marginalization processes, in Chapter 3 in terms particularly of the growing gap between poor and rich. Definitions of marginalization link human needs and rights in the pursuit of human flourishing. That process understanding of the freedom to be and to do, reflected in measurable outcomes, connects with reflections on explanations of gross inequalities. Chapter 4 takes the form of a brief case study of the overlap between marginalized communities and churches in Manchester, the double whammy of double whammies!

The third essay (Part 3), on making connections, explores ways of reconnecting Christian faith and church to people, communities and the public square, in response to the marginalization problematic. Chapter 5 does so with reference to the Church and theology, and Chapter 6 through developing a Christian political economy. They illustrate how developments in Christianity have constructive implications for secular life, for example in terms of empowering marginalized people and communities, a bias for inclusivity in public policy, the development of praxis-oriented disciplines, measuring marginalization, religious economic activities, and the role of economic-theological heresies.

The final essay epitomizes the task of the book, which can be summarized as 'a renewed attempt to demonstrate the value of theology not just in its own world but in the world of politics, economics, government and civil society'.[9] It is about making connections.

PART 1

ON CHANGE:
THE FIRST ESSAY

1

UNRESOLVED
DILEMMAS
Challenging Global Change

To say we face change on a scale and intensity never before experienced by humankind has been said too often. We've heard it all before. It's typical, too, of the arrogance of modernity. We are not the first to live through great change. Some 6,000 years before the birth of Christ, New Stone Age people made the momentous move from hunter-gathering to agriculture and livestock, thereby supporting growing populations living in towns and cities. Others, of course, will refuse to accept change, even if they fall over it. As the head of Warner Brothers said in 1927, 'Who the hell wants to hear actors talk?'

Despite these qualifications, the fact is we *are* living through the greatest changes in history not simply because of their scale and intensity, but also because of their global nature. To illustrate and justify that claim, I will explore four arenas of change: global economy, technology, demography and environment. That in itself is a major statement. Facing up to our changing context cannot be focused on globalization or environment, as though one or the other explains everything. There are always a number of different distinct integrities, even though they are always interacting with each other. There is never one problematic now.

Examining each area, I am confronted, time and time again, with the judgement that the order of change is both qualitative and quantitative. The startling observation is regularly made that more has been achieved since 1945 than in *all* previous history. Faced with that in world production, research and development, or population growth is thought-provoking enough. But add the disappearance of species and we are addressing not just the cumulative effects of change across all arenas, impinging globally on every locality and person. We are also, for the first time in earth history, encountering immoveable limits of the ecosystem, the ultimacy of finitude itself. Basic statistics of change in each of these four areas therefore become, in Keynes' words, *wild facts*, 'the assaults of thoughts upon the unthinking'.[10] It is a new global context of wild facts which produces *the new contextualism*,[11] the greatest challenge of unresolved dilemmas to all thought and practice.

Some will judge that rehearsing features of change in, say, the global economy and demography is to repeat what we all know from reading the quality press. I have maybe said enough to question that trite observation, 'we've heard it all before'. But there are four additional reasons why this initial essay has to reflect on the nature of contemporary change.

First, these changes are all decisively global in character. They therefore remind us that we can no longer restrict ourselves to localities as communities or nations. Our lives are increasingly bound up with global happenings. That means I can no longer reflect on Christian social thought and practice from the perspective of North West England. An extended stay in Sweden, surrounded by foreign language and customs, made me practise what I increasingly preach. We are all now cosmopolitan citizens. There is no 'local any more that is not touched by powerful outside forces . . . the local itself increasingly cannot be defined simply in territorial terms'.[12]

Second, examining any of the changes reveals far wider consequences. For example, they all have implications for the marginalization problematic, why many are so poor in such a rich world. The 11 September 2001 is about that global concern. Attempts to keep migrants out of our backyard is about global demographic change. Pension problems are about the global economy. They are all interlinked. They all affect marginalization processes, and, in turn, are affected by them.

Third, each arena exhibits global characteristics of change which need to influence ways we think and act. For example, they suggest the importance of complex reality, as multilayered, multicausal, as paradoxical, both cause and effect, and reformulating space and time. Every area of change profoundly interacts with the others. All raise ethical issues as much part of the empirical as the technical. Any engagement with problematics like marginalization must take such matters seriously, or henceforth be regarded as profoundly inadequate. That rules out much theology, which is why Christianity is increasingly marginalized from globally public arenas.

Fourth, if that is the case, engaging problematics informed by these characteristics becomes central to Christian life and witness. They become integral to any Christianity taking context seriously, because these matters must shape the agendas of all seeking human flourishing with environmental sustainability. The argument of this book is to reconnect marginalized churches to that global context of change through that marginalization problematic.

The Global Market Economy: Something Old Something New

> The bourgeoisie has through its exploitation of the world market given a cosmopolitan character to production and consumption in every country . . . In place of old wants, satisfied by the productions of the country, we find new wants, requiring for their satisfaction the products of distant lands and climes . . . In one word, it creates a world after its own image. (Karl Marx)[13]

What Marx discerns as a sign of emerging times is now dominant reality. The internationalization of production, trade and finance has become, in Sassen's words, 'a fundamental aspect of globalization',[14] particularly since 1945. Because of the growing dominance of economic interconnections, and its strong links to political, social and cultural life, from local to international levels, it is not surprising that the Anglican Lambeth Conference of 1998 described 'the globalization of the market economy' as 'the greatest single new force shaping the world'.[15] That concept of global market economy is itself a contested concept, and with the realities it describes, provokes strong opposition if not outright rejection. Growing anti-globalization protests will not go away. Yet global economic processes, particularly as the internationalizing of production, trade and finance, and as a formative influence of communication technologies, makes that impossible, even if desirable, to unravel.

At the heart of these long-term globalization trends lies the *market economy*, emerging in late eighteenth-century Europe, expanding worldwide, and now reinforced by the collapse in 1989 of the only feasible alternative of soviet command economies. Based on signals and information given by the market mechanism of changing consumer choices, technologies, efficiency and opportunity, and the incentives markets give to encourage suppliers to satisfy consumers, a welter of developments since 1945 resulted in an explosion of market economies producing what one commentator has vividly described as a 'climacteric'.[16] Expressed in the staggering increase in international production, trade and finance, it was undergirded by new international institutions like the World Bank (WB), the International Monetary Fund (IMF), and what was to become the World Trade Organization (WTO).

What emerged has been described as a *new capitalism*,[17] expressed particularly as neoliberal global capitalism, as the 'changing qualitative nature of economic integration' (as decentralized economies, less state intervention, privatization, deregulation, reducing tariffs, and deregulated financial markets).[18] It is the sheer thrusting power of these globalization processes of new capitalism which have been likened to 'a massive articulated lorry, or "juggernaut", careering down a mountain pass out of control, leaving havoc and destruction in its wake'.[19] For the global economy produces losers, from Amazonian rainforest to the peoples of Sub Saharan Africa, as well as winners, from financial speculators to the nations of North America and Western Europe. In other words, globalization is 'a paradox: while it is very beneficial to the few, it leaves out or marginalizes two-thirds of the world's population'.[20] Not surprisingly critical responses to such intrusive forces have varied from the protective reactive fundamentalism so splendidly described by Barber as *Jihad v McWorld*, to the growing consciousness and charting of global inequalities represented by the work of the United Nations Development Programme (UNDP) from 1990.[21]

Like all market economies, the global version centres on producing and trading goods and services developed to such a quantitative level as to suggest a qualitative leap or change.

Take world manufacturing output. A base of 100 in 1900 became 311 in 1930, 567 in 1953, 950 in 1963, and an astonishing 3,041 in 1980. So 'the global economy grew more since 1945 than in all world history prior to World War Two'. That means between 1950 and 1980, world real GNP grew fourfold from $2 trillion to $8 trillion, with Swiss per capita GNP reaching $36,300 in 1991. In stark contrast, India's per capita GNP was $360, differentials reflected in child mortality rates, life expectancy and access to education. Globally, 1.3 billion now live on less than $360 per annum, and that after 'nearly five decades of unprecedented global economic growth'.[22]

The supreme symbols of that wealth-creating capacity of the global economy, again since 1945, are transnational corporations (TNCs), great 'planetary organizations' epitomizing 'the new logic of the global market-place'.[23] TNCs represent long-term trends concentrating productive and trading resources in bigger and bigger units. Like the factory system of the nineteenth century, they do not dominate the global economy, yet they do determine 'the metabolism of the entire system' in terms of operating across national boundaries. Again, the story is of astonishing growth. So 7,000 TNCs in 1969 became 45,000 in 1997. Of the world's 100 largest economic entities, 51 are TNCs and only 49 are nation states. The annual sales of General Motors are bigger than Norway's GNP. NCs control 20% of world production and 70% of world trade.[24]

Linked to the growth of TNCs has been the expansion of world trade in goods, from $1.3 billion in 1977 to over $48 billion in 1990, and in services, including finance, from $3.3 billion to $325 billion. Deregulation, liberalization and reduction of tariffs played an important part in this global development, yet 80% of world trade is still between industrialized and developed nations. Exponentially growing trade in goods and services is again linked to the growing gap between richer and poorer nations. Sub Saharan Africa's share in world trade in manufactures, symbol of modernizing economies, *fell* from 0.4% to 0.2% between 1965 and 1986. The latest liberalizing mechanism, Trade Related Intellectual Property Rights (TRIPs), reinforces that marginalization, illustrating the unequal access to knowledge and technology, since the poorest nations possess only 3% of patents despite the South containing 90% of the world's biological wealth. Yet commitment to free trade remains at the centre of the global market economy, following the nineteenth-century economist Ricardo's great law of comparative advantage. In other words, each state should concentrate on what it is best at, trading with other nations' advantages. Yet despite the resultant breathtaking increases in *total* world trade and production, the law did not allow for the free flow of capital across national boundaries in pursuit of greatest profit. It assumed 'a world in which capitalists were fundamentally good Englishmen . . . not a world of cosmopolitan money managers and TNCs'. That is the order of change to a borderless global market economy.[25]

Yet even the power of TNCs is overshadowed by the financial sector of the global economy. For example, foreign direct investment (FDI) in the 1980s, much of it by TNCs, grew five times faster than world trade, and ten times faster than world output. Private FDI is now higher than government aid to developing nations, yet concentrated on a small number of nations. Of FDI flowing from the North to the South, China received 38% and Sub Saharan Africa only 2.2%. Most FDI goes from North to North, 91% going to 43% of the world's population in 1996. The neoliberal claim of a global free market to generate universal improvements in living standards is therefore met by the charge that 'it perpetuates and deepens economic unevenness'.[26]

That paradoxical nature of global capitalism is most stridently illustrated by the explosive growth of financial markets since 1945, supported by the deregulation of foreign exchange and domestic financial markets, and by computer networks. Trading across national boundaries now occurs 24 hours a day, centred particularly on London, New York and Tokyo. *Daily* foreign exchange turnover accelerated from $1 billion in the 1970s to an astonishing $1.5 trillion by the late 1990s, with over 90% accounted for by speculation, unrelated to trade or investment. The *daily* figure is overtaking the total of *all* national reserve bank holdings, illustrating the vulnerability of real economies to the speculative flows of casino capitalism. So the South Asian financial crisis of 1997 resulted in a fourfold increase in unemployment in South Korea, and a 50% increase in poverty in Indonesia.

It is becoming fashionable in many secular and theological circles to condemn globalization processes in general, and the global market economy in particular. The wild facts of TNCs, trade and financial speculation make that an understandable and morally obvious response, especially when those facts are connected to marginalization and environmental problematics.

Yet reflections on the nature of economic growth in the last decisive 200 years reveal a highly complex set of realities which illustrate key features of contemporary change. They belie simplistic univocal judgements. They therefore should and will inform the following interpretation of marginalization as complex processes requiring equally plural responses.

For example, statistics of production, trade and finance reveal a story of unparalleled economic growth in our generation. Without its earlier achievements in the nineteenth century, the increasing population of the West would not have survived. Yet we have also noted the profoundly paradoxical nature of that process in terms of creating great poverty alongside great wealth. Not surprisingly, therefore, analysis of economic growth reveals a multilayered and multicausal phenomenon. Most commentators identify at least three main complexes behind such economic growth. First, material resources include climate, raw materials, power, agriculture, technology, the demand from large prosperous markets, division of labour and good communications. Yet, second, there is also an increasing recognition of less quantifiable but nonetheless substantial non-material resources like the continuous accumulation of knowledge and know-how, acceptance of an ethos of rationality including cultivation of appropriate means to ends rather than reliance on magic and tradition, commitment to enterprise and innovation, and willingness to work hard and be open to continuous experiment. It is these more cultural factors which some have understandably hijacked for the Protestant work ethic of Western Europe and North America. Yet recent successes of South East Asian economies like Japan and Hong Kong illustrate how 'one does not have to be a Weberian Protestant to behave like one'.[27] Indeed, cultural factors, as Chapter 2 illustrates, are more likely to be solvents of religious traditions in the longer term, than being constructively informed by them in the earlier stages of economic growth processes.

Third, alongside these two explanatory layers of the global market economy's power is growing recognition of the central importance of good governance. This includes promoting administrative competence free from corruption, maintaining public order and stability, an independent legal system preserving civil and political liberties, and protecting private property and the individual and company's claim on gains from legitimate endeavour, and the ability to make economic decisions without arbitrary unpredictable political interference. Given the increasing importance of good governance in economic development in a global economy, no society will overcome marginalization processes without it. Yet it is governance as part of the complex multilayered multicausal reality of economic growth processes which is a decisive lesson of this reflection on global economic change. It is 'in the mode of production and government, in the social and institutional order, in the corpus of knowledge and in attitudes and values – that makes it possible for a society to hold its own' in the twenty-first century.[28]

Yet reflections on the nature of change in a global market economy reveal much more for our following considerations of marginalization. Clearly central to that, as for any other global problematic, is recognition that we are dealing increasingly with multilayered, multicausal phenomena. This decisively rejects the cherished illusion of theologians, economists and politicians that one good explanation should be enough, a tendency which the heteroclitical tradition examines in Chapter 6. For 'the determinants of complex processes are invariably plural and interrelated. Monocausal explanations will not work.'[29] Yet we are engaging with far more than multiple interacting forces of varying potency. For these processes are increasingly both cause and effect. So emerging mass populations at the end of the nineteenth century, with increasing purchasing power, generated bigger markets and demand. This was met by mass production systems, credit and selling techniques, which in themselves influenced consumption patterns. In other words, 'in the economic sphere, significant changes are almost invariably the resultant of a mutually sustaining conjuncture of factors, so that most variables are at once both cause and effect, independent and dependent'.[30] It is these productive *synergies* which make modern economic processes so exponentially fruitful.

From a quite different perspective it is crucial to note how integrative forces characterizing the global market economy do not become 'the end of history', as Fukuyama argues. 'The extension of modernity in globalization is not simply the imperial reach of the West in a new guise. What becomes ever clearer is that the global process creates plural modernities.'[31] The story is not simply about the global ambitions of the American neoliberal version of new capitalism. There are other stories, hopefully more important, of European and Asian capitalisms. This but reflects how modern economic growth processes have no uniformity of sequence, no single path, but rather a variety of ways of putting together material, non-material and political resources constituting the emerging global market economy. It is acknowledgement of the seminal influence of forces of integration *and* difference.

Such a formative characteristic of contemporary change is reflected in the centrality yet changing nature of governance in economic processes. Without good governance marginalized nations will not become effective participants in the global market economy. Yet that political factor is itself undergoing fundamental change. For globalization processes are putting increasing pressure on the nation state in terms of its ability to manage its economic, political and cultural life, what Sassen has so strikingly described as the 'unbundling of sovereignty'.[32] Yet that in turn pushes governments into regional alliances, like the European Union, and into international relationships like the WTO. It is there that sovereignty of governance, shared with others, can and will still be exercised for public good or harm. It is therefore about a global economy of inclusivity and difference, certainly about, yet more than, economics. It is about 'a world being re-cast through the impact of economic and technological forces into a shared economic and political space'.[33] It is therefore about *political economy*, and the Christian engagement with that, which Chapter 6 addresses.

The Genesis Factor: Technological Change

Technological development, as its description as genesis factor suggests, has been at the centre of change, whether economic, social or political, throughout recorded history. So the discovery of the mechanical clock in thirteenth and fourteenth-century Europe spawned a series of developments, including the 'very notion of productivity',[34] so integral, like clockmakers, to the later industrial revolution. As then, so now, technological developments interacted with other major areas of change, indeed increasingly so, acknowledging the modern quantum leap within technological and other change.

This seismic transformation in contemporary technology is

particularly illustrated by its accelerating speed. Developing the steam engine, at the heart of the industrial revolution, spanned well over one hundred years, from initial inventions of Savery and Newcomen at the beginning of the eighteenth century to Parsons' patenting of the steam turbine in the late nineteenth century. After the Second World War, nuclear power took less than a generation to move from theory to production.

This story is not simply about dramatic breakthroughs. It is equally about substantial but complementary incremental modificatory changes, contributing to the emergence of a culture of built-in change, of change begetting change through a whole series of interactions. So inventions in organic chemistry in the later nineteenth century move from dyes to cellulose, artificial fibres to plastics, splendidly illustrated by the title of a chemical firm's history, *One Thing Leads to Another*.[35] It is that symbiotic process, that dynamic synergy which produced foundational products from radio valve to internal combustion engine, repeatedly yielding rich harvests of 'forward and backward linkages'.[36] So car production was the consumer of semi-finished and finished intermediate products (steel, glass, paint) and components (tyres); it created demand for fuel; it generated services (repairs, sales); it stimulated investment (roads, bridges); and provoked new technological developments (in engineering).

Essential to the accelerating and comprehensive nature of technological change has been the concentration of resources particularly as growing interaction with scientific developments. Institutionalizing technological and scientific programmes since the late nineteenth century has been a remarkable journey. Not surprisingly, it was intimately linked to the growing role of education and training in the development and transmission of knowledge, including increasingly in theoretical sciences. It was this marriage of science and technology which opened up the era of what the economist Kuznets called 'modern economic growth'.[37] It is this concentration and interaction of resources which can now solve the most difficult technological problems in improbably short times. As much research and development (R&D) is now taking place around the world in any one year as the aggregate of all R&D up to the 1960s, supported by a 226-fold increase in scientists, technicians and engineers, between 1880 and 1955. The role of scientific enquiry is now particularly informative.

As the new 'cognitive factor', it has led to a 'stunning array of new products and techniques',[38] flowing, say, from the seismic discovery of DNA by Crick and Watson in the 1950s, and affecting more and more fields of enquiry and application, from criminology and medicine to agriculture and genetic engineering. Indeed some have argued that the apparently limitless possibilities of knowledge, and therefore of their application to solving global problematics, are what constitute the hope of the genesis factor. For the nature of such knowledge 'suggests no analogy with other economic resources whose supply may be supposed to be finite'. It could only be 'exhausted if it was total'.[39] Yet the genesis story is also about the limits to human endeavour of finitude and sin, a message remarkably and most disturbingly confirmed by emerging environmental crises. 'In sum, all the talk about knowledge and the mind as an ultimate resource that will offset limits imposed by finitude, entropy and ecological dependence seems to us to reflect incompetent use of the very organ alleged to have such unlimited powers.'[40]

Three stories illustrate these features of current technological change. They are chosen because they are connected to the three basic factors or resources for production, labour, land and capital, in mainstream neoclassical economics, the foundational theory of the global market economy. What we observe is that while each exhibits the impact of contemporary change, the order of change is such that a process of mutation may be occurring with profound implications for future theory and practice.

Take *labour* and the development of robotics. Again, this needs to be located in the historical context of industrialization, with its dependence on substituting machines for human skill, and inanimate for human and animal power, generating that breakthrough in productivity at the heart of modern economic growth. For Ure, contemporary commentator on the early factory system which transformed Manchester and then the world, 'It is, in fact, the constant aim and tendency of every improvement in machinery to supersede human labor altogether.'[41] That process has continued apace, with the current radical step of replacing 'man by machines that think as well as do'.[42] It is these intelligent robots, based on computerized machines using artificial intelligence and knowledge-based systems, which are beginning to solve problems in the way humans do. In contrast, industrial robots are for production purposes and remain the main development in this stage of replacing human effort. In 1988, Japan, with its ageing population, led the field with 176,000 industrial robots, Western Europe had 48,000 and the USA 33,000. As a new way of production by reducing workers' physical and then mental efforts, such robotics are likely to stimulate major social change, including new definitions of work. As part of ongoing trends to international competitiveness, increasing productivity, and therefore raising the per capita output and prosperity of nations and people, they contribute to that increasing wealth production so central to human well-being. Yet they also have consequences for further marginalization, not least because eroding the demand for labour is precisely that factor of production which the poorest nations have in increasing abundance: they could 'keep poorer countries at the bottom of the heap, or weaken them further'.[43]

Take *land*, and its transformation by biotechnologies. Demand for such change is growing in terms of feeding exploding populations, and the increasing pressure this puts on finite resources of agricultural land. Again, different aspects of biotechnologies illustrate their essential creative potential along with the problem of damaging consequences. For example, genetic engineering uses 'living organisms or processes to make or modify products, to improve plants or animals, or to develop micro organisms for specific uses'.[44] Genetic engineers firmly believe that in months or years they can achieve by genetic manipulation improvements in yields that took generations using traditional plant-breeding technologies. That is an essential development because there are likely to be at least a further two billion mouths to feed in less than a generation. Yet these processes can also contain damaging environmental consequences for the land itself and for species, including the human. Developments in the field of *in vitro* synthetic production of food in factory laboratories potentially constitute an even greater threat to land as a factor of production. For this technology offers the replacement, say, of genetically engineered tomatoes with synthetic products, thus reducing the pressure on land, but also on farmers, and therefore on a principal source of labour in the poorer nations of the South. The growing opportunity for technologically strong TNCs in these fields, with increasing vertical integration of their operations, and the use of patent law, is leading to a 'biological' and agricultural 'imperialism'. It is the cumulative effect of all these developments which for good reasons, like feeding people, restricting environmental damage, and promoting technological drives, are unlikely to be halted, and yet are equally likely to exacerbate marginalization processes. That has been part of industrialization from the beginning, as we will see in Chapter 3. What is disturbingly different are these technological consequences for the growing gap between North and South through precisely these traditional factors of production, land and labour, of which the South has an over-abundance. 'What *is* new is the sheer size of the imbalances, and of the populations affected by them.'[45]

Finally, take *capital*, and the contribution of information technologies (IT) to the increasing dislocation by capital movements of the 'real' economy of production and trade. With the integration of computers and telecommunications, the dynamic instant interconnectedness of IT transforms the global economy and the role of capital within it. These developments again follow the routine of change in terms of their roots in the historical context, say the discovery of the telegraph and then the valve in the late nineteenth century. Yet again they also illustrate the new speed, complexity and paradoxical nature of change. For example, current interactions between IT and capital involve the compression of space and time, indeed, the 'Great War of Independence' from them.[46] So on the one hand, instantaneous communication, including knowledge through the worldwide web, erodes the significance of *space*. This means that decision-makers, say in TNCs, are relieved of the territorial constraints of locality, becoming a contemporary form of absentee landlords. Space and territorial matters cease to be priorities, at least for those able to move with the speed of electronic messages. The technological annulment of spatial distances thereby also polarizes as well as homogenizes the human condition. Some are freed from territorial constraints, others are entrapped by them in ghettos. On the other hand, the compression of space interacts most powerfully and formatively with the erosion of time. It is Castells who most imaginatively captures this transformation of process in the advent of the informational city, describing how the space of flows replaces the tradition of the flows between spaces.[47] Its implications are immense. For the compression of time means events are now experienced instantaneously, links with the past are reduced, and the future becomes more short-term. 'Time becomes a present with an edge of the future, reminding us of the constant obsolescence of the past.'[48] Traditions, nation states, and identities are all eroded or transformed.

Religions, and our particular concern with Christianity, illustrate these impacts. For example, the dependence of churches on localities and associational forms based on the geography of propinquity, constitutes an over-dependence on the past flows between spaces, not the emerging space of flows, of networking. The traditional theologies of the importance of land for faith, as expounded by Brueggemann,[49] are equally now under threat by such technological change. Yet the challenges are even greater, reinforcing once again marginalization processes. For the digital revolution is also the digital divide. Information technologies of the global market economy are linked to Castells' 'dehumanisation of Africa', the 'black holes of informational capitalism'.[50] So the dramatic increase in internet users from 16 million in 1995 to 304 million in 2000, was reflected in equally dramatic differences in regional access: in 1998 26% surfed the net in the USA, 0.8% in Latin America and the Caribbean, and 0.1% in Sub Saharan Africa.

Such is the explosion of technological change, such is the acceleration in wealth creation, such are the paradoxes. What of the future? The lesson of these changes is that there is no going back. There is no stopping them. For that judgement go to the stories of the origin of the genesis factor. So 'Adam and Eve lost Paradise for having eaten of the fruit of the Tree of Knowledge; but they retained the knowledge . . . the myths warn us that wrestling and exploitation of knowledge are perilous acts, but man must and will know, and once knowing, will not forget.'[51]

The Malthusian Nightmare: The Demographic Explosion

Since the industrial and urban revolutions of the late eighteenth century, accelerating populations have both reflected the nature and importance of dramatic change and its forceful interaction with other variables. Its early history illustrates these judgements, and provides rich connections with the rest of this chapter and book. It reminds us that such problematics as population are so significant that they must be addressed independently of variables like global economy and environment.

The Revd Thomas Malthus (1766–1834) wrote his classic *Essay on the Principle of Population* in 1798, in response to that problematic which also lies at the heart of marginalization processes. His foundational thesis was 'that the power of population is indefinitely greater than the power in the earth to produce subsistence for man'.[52] That tendency of increasing population to put unsustainable pressure on resources needed to support it would be averted by disasters of war, famine or plague, unless education or moral restraint controlled fertility. He therefore highlighted the issue of scarcity for the emerging discipline of economics: how do you allocate scarce resources among competing wants? It was this 'iron law of necessity' which challenged the utopianism of Godwin and Condorcet in the 1790s, that the problem of scarcity could be avoided by removing unjust institutions and so releasing the human potential for perfection. Yet Malthus' 'dismal' projections were wrong for different and more significant reasons. He quite underestimated the contribution of technology and production to economic growth, and thus to sustaining increased population. So the latter rose fourfold in Britain in the nineteenth century, but GNP rose fourteenfold. Yet as the current demographic story unfolds, that nightmare of demand exceeding supply will recur, but more significantly as a new awareness of the constraints of finitude, as expanding resources and demand break against environmental limits.

Malthus died in 1834, by which time world population had reached one billion. What had taken all history to achieve was then attained in only one hundred years, when population reached two billion in 1925. By 1975, it had doubled again to four billion, and in only 25 years, by 2000, it had reached six billion. It is likely to be eight to nine billion by 2025. By 2050, it is hoped populations will stabilize, because of the impact of economic growth and rising living standards on fertility rates. It is a most astonishing illustration of the speed and extent of change. Yet it becomes even more informative and influential when subjected to more detailed analysis.

For example, take the *location* of the recent demographic explosion. This is overwhelmingly in the poorer nations of the South, with the richer North experiencing little population growth, and therefore the 'greying' of the population, with all the different problems that creates. In 2025, 95% of population growth will be in developing economies. So, in 1950, Africa's population was half the European. By 2025, it is likely to be three times as much, rising to 1.5 billion, with Kenya moving from 25 to 77 million. The problem is that the growth is unlikely to be supported by an equivalent or greater increase in resources, as happened in Europe in the nineteenth century. And that is a fundamental cause of marginalization. For reducing that is dependent on productivity and economic growth (as GNP per capita) outstripping population growth.

It is not just a matter of balance in terms of where the population explosion occurs, but also the effects on the population itself. For the South, it means rapidly increasing proportions of young people, with their demands for education, job opportunities and social cohesion. Many nations will have over 50% under 15. What does that mean for memory and tradition as community identity? Will those Western values of democracy, market economy, human rights and liberal social culture maintain their position in the world if it is increasingly populated by societies which 'did not experience the rational scientific and liberal assumptions of the Enlightenment'?[53]

Even more disturbing is the pandemic of HIV/Aids, the epitomy of marginalization and social crisis in a global context, with profound consequences for mortality, life expectancy and economic growth. The intense burden of suffering which figures do not communicate is unimaginable. In 2000, Sub Saharan Africa had 24.5 million suffering from HIV/Aids, South and South East Asia 5.6 million, Western Europe 0.52 million. Most disturbingly, it targets young people, so common in the over-populated South. Aids could eventually kill 50% of Ethiopian and South African boys now aged 15. It is the great spotlight on 'marginalization, poverty and violence, the oppression of women and the exclusion of minorities'. It is profoundly linked to 'lack of ability to resist global economic forces'.[54]

But such a demographic explosion has other linkages affecting North as well as South. For example, migration has long been a strong feature of industrial history. So 20 million emigrated from Britain between 1815 and 1914, mostly to the USA. The modern phenomenon has been particularly disruptive. In 1995, 27 million migrants and refugees were in the care of the UN High Commission for Refugees. Yet it is the migration from South to North which elicits greatest unease, particularly in the latter. Along with the globalization of capital, Sassen regards such migration as 'a fundamental aspect of globalization',[55] even though the only freedom ironically rejected by economic liberals. Despite that highly selective barrier, as one commentator observes, '"people now, even if they are very poor, know how people live in other parts of the world" and will attempt to get there by land, sea or air'.[56]

Upheavals resulting from such population movements are reinforced by growing threats to order which over-population generates as conflicts over resources, politics and ethnic tensions. The former is recognition that enormous population pressures on land and economies least able to support them constitute an enormous threat to environmental integrity. The latter is connected particularly to war in all its forms. In the 1990s, five million died in intra-state conflicts, and 50 million were forced to flee their homes. The potential for future conflicts is inbuilt in emerging demographic imbalances, say with a population density per square mile of 4,206 in the Gaza strip and 530 in Israel. The current disturbing consequences of such conflict is the diversion of precious resources by poorer nations to military spending. For Low Income Countries with a per capita income of $700 or less, this rose from $36 billion in 1995 to $43 billion in 1998.

Since the late eighteenth century, rapid population increase has also been associated with continuous urbanization to the extent that 'The world is now an urban place.'[57] As recent as the 1950s, only 25% of world population lived in towns and cities. Only London and New York had over eight million inhabitants. By 2010, 75% will live in urban communities, and the ultimate figure is likely to reach 95%. Even by the first decade of this new century, there were 20 megacities of over 11 million, 17 in developing countries, with the biggest, Mexico City, having over 24 million. For the first time since the Stone Age, peasants are now a minority; we are all becoming urban. That is the challenge to the global community, and particularly to churches, not least because the urban is the primary location of the decline of the churches in the West. That is the problem with which this book started, and which will figure prominently in Chapters 2 and 4.

It is that association of demographic explosion with urbanization which particularly embodies the paradoxical nature of change and contributes to the marginalization problematic. For cities, like globalization, are 'an amalgamation of the most significant forces shaping our urban areas and our world today'. They thereby become the locations of contradictory pressures characterizing such processes.[58] So cities have been valued for their energy, cultural diversity, technological complexity and multiplicity of activities. Yet equally they have been seen as places of decay, poverty and crime. Whichever it is, and in whatever combination, they increasingly act as magnets in the South, attracting millions from rural contexts. There they 'gravitate out to the peripheral slums, the bustees or favelas, which squat on high-risk, hazardous sites without the support of legality, sewerage, infrastructure or secure tenure . . . more than a third of all the urban dwellers of the developing world have to eke out a life in these abysmal circumstances'.[59] So the cities of the South increasingly become centres of poverty and social collapse. Lagos (Nigeria) has 143,000 people per square mile in contrast to New York's 11,401. It is 'inconceivable that their inhabitants will enjoy the benefits offered by traditional European cities'.[60] Yet urban migrations of the poor in the South now also extend to the North, putting additional pressures on hard-pressed inner cities. It is a salutary reminder that none can escape the forces of contemporary change.

Cities also increasingly embody the forces of post-modernity in globalization, for example in terms of trends towards the space of flows. These are repeatedly generating new hierarchies in marginalization processes between and within cities, what Sassen describes as 'a new geography of centrality and marginality, which reproduces many of the old inequalities in new clusters, with little regard for national frontiers or regional geography'.[61] So the new global hierarchies of cities locates the financial centres of New York, London, Tokyo and Hong Kong at the top of the tree, with way beneath them the cities of the South, including Sao Paulo, Buenos Aires, Bombay and Mexico City. African cities are just not in this hierarchy. They are 'increasingly peripheral, increasingly excluded from the major economic processes that fuel economic growth in the new global economy'. It is about the 'disinformation of Africa', a 'technological and economic apartheid' of a whole region.[62]

Alongside these global hierarchies, hierarchies *within* cities are reformulated, deeply embedded in spatial segregations. These grave inequalities are increasingly 'read on the face of buildings, neighbourhoods and towns', ghettos of the underclass where none should live, often 'a stone's throw from opulent headquarters or luxurious condominiums', the gated enclosures of the rich.[63] It is this connection between demographic explosion and urbanization which manifests most stridently the emerging character of marginalization processes.

Threatening Creation: Environmental Crisis

Each time we examine an issue like the global market economy, technology and demography we imagine the wild facts of the matter can't get wilder, we assume marginalization processes can't be deepened even more. And each issue we have considered does precisely that. And the global environment is no different. Indeed, a consideration of the life-sustaining ecosystem communicates a sense of ultimacy, of reaching the End. The liberation theologian Boff rightly connects the marginalization of the deprived to the marginalization of environment, cry of the poor to cry of the earth.[64] This book is about that breadth of marginalization, extended to include the marginalization of Christianity to all that.

This problematic is essentially set by the nature of God's created order, the life of and on this planet earth. For the earth is clothed by a thin film of matter; thermodynamically it is a *closed* system, with no materials entering or leaving it, other than the sun's energy. Consequently, the only processes occurring are materials changed from one form to another, as self-sustaining cycle of life, as total ecosystem. The earth's thin film of life is therefore entire and interconnected, so damage inflicted on one part has effects not just locally but elsewhere. And that damage can take two forms. First, the injection into the ecosystem of waste from economic activity (as matter and heat) beyond the planet's capacity to absorb without cumulatively harmful consequences for humans and living organisms. Global warming and damage to the ozone layer illustrate this. But then second, extraction from the earth of increasingly irreplaceable resource and life forms. The destruction of topsoil, forests and species illustrates this. It is the cumulative effect of such damage on and in such an ecosystem which is beginning to communicate a sense of ultimacy, 'a concrete sense of running up against some kind of physical limitation in the absolute capacity of our planet to absorb the kind of punishment we are dishing out'.[65]

That ultimate threat, that ultimate marginalization of and from the ecosystem itself, is deeply embedded in modernization forces, in the industrialization and urbanization that have dominated this essay so far. For the complexity, rate and extent of such change, summarized in doubling world population and quadrupling world economic activity between only 1950 and 1990, is putting unsustainable pressures on the environment. The results are the starkest of wild facts.

Take destructive inputs into the ecosystem. Global warming is essentially about reradiated heat being trapped, as in a greenhouse, and therefore warming up atmospheric gases. It is caused by the release of carbon dioxide, through burning coal and oil, classic signs of economic activity, into the atmosphere. The resulting rise in global temperature affects sea levels, among other things. This will have devastating consequences for developing economies like Egypt, Bangladesh and China, with high population densities in low-lying delta regions. Damage done by releasing CFCs into the earth's protective shield of ozone is a similar order of problem. The hole thereby created means more ultra violet radiation now reaches the earth's surface, causing increases in skin cancer, and damage to crop growth and the human immune system.

Significantly these examples illustrate how developing economies of the South are increasingly and inevitably contributing to the environmental crisis as they struggle to raise living standards. China increased its coal output twentyfold between 1948 and 1982, and if every household acquires a car and a fridge, the threat to environmental integrity is awesome. That is the likely outcome of the industrial ambitions of China and India, because by 2025, they will house 35% of the world's population, all demanding improved living standards. Yet despite these trends in the South, the developed economies of the North continue to bear disproportionate responsibility for the environmental crisis. The USA, with 4% of world population, emits 17% of greenhouse gases. That is some indication of the emerging complexity of the marginalization problem.

Or take damage done to irreplaceable life forms. Between 1950 and 1990, the world lost 20% of topsoil from its croplands. In 1950,

238 million Africans had 272 million livestock. By 1987, that had risen to 604 million with 543 million livestock. Resulting overgrazing led to grassland deterioration, and then soil erosion, 'the self-reinforcing cycle of ecological degradation and deepening human poverty'.[66] In that same period we lost 20% of tropical rainforest, including 15% of the biggest in South America, the world's largest CO_2 filter, and great temple of biodiversity. The latter is a reminder that we are now losing one species every day (compared to one every year from 1850 to 1950, and one every ten years, from 1500 to 1850). And all in a generation: 'What Nature created in the course of millions of years will be destroyed by us in little more than forty years.'[67]

There are four features of such change which need to inform our reflections in the final essay (Part 3). First, the challenge of the ecosystem to economic growth. The issue here is whether a self-contained and therefore finite ecosystem can sustain the accelerating demands of an economic system with increasingly damaging consequences for the environment. It is essentially a reformulation of Malthus' iron law of necessity of economic scarcity in conflict with expanding population demand. It is recognition that the scale of human activity, as population growth and supportive economic activity, may be expanding too much for the biosphere on which it ultimately depends.

Second, reflections on the ecosystem and human activity confirm the profound interrelationship of living and non-living systems among themselves and with their environment. It confirms and deepens our understanding of the interactive nature of change, such a striking feature of this study so far. It suggests and demands an interconnected interpretation of knowledge, reflecting 'the way in which all beings are dependent upon one another, constituting the vast fabric of their interdependencies'.[68] Reflections on a reformulated interdisciplinary and interactive understanding of praxis in Chapter 5 is profoundly influenced by this experience of change.

Third, the consequences of population and economic growth in this historic generation are clearly affecting our environment and lives. They are measured in decades rather than centuries. They will therefore require taking account of perhaps the most difficult lesson of contemporary change, that our thinking and practising will need to become increasingly *intergenerational*. The

environmental crisis is profoundly about conflict between immed-
iate gratification and long-term gain. That is a most difficult
lesson to learn politically.

Fourth, we are therefore once again faced with the issue of
politics, of good *governance*, certainly within nations, as the lessons
of economic growth and the overcoming of marginalization
remind us. Yet that problematic of marginalization, when connected to the environmental problematic, as it demonstrably is,
will increasingly require the development of inter-nation institutions and processes of governance. Global problematics demand
global responses. At the heart of that will certainly be managing
economic life and the discipline of economics, but equally their
interaction with the ecosystem, and therefore with the practice
and discipline of an expanded political economy.

These reflections on the nature of contemporary change constitute an essential prerequisite for engaging such global problematics as marginalization between and within nations, and between
them and their environment. Indeed, their cumulative effect
confirms the new importance of the interaction between how we
do things and what we strive to do, between process and problematic identified in the Introduction. For Boff, reflecting on the
relationship between poverty and environment, the challenge is to
reject closed ideas, to 'mistrust one-way causality, to strive to be
inclusive in the face of all exclusions, to be unifying in the face of
all disjunctions, to take a holistic approach in the face of all reduc-
tionisms, and to appreciate complexity in the face of all over-
simplifications'.[69] That requirement for new ways of thinking and
doing is now incumbent on us all, whatever problematic is
addressed in the future. That is the challenge of contemporary
global change.

DEATH OR MUTATION
Changing Christianity

Dr Johnson is once reported to have remarked that facing death at the executioner's hand next morning certainly cleared the mind. Calum Brown begins his latest publication with equally dramatic words: 'This book is about the death of Christian Britain.'[70] That is no idle speculation. The Church of Scotland has declared it will cease to exist by 2033 if present trends continue. My analysis of the Anglican Diocese of Manchester's performance suggests its death by 2040.

These are wild facts of change affecting Christianity in Britain and Western Europe. What took many centuries to construct may have been dealt a terminal blow in only forty years – that same astonishing generation, beginning in the 1960s, of global change recounted in Chapter 1.

This chapter explores such religious change, as essentially an extension of the first chapter, and therefore frequently resonating with it. It is a study of death or mutation as the reaction to changing national and global contexts. Such is the choice we face, given such change.

Although this is a case study of British Christianity, it is not parochial. It is certainly about a dramatically transforming national identity, ending centuries of major influence by churches. Different ways of continuing that Christian contribution are explored at the end of these reflections. That concerns the mutation of religion. Yet this is against the backcloth of dramatic church decline, about the option of death if present trends continue. That story is also acknowledged by examining explanations of such religious change. Although it involves engagement with the sociology of religion, this discussion is conducted from the perspective of Christian social ethics, requiring conversation with such disciplines but broadened to include history and economics.

It is through that exploration of the explanation of religious decline through secularization theory that this discussion assumes wider significance. As urban-industrial processes cascaded globally from British origins, will this experience of religious change follow the same route? Grace Davie has rightly warned against regarding British and European experience as a prototype for global religiosity.[71] In Africa and Latin America, the stories are of astonishing growth, particularly in the hopelessly bourgeoning cities. The Assemblies of God in Brazil grew at the yearly rate of nearly one million members in the early 1990s; Rio de Janeiro planted five new Pentecostal churches a week during the same period. Even in the USA, the most modern, commercial, materialist, secular and plural of societies, 40% still go to church regularly. And the rise of religious fundamentalism in Judaism, Christianity, Islam and Hinduism only confirms that reality of a world as 'furiously religious as ever'.[72]

Yet no one can remain unaffected by the changes set out in Chapter 1. They are increasingly global in character, and will inevitably influence religious life. What is happening in Britain and Europe is likely to be of profound importance for these wider international contexts. As the origin and continuing heartland of such change, it is unlikely that certain patterns of experience will not recur on a wider scale in the coming generation. That is not about regarding British Christianity as a global prototype. It is about recognizing that global changes are likely to generate *different* models of response but with substantially increasing shared experiences.

A brief account of the decline and mutation of British Christianity facing such change is therefore of particular and wider relevance. It is about its growing marginalization from public and individual lives, about churches being 'pushed to the margins of social significance'. And that is because 'In unprecedented numbers, the British people since the 1960s have stopped going to church.'[73] The construction of identity is no longer influenced significantly by Christianity. Its reconstruction proceeds apace without it. Reconnecting Christianity to that is the task before us.

Exploring Religious Change: The Experience of British Churches in the Great Generation of Change

The wild facts of church decline in that historic generation from the 1960s are another breathtaking illustration of contemporary change in terms of speed, depth and extent. A century of gentle decline (overall church membership only moving from 19.3% in 1900 to 17.6% in 1956) was abruptly reversed after the Second World War, with substantial surges in churchgoing, baptisms and Sunday Schools, and Billy Graham campaigns attracting millions. Yet this only served to heighten what followed.

So in 1960, Britain remained a highly religious nation of church-going, with religious rules for conduct, and a central role of Christian piety in the formation of national character and society, and family and individual life. But then all hell was let loose. In only forty years, churches experienced dramatic drops in membership and attendances. People and nation were increasingly reimagining themselves in ways no longer significantly informed by the churches. The death of Christian Britain began to appear as a realistic option.

Statistics tell this amazing story in bare unequivocal outline, showing a 50% loss of organizational effectiveness in one short generation. By 2000:

- less than 8% attended Sunday worship in any week;
- less than 25% were members of any church;
- less than 10% of children attended Sunday School (75% in the late nineteenth century);
- less than 50% got married in church;
- only 20% of babies were baptized in the Church of England (two thirds in 1960);
- in most English counties, non-churchgoers were over 90% of the population.

And the figures continue to decline, most disturbingly, with Christian faith and churchgoing no longer being transmitted to young people, producing a generation of widespread religious illiteracy. The changing role of women in this transformation has been particularly emphasized by Brown. Occupying a central place in churchgoing and the transmission of belief to new generations, women played a dominant part in the church and religious life of the nation from 1800 to 1960. That feminization of piety, and pietizing of femininity was transformed in our generation with the liberation of women from restrictive sexual and family roles, and their growing participation in the workplace. By the 1980s there had occurred 'an unprecedented breaking of a fundamental tradition which had previously passed unbroken from generation to generation'.[74] Women no longer went to church in numbers, sent their children to Sunday School, taught prayers in the home, had their children baptized and confirmed, and were increasingly no longer married in church.

Statistics from the Diocese of Manchester only confirm that picture of decline, indeed more alarmingly so, if that were possible:

- Baptisms fell from 19,423 (1960) to 4,210 (2000).
- Confirmations fell from 10,571 (1960) to 1,345 (1999).
- Easter day communicants fell from 92,450 (1960) to 29,800 (2000).
- Electoral roll membership fell from 128,748 (1960) to 39,600 (2000).
- Usual Sunday attendances (six consecutive Sundays) fell during 1997–99, from 159,669 to 136,963 (14.7% decline in three years).

On the latter figure's projection, generously extrapolated to a 15% decline in attendances every five years, then by 2040, the Diocesan Church will no longer exist in any significant way. Current national Methodist losses are running at 7% in three years but from a much lower base line.

Bleak as these wild facts are, some seek comfort from the persistence of widespread belief in God, with over 67% expressing faith in the existence of some kind of God. This important phenomenon of believing not belonging, although it clearly questions ideological assumptions by secularization theory of the disappearance of theism, may have insecure foundations if the supportive basis of strong churchgoing levels is removed. Is dramatically declining church membership now falling below a level which will threaten the survival of that common religion? 'How far can the present structures of religious life in this country maintain themselves if increasing numbers of people in British society prefer a passive rather than active relationship to these structures?'[75] Some 47% of the Dutch no longer believe in God and have no religion (an increase from 18% in 1960). Will belief in God follow the route of churchgoing, becoming a 'culturally isolated activity as well'?[76]

In rehearsing statistics of change for the British, and particularly the Anglican Church, remember similar patterns of decline affect all denominations, in varying degrees and chronologies. For example, the Roman Catholic Church did not begin the decline process until the 1970s, but now is set to catch up with everyone else. More importantly, they reflect a European-wide phenomenon. Dutch weekly Catholic mass attendance dropped from 64% in 1960 to 35% in 1974, with French attendance falling from 23% in 1968 to 17% in 1972. McLeod's story of the village of Limerzel, a typical French Catholic stronghold, is a remarkable account of unheard of decline even in the supposedly more religious-friendly rural context. In 1958, 92% of adults were regular practising Catholics. By 1985, it was 35%–40%.[77]

Now the cumulative effect of such focused religious change cannot be isolated from whole series of changes, affecting all areas of life in the global context, which Chapter 1 so vividly recounted. For example, collapsing time and space through information technologies, replacing flows between spaces by space of flows, challenges religious traditions which place high premiums on land, community and locally based associations. Demographic explosions, and the eruption of great cities and towns in the poor South, have seen the rise of religions like Christianity and Islam partly because of the attraction of maintaining identity that such warm communities offer to those displaced from settled rural communities into threatening urban vastness. So it was with Methodism in urban Britain in the nineteenth century. Yet will these same separated communities resist the later onslaughts of the more consumption-oriented choice-driven societies of the global economy? Will the Jihad succeed against McWorld in the long run?

As if that were not enough. Yet onto that pattern of global change needs to be bolted a series of other changes, strongly interacting with the first, but played out in the British context itself. Again, transformations since the 1960s confirm the seminal significance of the generation through which we are now living. Again, the changes affect every area of life. For example, take the economy with the transition from industrial society, dominated by mills, factories and mines and full-time male manual worker jobs for life, to post-industrial society of superstores, out-of-town shopping malls, and female part-time employment. It marks movement from a production to consumption-oriented economy and society, with extensive implications for previous understandings of work, community and class. Their forceful contribution to our understanding of identity is now being replaced by more plural identities and communities.

Or what about the transformation of personal and family life? From the 1960s, this journey too has been epoch-making, from dominance of marriage for ever, with superiority of husband over wife, and children born in marriage, to a plurality and greater equality of relationships, genders and ages, with a reduction of marriages, and increase of divorce, remarriage, cohabitation and single-parent families, with over 30% of children born outside marriage, and the rise of same sex relationships.

A similar order of change in terms of speed, extent and complexity has equally informed the cultural arena, with the replacement of grand narratives, seeking to explain everything, by a plurality of competing understandings none of which claims priority, all of which are now relative. Post-modernism, as the great symbol of contemporary cultural change, profoundly influencing and questioning our understanding of the absolute nature and claims of religion, has its parallel in the political arena with what I call Blatcherism. By this is meant the movement from the Butskellism of the post-war consensus, based on the convergence of the Conservative left of Rab Butler and Labour right of Hugh Gaitskell, and promoting strong intrusive national and local government, nationalization and welfare state, to a new consensus begun by Thatcher and continued by Blair, and centred on a much more market-oriented society of competing individuals, reflected in privatization, dismantling of local government, and marketizing education, health and welfare. Symbolic of that commodification of life is growing demand for measurement and league tables, affecting even religion as we shall see later.

With such global layers of change upon national layers, is it surprising that equivalent transformations have turned churches and Christianity in Britain upside down and inside out? It is certainly a matter of 'Society . . . changing rather than simply the religious sector within this.'[78] As one villager of Limerzel told the sociologist Yves Lambert, 'Everything is changing, so why not religion too?'[79] But that does not detract from the awesome power of the changes experienced by British Christianity and churches and their European partners.

Contributions of Secularization Theory to Understanding Religious Change

Although wider global and national changes cannot alone account for religious change, their influence becomes more obvious and identifiable when connected to the secularization theory of religious decline. For example, the theory's recognition of rationality in modernization processes as profound solvent of religious beliefs is an integral part of today's global economy and technology. This is in no way to accept the comprehensive claims of the secularization theory's proponents with their tendency to persist with the universal claims of a grand narrative, that their theory is the one key to open all doors. Complexity and plurality of contemporary change, including its multicausal nature and so much more, profoundly question such claims as we shall see.

The secularization thesis, however, has a certain plausibility, particularly as an explanation of the likely long-term corrosive influence of modernization processes on religious traditions in general, and on Western Christianity and churches in particular. Emerging in the 1950s and 1960s, as central to the discipline of the sociology of religion, it postulated 'the necessary connections between the onset of modernity and the demise of traditional forms of life'.[80] The rise of individualism and rationality, initially linked to Reformation, Renaissance, Enlightenment and Scientific Revolution, was seen as rendering the supernatural claims of Christian belief increasingly implausible. The 'over-arching sacred canopy',[81] which Christianity had provided for centuries as the principal framework for living for individuals and nations, would be systematically replaced by autonomous secular interpretations.

The thesis is therefore profoundly pessimistic over the nature and possibilities of religion in increasingly urban-industrial societies. It is firmly committed to the argument that 'the world was in the grip of an irreversible process of secularization', and therefore 'religion was in decline'. For Bryan Wilson, leading exponent of the theory,

> Secularisation relates to the diminution in the social significance of religion. Its application covers such things as: the sequestration by political powers of the property and facilities of religious agencies; the shift from religious to secular control of various of the erstwhile activities and functions of religion; the decline in the proportion of their time, energy and resources which men devote to super-empirical concerns; the decay of religious institutions; the supplanting, in matters of behaviour, of religious precepts by demands that accord with strictly technical criteria.[82]

Certain features of this explanatory framework of religious change have been of particular importance, not least because they resonated with other perspectives, including as expressed by contemporary commentators in the nineteenth and twentieth centuries. For example, the emergence of industrial towns and cities from the late eighteenth century, spearheaded by the great cottonopolis of Manchester, was quickly regarded as a formidable threat to traditional theories and practices, including Christianity. Their dynamic growth, explosive mixture of novelty, choice and temptation, and their paradoxical nature as centres of civilization and hell on earth, meant that they were quickly regarded as destructive of Christian values, life-styles and parochial organization. It became the other side of the coin of church and faith as more naturally at home in pre-industrial traditional rural societies. That view has been the basis of the romantic tradition's rejection of urban-industrial societies, epitomized by the poetic claim that 'God made the country and man made the town.'

That view of the city as obdurate obstacle to Christian faith and churches was only confirmed by the emergence of the working classes, central to the development of modern urban-industrial societies. For the industrial proletariats, and particularly the more unskilled, were regarded as especially unreceptive of the Christian message, and therefore noticeable by their absence from churches built in increasing numbers to house them in the later nineteenth century, and rarely full. It was Ted Wickham, founder of the Sheffield industrial mission in the 1940s, and author of the seminal study of Sheffield, *Church and People in an Industrial City* (1957), who brought these two features of class and city into the academy. His detailed studies drove him to conclude: 'From the emergence of the industrial towns in the eighteenth century, the working class, the labouring poor, the common people, as a class, substantively, as adults, have been outside the churches.' As a clergyman had declared in 1890, 'it is not that the Church of God has lost the great towns; it has never had them'.[83]

It is these understandings of city and class which fed into the emerging secularization theory's explanation of religious change and decline. It is a view of modernization processes as historically inevitable solvents of traditional religious beliefs and practices. For the great political philosopher Edmund Burke, the very beginning of these processes provoked the judgement that such 'a world constructed on commercial foundations was vulnerable to the demise of the "spirit of a gentleman and the spirit of religion" '. For Steve Bruce writing today, the sacred canopy now reflects

> competing conceptions of the supernatural world which have little to do with how we perform our social roles in what is now a largely anonymous and impersonal public domain and more to do with how we live our domestic lives. Religion may retain subjective plausibility, but it does so at the price of its objective taken-for-grantedness. Religion becomes privatised and is pushed to the margins and interstices of the social order.[84]

Whichever way you look at it, whether you start at the beginning or now, we are addressing the marginalization of Christianity from the contemporary world. If that is secularization thesis, so be it.

Critical Learning from Secularization Theory

Having encountered the complex multicausal nature of change in Chapter 1, it is not surprising that the claims of the secularization thesis to alone account for church decline in Britain have been challenged since the 1970s and thereby changed for the better. Essentially criticisms have highlighted the failure of the thesis to account for, on the one hand, the success of church growth throughout the intensive industrialization and urbanization of the nineteenth century, and on the other hand, the widespread persistence and mutation of religious beliefs in Britain today. It is these developments of more plural explanations of religious change which also suggest directions for the task of reconnecting church to emerging context in terms of individual and public life.

Building a highly religious nation

The strong religious patterns established in Europe following the French and industrial revolutions persisted until the 1960s. What has happened since then is equally remarkable for the significant dismantling of that dominant position of Christianity and churches. Yet the previous 160 years of modernization processes were quite the opposite and flatly contradict the assumptions by secularization thesis of inevitable religious decline in the face of such processes. In Britain, in the industrial and urban heartlands of West Yorkshire, by the late nineteenth century, about 40% of the population attended church and 75% of 5–20 year olds attended Sunday School, a great proportion of whom came from the working classes. Church membership peaked around 1900 at just under 20%. That major growth was certainly the story of the Manchester diocese. Bishop Fraser (1870–85) consecrated 105 new churches, and 117 new parishes or districts were formed. The experience of rapid expansion was repeated across the country. For example, in West Yorkshire, between 1831 and 1871, the Devonshire Street Congregational Church in Keighley typically grew fourfold, against the population growth of 2.5. Such optimism, in stark contrast to the pessimism of secularization theories, was closely linked to great evangelical revivals affecting all denominations. It generated a sacred progress measurable by growing memberships and attendances, but particularly by bricks and mortar. In 1801, Halifax had 7 churches or chapels, by 1900 it had 99. This astonishing growth of the urban church in the nineteenth century, embodied particularly in church plant (churches, Sunday Schools, halls, and schools), reflected a particular religious confidence and conviction, which is easy to decry today, when we have to find ways of demolishing or selling such buildings. But this is partly because we no longer have the confidence and conviction of nineteenth-century Christians. For the historian Green such expansion and building meant that 'they took the spiritual and moral socialisation of the people to be their especial, organisational task. . . . Becoming self-consciously inclusive churches, they went to inordinate lengths to find out precisely who in the community was not largely or regularly of their number. Then they undertook sustained and sacrificial efforts to make them so'.[85]

Such committed and connected churches became an intimate part of nineteenth-century society, no longer aloof from it, but the most socially accessible institution after pub and corner shop. With their panoply of organizations, with a majority of working-class members in cities, they became central to the social life of industrial towns and cities. They were the most accessible of voluntary organizations in urban society, not least because they were the most ambitious. Where secular societies traditionally limited their purposes to specific goals, sacred organizations interpreted salvation in the widest possible institutional framework – in terms of the mission of the church for God. The Northgate End Unitarian Church in 1890 in Halifax, besides a thriving worshipping congregation, had a large choir, a strangers committee, a poor fund, a Sunday School, a Band of Hope, a Penny Bank, Elocution Society, Guild of St Christopher, a Rambling Society, an Orchestral Society and a Mutual Improvement Society. Through the committed individual, embodied in a religious community, it pursued the goal of a Christianized people. And, to a significant degree, that is precisely what it achieved against all the arguments of secularization theorists. It was a remarkable achievement by the urban church, constructing 'a highly religious nation',[86] and providing a framework for national and individual identity, based on regular churchgoing, religious organizations, Christian piety informing personal and public behaviour, and with the strong support of women. And that persisted, with only a modest reduction, until the 1960s.

Reflecting on these achievements, four lessons emerge embodying strengths and limitations of that journey. They are of particular significance because they connect to subsequent major decline, thereby reflecting the complex nature of change, yet also suggest possibilities for facing up to change.

First, the ability to grasp change. In the later nineteenth century, the churches and their leaderships possessed confidence and optimism to Christianize society and individuals. That ambitious belief was embodied in organizations, buildings and social outreach. From around 1900, the mood of confident optimism began to change. By the 1920s, there was growing recognition that one of the great eras of ecclesiastical expansion was coming to an end: 'Sometime during the 1920s the local religious classes lost heart. They ceased to believe in their mission to evangelise the nation. Not, of course, in its necessity; only its practicality. It no longer seemed possible.'[87] At the same time, a perceptive commentator on the US context observed the passing *from* 'a pain or deficit economy', so intimately linked to the nineteenth-century evangelical age of atonement, with its view of life as a struggle for and to a salvation economy, *to* 'a pleasure or surplus economy'. As a result, 'religiously-sanctioned moral restrictions that had been appropriate to harsher times now seemed an unnecessary burden'.[88]

It is the correlation between such changing context and religious convictions and policies that develops into formative explanations of religious change. For in the remaining decades of the twentieth century, these contextual changes gathered momentum, with the emergence of a much more consumption-oriented society, full of pluralities and choice, reinforcing a pick-and-mix style of individualized living. These transformations were never grasped by churches, in ways their evangelical atonement theology had engaged with the voluntarism of the free market and its enterprise, and with the mutual self-help of friendly societies and associations. Even the seminal report, *Faith in the City* (1985), failed to address the depth of marginalization and social atomism occurring then and since. As Ward rightly observes in his *Cities of God*, the report's use of terms like community, locality, and fellow-citizens betrayed its belief in a social order into which it could tap yet which no longer existed:

> It never asked whether the social atomism of city-life had moved beyond being able to collaborate; it never asked who contributed and why, and who couldn't or wouldn't contribute; it never asked about the growing numbers who have already opted out – who have already opted for a virtual reality (in drugs, in drink, in interactive computer games, in play-station fantasies, in film, in televiewing).

In other words, the Church had failed to understand the emerging new context; it therefore inevitably lacked confidence to do anything about it; it was increasingly disconnected from public and private lives. 'The Church, albeit in a different way, is as marginal as so many of the poor it portrayed.' [89] To change that by learning from it is our agenda.

Second, there is a recurring theme through the nineteenth and twentieth centuries of the marginalization of churches from marginalized urban working classes, a double marginalization. That problematic is an important part of the secularization thesis, and its explanation of religious decline. We have seen how the story of church growth, and its strong links with urban working classes, is a significant modification of that thesis. Yet as McLeod has reminded us, more unskilled and poorer urban groups were traditionally much less likely to go to church. So in 1902–3, in London, 'Anglican congregations averaged 4% of total population in the poorest districts, but 22% in wealthy West End parishes.' In Bordeaux, in France, as late as the 1950s and 1960s, 3% of working-class adults were mass-goers as against 32% of professional classes.[90] Now this is not to argue that the marginalization of churches is predominantly explained by reference to class alone, yet it is to recognize that class is part of the total explanatory picture of religious decline, as Chapter 4 illustrates. The churches still facing most difficulties in Manchester today continue to be located very disproportionately in the most deprived communities. The research question which provoked the journey of this book, that there was something about the urban which contributes to the marginalization of the Church, is confirmed, but only as part of much more complex patterns of change.

Third, the changing nature of the urban is connected to the changing nature and importance of associationalism, and has profound implications for church life. Through the nineteenth century up to the Second World War, churches were organized increasingly around buildings, memberships and organizations. Women brought up in the 1920s refer time and time again to the dominant position churches played in their lives, with Sunday given to church attendance, and then church organizations two or three times a week. Membership and attendance at church and its multitude of associations became the badge of Christian belief and conviction. It was essentially total commitment to community and organization as propinquity. It confirmed Brueggemann's theological conviction that 'a sense of place' is 'a primary category of faith'. It is a connection recognized by Gill's latest research confirming churchgoing as a primary influence on the formation of Christian beliefs, practices and virtues. So if churchgoing and the link to church organizations like Sunday Schools decline, there is likely to be a decline in Christian beliefs and practices. It is this empirical evidence which questions the claims of secularization thesis chronology that modernization's erosion of beliefs leads to a crisis in churchgoing.

Yet it is precisely the changing context of modernization processes evolving through the twentieth century, and particularly in this generation, which revealed the profound limitations of that overdependence of churches on such spatial associational forms. Essentially they shared in a crisis of long established patterns of thought and institutions in a period of intense and continuing change. The strength of that spatial and membership associationalism, with the nineteenth and early twentieth-century churches 'the most socially accessible institution after the pub and corner shop', became that major weakness reflected in the demise of pub, corner shop and church by the end of the twentieth century. That trend is confirmed by the destruction of space and time by new technologies with the replacement of flows between spaces by the space of flows. When linked to the rise of privatized individualism and choice, such new patterns compel churches to find new ways of expressing belief and belonging no longer so dependent on traditional spatial associations. Yet they continue to predominantly promote old models of association, and pay a heavy price for so doing.

Fourth, religious change has always been influenced by endogenous factors, by changes within religious life itself, including the trend to more introverted church life, and conversely to church disengagement from urban society. Take the former, the move to more church-centred life. The churches' strength in the mid nineteenth century in the new threatening urban context was linked to their ability to reach individuals and attract them into the associational forms of churches. It was a sacrificial way of life for individuals in their associations. That strength of the urban church was linked to their soteriological doctrines, recruitment technologies, and church building programmes. Yet in the earlier twentieth century the attraction to individuals of associational forms began to fade. Why? One reason may well have been a growing change of emphasis in church life itself, to a more church-centred, self-absorbed programme and character. For one historian: 'as the conventional boundaries of the urban landscape moved outwards, both in Halifax and Keighley, so the associational priorities of local voluntary religious organizations turned inwards',[91] and have continued to do so to this day. The priority became liturgical orderliness, and developing Sunday Schools into narrow preparation for church membership rather than broader schools for coping with urban living and Christian citizenship.

The other side of the coin to more church-centred life was the trend of church disengagement with urban society. This is not about intentionally abandoning significant urban programmes. *Faith in the City* and the Church Urban Fund show that is not the case. Yet just as churches have never grasped the nature of contemporary change, so they never understood the primacy of the urban, that we are all urban now. So they pursue their seemingly virtuous agendas, supposedly fostering their domestic life, but with 'unforeseen consequences' which accentuate the growing gulf between urban society and people and such religious associational life. Take the Church of England. Its periodic bursts of necessary reform may have improved its organizational effectiveness and increased its self-governing capacity *vis-à-vis* the state, yet the unforeseen cost has been the separation of the Church from common life of people and society. For Hastings, 'There looks to be an almost inexorable law that every effective measure of Anglican pastoral reform also contributes to a narrowing in the Church's sphere of influence, as well as undermining just those institutions and observances which have hitherto provided some sort of bridge to the poorer classes.'[92] So making the Eucharist the only service in most churches (with Confirmation as the badge of dwindling admission), producing synodical government excluding the common people of the parish from participation, and moving to national and diocesan self-government, all represent a profound narrowing of the character of a supposedly national Church. It erodes the federal nature of Anglican ethos, and puts power in the hands of essentially unaccountable mediocre bureaucracies, narrowly elected elites, and at best good average managerialist episcopacy. So the classic current virtuous resort to shared ministry and training programmes spreads more jobs among fewer people, essentially in running the Church. It confirms the judgement that periodic attempts to reform the Church are linked to their failure to achieve much, particularly in terms of halting, never mind reversing, grave decline. It is as though the Church has never understood what has been happening to society, and therefore to itself. Maybe dramatic decline in this generation is the heavy price being exacted for that failure.

Recognizing mutating religion

The secularization explanation of religious change is rightly challenged by its failure to account for the astonishing success of churches confronted by the disruptive forces of early industrialization and urbanization in the nineteenth century. It was an achievement reminiscent of evangelical triumphs in urban Africa and Latin America today. Yet the secularization thesis is also held to account for failing to explain the persistence of religion in contemporary British and European contexts. Clearly the thesis does contribute to explanations of recent church decline. Yet it does not account for the widespread persistence of religious belief, including in new forms. Religion is declining as churchgoing, yet it is also persisting through mutation. Three areas of current religious experience illustrate this interpretation of religious change: common religion, New Age religion, and a plurality of faiths.

The remarkable survival of common religion (as private choice) and civil religion (as public function of religion in society) is well documented. For example, despite the collapse of churchgoing, 67% of British people still believe in God (down from 79% in the 1960s). Such high levels of belief and low levels of practice, as already noted, are described as the phenomenon of believing not belonging. As privatized religion, it is the most prevalent form of religiosity in Britain and Western Europe at the beginning of the new millennium. In a more consumption-oriented society, it reflects a pick-and-mix approach to religious belief, drifting further away from Christian orthodoxies. So although people still believe in God, there is evidence of increasing disconnection from such fundamental church credal beliefs as the virgin birth, resurrection, ascension and divinity of Christ. The strength of civil religion, reinforced by events commemorating the death of Princess 'Di' and national tragedies, supports the continuing public role of particularly the established Church to function vicariously on behalf of society as a whole. Yet that strength of common and civil religion is itself under threat from the decline of churchgoing below the threshold necessary to sustain it. Gill's argument that wider societal beliefs depend on regular church-going, and diminishing support for even belief in God among younger people, give strong support to such unease.

New Age religion is particularly associated with the rise of post-modern and post-industrial societies since the 1960s. It represents a complex of perspectives on belief and spiritual life, from astro-logy and horoscopes to reincarnation and alternative therapies. Linking these different activities are holistic commitments to the interrelationship of body, mind and spirit, supported by broad and diverse spiritualities, individually interpreted and appropri-ated. This is reinforced by willingness to draw on different religious traditions from East and West, and cutting and pasting by each individual to construct personal spiritual portfolios.

The trend to diversity and plurality is particularly reinforced by the arrival and growth in Europe of the other great faiths, par-ticularly Islam. There are now over six million Muslims in Western Europe, France having over 1,000 mosques. It confirms, with common and New Age religions, the emergence of post-Christian rather than non-Christian Europe. It substantiates the argument that 'dechristianisation is not entirely coextensive with secularization'.[93]

It is the significance of common and New Age religion which begins to suggest an emerging religious profile individually and privately created and expressed, even though likely to have some connection to and dependence on traditional churchgoing and beliefs: 'European individuals increasingly discover their own religious agendas independently of the institutional churches, while the latter continue to offer significant points of reference.'[94] It represents a shift from Christian nation to spiritually plural society, reflecting the individualism of post-modern and post-industrial society as consumption-oriented pick-and-mix religion. Yet these developments also indicate people discovering their own religious agendas, including spiritualities of more diverse kinds. They embody simpler, more human sides of living, belief that 'we are more than the sum of our shopping'.[95] It represents the mutation not decline of religion.

The secularization thesis as explanation of religious change in

Britain has therefore been rightly modified by recognizing the achievements of the churches in the nineteenth and early twentieth centuries, and the persistence today of more diverse spiritualities, religious beliefs and practices. It is the latter, alongside the existing survival of churches certainly in the short to medium term, which together begin to portray British and European religious experience as a type to be set alongside other experiences in the rest of the world. Just as there are varieties of capitalism in the global economy, so there are varieties of religious experience, each interacting with the others, with maybe one becoming more dominant at certain times and places. As the changes outlined in Chapter 1 proceed apace, as they will, the features of the British-European model are likely to exert more influence on African and Latin American models.

The constitution of a religious type incorporating relationships between declining churchgoing and mutating religion is interestingly reflected in the problem of how to measure such phenomena. Measuring what you value, whether education, healthcare or supermarket shopping, is increasingly symptomatic of the commodification of life in a global market economy. Yet the origins of that approach lie deep in modernization processes, including as applied to religious life. It was at the end of the eighteenth and in the early nineteenth centuries that churches in Britain became increasingly committed to measuring religious belief as expressed in churchgoing. Rising industrial cities and towns were seen as constituting particular threats to church life. So it was that Thomas Chalmers, theologian, Christian political economist and urban missioner, provided important connections between quantifying methods of early political economy and the need to calculate the effectiveness of church mission performances. In his *The Christian and Civic Economy of Large Towns* (1821–26), he develops an ecclesiastical economy to promote the social study of religion as a science, much as Adam Smith's political economy had done for commerce and demography. Rules were therefore drawn up by which religions could be defined like economies – what was it to be 'religiously rich' or 'religiously poor'? So emerges the whole system of church performance measurements relating to attendances and memberships which have played such a central part in the development of the secularization thesis and its explanation of religious change as decline.

Though essential for describing church effectiveness, such understandings and measuring of religious change also have significant limitations. Non-attendance at church does not equate with irreligion. The persistence and mutation of religious belief today illustrates that problem. Any adequate account of current religious life in Britain therefore has to incorporate the less tangible, and therefore less measurable yet equally real diverse nature of contemporary religiosity. Understanding, interpreting and measuring church decline now has to stand alongside such accounts. It is a tangible illustration, explored through religious life, of the complex nature of change in today's world and its implications for human living. And it will link to important debates, now to be explored, of how to understand and measure marginalization and our responses to it through reformulated Christian political economy.

PART 2

ON MARGINALIZATION: THE SECOND ESSAY

3

MARGINALIZATION

Why Some are Rich and More are Poor

James Wolfensohn, President of the World Bank, saw significance in the events of 11 September 2001 way beyond American concern with security: 'Many people . . . grew up in developed countries thinking . . . there was a wall round the developed world. They thought that poor people had no relevance to us. What happened on September 11th was that anybody who thought there was a wall now knows there is no wall.'[96] On that tragic day, 3,000 people died in New York and Washington, yet on every day, 40,000 children die, and one species is lost from this earth for ever. These wild facts are intimately connected to the growing gap between richest and poorest in our world. They reflect the disconnecting of whole nations and peoples from emerging global economy. They are recognition that 'The perils and promise of globalization make inequality a crucial consideration.'[97] They form the basis of marginalization processes, 'the greatest single problem and danger facing the world of the Third Millennium.'[98] It is that problematic which is the subject of this enquiry.

What gives added importance is that it continues a long historical tradition. It was the Revd Thomas Malthus, arguably the founder of Christian political economy, in correspondence with another great economist, Ricardo, in 1817, who proclaimed: 'the causes of the wealth and poverty of nations – the grand object of all enquiries in Political Economy'.[99] In this, he was developing the convictions of the founder of modern economics, the moral philosopher, Adam Smith and his *An Inquiry into the Nature and Causes of the Wealth of Nations* (1776). That moral concern to overcome poverty recurred as an important agenda for political economists in the later nineteenth century, including J. S. Mill and

Alfred Marshall. It is a reminder to locate our contemporary concern in wider historical contexts. Even more significant, the historic engagement of economists with the agenda of wealth and poverty may in itself be part of the explanation of why that problematic has persisted. The very programmes of modernization may themselves contain reasons why some continue to be rich and most are poor. It is the entirety of these processes, focused on the historic and contemporary divisions between rich and poor, which become a *metaphor* for wider marginalization processes in today's world, as the marginalization within and between nations, between peoples and their environment, and then the marginalization of Christianity from that.

Why an inquiry into what is clearly an historic problematic? To revisit such an agenda today is justified, indeed required, by the scale and extent of contemporary change. We have seen how its cumulative effects mark a decisive transformation of the contemporary context in this short generation. That applies equally to divisions between richest and poorest in our world. They have increased to an unprecedented degree since the 1960s, accelerating the closer we got to the year 2000. Was 11 September 2001 really a surprise? For whichever change we examine, whether global economy, technology, demography or environment, they contribute, among other consequences, to marginalization processes. They make them worse. But in addition, their characteristics inevitably inform any understanding of such problematics. Interpreting and engaging marginalization processes in that context means dealing with a complex, multilayered, multicausal phenomenon. The following definitions and explanations illustrate this profoundly.

The recurring centrality of this problematic to human and theological concern can be illustrated from my own story. My first book, *The Scandal of Poverty* (1983), emerged out of years of research and immersion in marginalized communities, from the Gorbals in Glasgow to Hulme in Manchester. This led to my consultancy involvement with the church enquiry into marginalization processes in Britain, embodied in the gulf between inner cities and suburbia, leading to the seminal report *Faith in the City* (1985). Out of these interests emerged the concern to explore the central economic character of that problem of poverty, necessarily moving into wider economic and political affairs. *Faith in the*

Nation (1988) and *Christianity and the Market* (1992) represented that stage of the journey. In my last book, *Public Theology for Changing Times* (2000), marginalization then re-emerged as a key part of the emerging British and global context. What this project addresses are these marginalization processes. Their intransigence, not least reflected in the way they have continued to dominate my own personal agenda, and the way they are connected to other dominant global issues, now lead me to regard them as one of the great problematics we now face on this planet. It is almost as though whichever issue I now address, I return to marginalization as one of the great keys to open so many doors. And it becomes a matter of central theological significance because of that foundational character and importance, an imperative conjoining with religious and Christian concern for the excluded in general and poor in particular. It reflects the Judaeo-Christian belief, in R. H. Tawney's words, that there is 'no touchstone, except the treatment of childhood, which reveals the true character of a social philosophy more clearly than the spirit in which it regards the misfortunes of those of its members who fall by the way'.[100] In these ways, it becomes one of the great invitations to pilgrimage. Indeed, it is now much more. It is, in words adapted from Emil Brunner's great book, *A New Divine Imperative*. Yet that religious challenge is now made in and to a world transformed from the Tawney–Temple era, although some, like Forrester in his important contribution in this field, *On Human Worth*, still cling onto their theological exclusivism. For before the 1960s, William Temple could still argue that Christianity had the answers. For him, 'apart from faith in God, there is really nothing to be said for the notion of equality'.[101] After forty years of relentless church decline and increasing marginalizing of Christianity, how we develop the theological contribution to such public problematics will be quite different. It will necessarily be a significant and integral part of an interdisciplinary project, implicitly part of the great conversation of human kind which marginalization processes so clearly now require. That is the new divine imperative, to be part of that great journey, as that great journey.

What is required in this essay, therefore, is significant movement of thought from my previous work. The increasingly changing context will demand that at least. Marginalization is not the same as it was then, or certainly twenty or forty years ago. There was no one more infuriating than Ronald Preston, whose life spanned most of the twentieth century, claiming that he'd heard it all before. So what is new in this essay is the use of seminal under-standings of the human, developed by United Nations Human Development Reports (UNHDR) and by the economist Amartya Sen, as foundational critiques of marginalization processes. Allied to that is the Swedish adaptation of the Rawls theory of justice to address marginalization in the context of a global market economy. In addition, growing recognition of the problem of modernization, even though an essential contributor to human development, is particularly illuminated by the contributions of feminist political philosophy and theology, particularly the justice theory of Iris Young.

Any contribution to such a problematic is inevitably greatly influenced by the perspective of voice location. Where you stand on wealth and poverty essentially determines your interpretation and response. The voices of the IMF, WB and WTO are not voices of the poor. What is equally clear is that any credible theology must take most serious account of the experiences and concerns of the poor. Beginning with the problematic of marginalization, with 1.3 billion men, women and children living on less than $1 a day, is my way of doing that. It is central to my reformulation of church, praxis and economics in the third essay (Part 3). Yet this essay also recognizes that such foundational experiences and insights necessarily have to interact with themes and understand-ings emerging from the first essay on change as interdisciplinary project (Part 1). I make no excuses whatsoever for that process of interaction of experience and critical theory. The marginalization problematic is too complex and important – truly a matter of life and death for people and environment – not to make full use of all these experiences and insights.

The essay itself forms three sections and an addendum. The first is a definitional interpretation of marginalization, with particular reference to ways of interpreting what it means to be human and just in a global context. The second is a statistical profile of marginalization, the wild facts, as it were. Finally, there is an exploration of the explanations of marginalization as through and beyond the paradox of Marx's view of modernization processes as inverse alchemy. Chapter 4 completes the essay with regard to the link between marginalization processes and churches.

Defining Marginalization: Human Well-being and Justice in Global Context

In our world, 1.3 out of 6 billion people are compelled to live on less than US$1 a day. That means, as the President of the World Bank has rightly acknowledged, that 'when you live on a dollar a day it's a question of life and death'.[102] For many, that is the story, as Forrester powerfully tells it, of the Indian Munuswamy,

> a beggar, a burnt-out leper, with a clawed hand and hardly any toes, [who] regularly begged on the footbridge over the railway outside the college . . . with his broken life, his physical frailty, his illiteracy, his poor self-image . . . Munuswamy lived in the tiny, circumscribed world of the railway bridge and his little mud hut, full of uncertainties about survival, dependent on the alms of others, his life a constant humiliation.

That seems to be an extreme case, but it is not. It is the tip of a very large iceberg of 'the normality of suffering' of over one billion human beings. Add the three billion with not enough to eat, and the 60 million who die of hunger and hunger-related diseases each year, and we begin to approach the scale of the contemporary problem of poverty.[103] For Amartya Sen, economist, moral philosopher and Nobel Prize Winner, it is

> a world with remarkable deprivation, destitution and oppression. There are many new problems as well as old ones, including persistence of poverty and unfulfilled elementary needs, occurrence of famines and widespread hunger, violation of elementary political freedoms as well as of basic liberties, extensive neglect of the interests and agency of women, and worsening threats to our environment and to the sustainability of our economic and social lives.[104]

With the UNHD Reports, Sen has been instrumental in ensuring the marginalization problematic becomes *people centred*, and so programmes to overcome it are centrally concerned with promoting the human well-being of all. What that means, in all its fullness, lies at the heart of this essay.

Although poverty remains the commonest reason for people's

exclusion from social flourishing, marginalization is a much more multilayered and multifaceted phenomenon. It affects different groups, including sexual, gender-based, racial and ethnic, even though relative deprivation is a recurring feature of them all. This essay focuses on marginalization particularly in terms of why some are rich and more are poor, while recognizing that no one single form can be assigned moral primacy, and many belong to more than one group. As Sen has acknowledged, that in turn will involve recognizing, with the UNHD Reports, that the majority of the poor are women, and they constitute a central part of any effective response to it. For this reason, conversations with feminist political philosophers, economists and theologians are essential.

Yet such marginalization is about more than poverty. It becomes an even greater problematic when located in that world of unprecedented wealth creation which the emergence of the global market economy since 1945 has revealed. That growing division between richest and poorest is most starkly illustrated by the fact that the assets of the world's three richest billionaires exceed the Gross National Product (GNP) of the 49 Least Developed Countries, with a combined population of 668 million people. The 225 wealthiest individuals have assets equivalent to a third of the world's population (two billion people). It is the divisions exemplified by such wild facts which complete this initial account of the marginalization problematic. They constitute processes of the exclusion of billions of people from proper participation in society and world, with the latter global dimension becoming of increasing significance.

Now it is that new global context which involves all of us in this problematic. From one perspective that has been argued consistently by those who see rich and poor as two sides of the same coin, bound inextricably together. So, in 1903 Caird, Master of Balliol College, Oxford, challenged three young students of extraordinary promise, R. H. Tawney, William Beveridge, and William Temple, to 'Go to the East End of London, and find out what poverty is, and why in Britain there is so much grinding poverty alongside great wealth, and work out what can be done about it.' Tawney's classic answer was to be found in advice given to the student of poverty 'to start much higher up the stream than the point he wishes to reach; but what thoughtful rich people call the problem of poverty, thoughtful poor people call with equal justice the problem of riches'.[105] Along with the complex tradition of connecting political economy and ethics, and Christianity's contribution to it, the language of the enquiries of the UNHD Reports and Sen then binds us even more into the marginalization problematic because of the overriding concern with that human flourishing in which all people, both rich and poor, have a stake.

Beginning with such an account of marginalization is of fundamental importance. It is unequivocal recognition that any such enquiry must start from an actual problematic clearly located in the contemporary context. It does not begin by considering a theory of justice, or of the human. It begins with people and their predicaments. It is about listening to 1.3 billion people on less than $1 a day. From that the sense of humanity, justice, emerges. For 'one speaks only inasmuch as one listens, that is, one speaks as a listener'.[106] The following reflections develop from such a basis, deeply influencing the final essay (Part 3), including the reformulation of praxis in Christian ethics. They therefore emerge from a hearing, from a recognition that 'The call to "be just" is always situated in concrete social and political practices that precede and exceed the philosopher.'[107]

Definitional explorations: problematic as people centred, relational and paradoxical

Why use the particular concept of marginalization to describe such realities? Why not remain with the concern for poverty in the midst of such wealth in the tradition of Adam Smith, Malthus and Caird? This has certainly stood the test of time, and is centrally part of the interpretations of contemporary divisions in this essay. Alternatively, why not work with the great historic concern for equality and against inequality? That course is adopted by two of the best contemporary works in this field, Hicks' *Inequality and Christian Ethics*, and Forrester's *On Human Worth: A Christian Vindication of Equality*. Both have influenced this essay. For example, I owe the moving story of Munuswamy (page 57) to Forrester, and the Inequality Adjusted Human Development Index in Chapter 6 to Hicks, and much more. Accepting these constructive contributions, I have nonetheless chosen the concept of marginalization processes because it more adequately and feasibly describes the complex nature of contemporary divisions and the hope of reducing them, including, but not only, poverty and wealth. It does so, too, in ways which connect with the traditional engagement with the latter. Yet, unlike the commitment to equality, it offers the possibility of more likely achievement in terms of the pursuit of a more inclusive society and world. Let me elaborate this definitional concern a little further.

Marginalization relates profoundly to the nature of the divisions consequent upon the presence of undue inequalities between poor and rich. It is thereby productive of separating the poor from the ability to participate reasonably in contemporary society. Its value is also enhanced as a concept by its ability to encompass the profoundly multilayered nature of that relative deprivation. Income and economics clearly and inevitably continue to be at the centre of the wealth–poverty debate. Yet there is growing recognition that such concepts as marginalization processes are more able to also embrace such critical areas of human living as health, education, gender and race in terms of excluding processes and conversely commitment to broad-based inclusivity.

Like inequality, the concept is essentially relational in character, connecting to the issue of maldistribution of resources, and its profound consequences for human living and the environment within our world. The emergence of the UN Development Programme in the 1990s, including its commitment to explore ways of measuring such global marginalization, confirms the importance of this global conceptual concern.

Clearly, any consideration of relative deprivation has to acknowledge the presence and significance of absolute poverty as one end of a spectrum of deprivation. As starvation, it is the ultimate marginalization because it threatens life itself. Throughout the twentieth and into the twenty-first century famines have occurred particularly in Africa, though not exclusively. The most horrific occurred in China from 1958–61 under chairman Mao, with the unnecessary deaths of 30 million people. Recent recurrences of this historic threat to life have revealed the contrived complex nature of such extreme marginalization. Studies of the Bengal (1943), Ethiopian (1972–74) and Sahal (1968–73) famines have questioned Malthus' premise, in his *An Essay on the Principle of Population* (1798), that starvation is caused by population growing beyond the resources required to sustain it. Current and projected demographic explosions, described in Chapter 1, still lend themselves to that diagnosis. Yet evidence accumulated by Sen and others points to the presence of substantial food reserves in such societies. The problem is rather that groups most vulnerable to the threat of famine lacked entitlement to grow or purchase available food. The problem focuses on 'a person's ability to command commodities in general and food in particular'.[108] It is that enforced lack of the fundamental capability to function as a human being which Sen later challengingly connects with the absence of democratically elected governments. Another, less extreme manifestation of such absolute poverty, again connected to demographic explosion, but now manifested in rapid urbanization, is found in 'cardboard and metal shelters that characterize nearly every city of the developing world'.[109]

Importantly, the profoundly relational character of marginalization as deprivation has also become a formative part of our understanding of poverty in advanced economies, confirming and substantiating increasing linkages between marginalization processes operating within and between developed and developing economies. So Townsend's magisterial enquiry into *Poverty in the UK* (1979) convincingly argues that

> Poverty can be defined objectively and applied consistently only in terms of the concept of relative deprivation . . . understood objectively rather than subjectively. Individuals, families and groups in the population can be said to be in poverty when they lack the resources to obtain the types of diet, participate in the activities and have the living conditions and amenities which are customary, or at least widely encouraged or approved, in the societies to which they belong.

He then continues his definition of relative poverty by connecting it rightly to marginalization processes by noting that the resources of the poor 'are so seriously below those commanded by the average individual or family that they are, in effect, excluded from ordinary living patterns and activities'.[110] Wedderburn's study of *Poverty, Inequality and Class Structure* (1974) confirms that definition in terms of 'where people possess less of some desired attribute, be it income, favourable conditions or power, than do others'.[111]

These foundational understandings of poverty as essentially

relational reality, and therefore leading directly into the concept of marginalization processes, reflect a long tradition. For example, they are centrally part of Adam Smith's original inquiry into wealth and poverty. So, 'By necessaries I understand not only the commodities which are indispensably necessary for the support of life, but what ever the custom of the country renders it indecent for creditable people, even the lowest order, to be without.' That interpretation is confirmed later by Marx's recognition of the historical and moral element in the concept of subsistence when he argues that 'nevertheless in a given country, at a given period, the average quantity of the means of subsistence necessary for the labourer is practically known'.[112]

Of course, some will question the use of marginalization to describe a problem so overarching by sheer quantity, extent and intractability. If half the world is hungry when does it cease to be usefully identified as a margin? Yet whether referring to 1.3 billion people living on below $1 a day, or to the poorest area in England, a large council estate, those realities are concerned with processes intrinsically part of nation and world. They are symptomatic of the whole character of society and world. 'If there are sinful structures of exclusion and social deprivation these are not limited to particular districts within cities but effect, perhaps I should say "infect" the city as a whole both as built space and human community.'[113]

That recognition of the relevance and accuracy of marginalization to describe and account for growing contemporary divisions between the poor and the rest is confirmed, critically elaborated and enriched by insights from Christian tradition. For Michael Taylor, marginalization should focus on more than justice. Christian teaching has much more to say than what are the right things to do. It is also profoundly concerned with the nature of things. 'It talks about what "is" the case as well as what "ought to be".' It is that recognition of indicative as against imperative mood, which allows him to interpret Christ's actions in terms of the actual processes of marginalization and inclusion. Christ's death 'had no particular merit in itself . . . It was his ministry that was required: to the weak and the powerful, to the insider and the outsider'. So for Beverley Harrison, 'Jesus was radical not in his lust for sacrifice but in his power of mutuality. Jesus' death on the cross . . . was no abstract exercise in moral virtue. His death was the price he paid for refusing to abandon the radical activity of love – of expressing solidarity and reciprocity with the excluded ones in his community.'[114] Now it is that understanding of the marginalized which reflects broader understandings of sin by gospel writers. For them, a sinner was one who stands on the margins, outcast from society, vulnerable because of lack of health, social standing or economic status: 'a sinner, in the Gospel texts, is one who has been rejected and marginalized, one who appears to be outside the protective care of God's covenant stead-fast love'. Yet in no way are they responsible for their plight. They are there because society has consigned them to the margins. And it is precisely to such sinners, such marginalized, that Christ is sent. He identifies with that marginalization, those who bear it, and therefore redeems them.[115] It is that ministry to those margins, to and by a church now on the edges, which is described in Chapters 4 and 5, that fulfils the prophet Micah's calling, which is 'to do justice, and to love kindness, and to walk humbly with your God'. (Micah 6.8)

That process of filling out the concept of marginalization, of developing its meaning to connect with the nature of contemporary secular and religious change, is further elaborated by acknow-ledging its resonances with economic theory. For economics and economies are at the centre of globalization and therefore marginalization. And, in mainstream neoclassical economics, the *margin* is 'the locus of economic choice', because it is the marginal or least important use value of goods or services that determine the exchange value. In other words what and how much is produced is what happens at the margins, that makes it more expensive, or cheaper. Following the law of diminishing marginal utility, people satisfy their most pressing needs first, so each addi-tional unit of income added is used to satisfy a less pressing want. As we observed with the global market economy, at its heart is this market mechanism, the most effective wealth-creating construct. There is no going back from that, as the radicals Cobb and Daly have recognized: 'We have no hesitation in opting for the market as the basic institution of resource allocation.'[116] But like them, we also recognize the deeply paradoxical nature of such economics. For, according to economists following that law of marginal utili-ty, we cannot say food for the hungry generates more utility than a second car for a richer family. There is the global connection between marginalization and economics as margins and as exclusion. In that concept of marginalization are therefore embedded too many insights from too many experiences and disciplines not to satisfy its continued use as working tool. The following reflections continue that task.

Defining the human as capability for flourishing, rights and justice: towards an international ethic for engaging marginalization.

The early stages of this enquiry into marginalization have begun to raise questions concerning what kind of people and societies need to be promoted in order to overcome its damaging consequences. For marginalization is essentially about the exclusion of people from the ability to lead fulfilled lives in terms of adequate health, education and income, and from participation in the life of community and society, including its governance. Now it is that concern for a more inclusive society and world as the normative vision which connects us to major contemporary debates in philosophy, economics, politics and theology, about what is required for greater human and social well-being. It addresses what Elizabeth Anderson refers to as those characteristics or attributes, the absence of which reflects people's marginalization, and which are therefore, in turn needed for their inclusion in society.[117] For example, for utilitarianism (a philosophy so central to modern economics), these inclusive characteristics refer to the pleasure or happiness of each person, the sum total of which constitutes a good society. It therefore focuses on each person's utility. So a marginalized unjust society is one with an aggregate loss of utilities, a society in which people are less happy than they need to be. It therefore focuses on each person; it is not interpersonal; it is indifferent to distributional concerns or human rights, seeing only the aggregate of individual utilities.

Another major philosophical school, Nozick and the libertarians (linked to the neoliberal global free market advocates), promotes the priority of individual rights, including private property. The entitlements we have are exercised through these rights which are judged not by their consequences, leading to an inclusive society, but in relation to their intrinsic value; therefore you can starve because your entitlements yield insufficient food. It is about procedural rules irrespective of consequences.

Neither utilitarianism nor libertarianism therefore address marginalization or the social well-being of all. It is at this point that a more adequate response is developed by John Rawls. He focuses on primary goods as a broader view of the resources *all* people need to achieve their self-chosen purposes. These goods include 'rights, liberties and opportunities, income and wealth, and the social bases of self-respect'.[118] Yet although distributionally just, because Rawls clearly addresses the need to ensure no one falls below the minimum level of goods required for supporting human well-being, his work contains a fundamental flaw.

How that is addressed leads us into the work of UNHD Reports and Sen. For they rightly argue that individual capabilities to exploit such goods can vary so much as to generate profoundly unequal outcomes. The freedom of poor people from famine and undernourishment depends on the availability of Rawls' primary goods as income to purchase food. Yet it *also* depends on people's metabolic rates, gender, pregnancy, climate and exposure to parasitic diseases. Thus, *to address marginalization effectively is about more than fair distribution of resources.* We have also to address the 'relevant personal characteristics that govern the conversion of primary goods into the person's ability to promote her ends'.[119] The disabled may therefore need more resources to achieve their self-chosen purposes.

Attention is consequently focused, in the tradition of Mahbub un Haq and the UNDP from 1990, on the *freedom* generated by commodities rather than on the commodities themselves. Marginalization, as poverty, therefore becomes for Sen

the deprivation of human freedom: among the factors that can make us substantively less free there are a number of considerations including lowness of income, lack of basic education, lack of arrangements for healthcare, on the one side; but also on the other an adverse environment, a depleted natural resource base, foul air to breathe, or polluted rivers to get your water from. So each comes into the notion of poverty in a big way.[120]

It is that breadth of understanding of poverty, from primary goods to environment, which I will now pursue. For we are beginning to see what the beggar Munuswamy has been deprived of as a human being. For the pursuit of human fulfilment, of individual and social well-being, is intimately about having the *freedom, and therefore the capability, to be and to do, to pursue one's self-chosen purposes*. It is that understanding of the capability to function which is now central to the understanding and promotion of the human in our context. It means that 'an individual's advantage, according to the capability approach, is not judged by his/her subjective individual happiness, nor by the set of external resources at his/her command, but what those resources would allow the person to be or to do'.[121] That is certainly about achieving the functionings necessary for such a pursuit already identified, and including primary goods. But it is equally about recognizing the capabilities of people to pursue their well-being. Fortunately, since capabilities and functionings are intimately connected this allows for their measurement, including as inequalities the extent to which they are not achieved. How do you evaluate the freedom or capability to achieve such functionings other than by linking them to actual achievements? For the 1997 UNHDR, it became a matter of identifying not what you don't have, but what you can't or can do. Translated into its Human Development Index (to be elaborated in the third essay (Part 3)), it uses three measurements to identify such inter-national deprivation in essential capabilities, of a healthy life, knowledge measured by literacy, and economic provisioning. That breadth of functionings is a reminder of the multifaceted nature of poverty, even though economic resources remain fundamental to overcoming it: 'It so happens that the enhancement of human capabilities also tends to go with an expansion of productivities and earning power.'[122]

The international value of this broad-measurement accessible interpretation of the human is that it is able to speak across divisions between North and South, and advanced and developing economies, through the global processes of marginalization. Since that human freedom to be and to do is related to the in-equality of functioning rather than achievement, the size of income alone does not determine that capacity. So black men in Harlem, New York, have less chance of reaching forty years old than Bangladeshi men not because of income but because of poor healthcare and higher urban crime. In other words, the extent of capability deprivation 'can be quite remarkably high in the world's most affluent countries'.[123]

The importance of that difference in capability to function as a human being is therefore confirmed for understanding marginalization as definition and measurement in the global context. For we have seen how equality of primary goods, including incomes may not lead to equality of well-being because of personal variations in our ability to convert such resources into the freedoms of well-being. That criteria, as we have begun to see, applies within as well as between nations, and significantly equally within advanced economies. For example, in Britain,

> many of those who are poor in terms of income and other primary goods also have characteristics – age, disability, disease-proneness, etc – that make it more difficult for them to *convert* primary goods into basic capabilities, for example, being able to move about, to lead a healthy life, to take part in the life of the community. Neither primary goods, nor resources more broadly defined, can represent the capability a person actually enjoys.[124]

Yet this recognition of the profound individual differences of the human does not detract from the equal importance that marginalization also represents 'a set of predicaments common to all humans'.[125] That commonality is reflected in the agreed bundle of basic functionings used by the UNHDR in relation to education, health and income as foundational for the effective pursuit of human fulfilment in the contemporary global context.

This critical and creative interaction between difference and commonality in interpreting human fulfilment through capability functioning is confirmed and further developed by the concept of basic human needs. This highlights the threshold below which people's capabilities are so impoverished that they cease to function in any significant way as human beings. Emerging in 1976 through the work of the International Labour Organization, it became an important part of the development debate. Its elaboration avoids, on the one hand, the universalism and foundationalism of a common human essence, and on the other hand, the MacIntyre post-modernism of rival and incommensurable moral premises. Instead, like the UNHDR, it has acknowledged a shared recognition of the importance of basic needs for human flourishing, faced with common threats, epitomized, for example, by starvation and undernourishment. But it then moves to embrace particular fundamental needs in healthcare, education and economic resources, individually expressed within each context.

As this interpretation of human fulfilment begins to emerge, it is expressed in the empirical realities of income, health and education, but is also grounded in moral discourse. For example, the work of the UNHD Reports, and of political philosophy across a wide spectrum of understandings, from Nozick to Rawls, all recognize the importance of equality for interpreting basic freedoms required for human flourishing. The historic and contemporary breadth of this egalitarian understanding of what it means to be human, and what is therefore required to promote it, draws from a variety of sources from classical Greek and Asian philosophies, through the Enlightenment, including French and American revolutions, to current UN and regional Declarations of Human Rights and other associated protocols. Many of these statements were and are deeply influenced by the Judaeo-Christian tradition, with its recognition that God gives life to all people so that they may have it more abundantly. It is that dignity of each individual person, including therefore a shared humanity, which flows into a whole series of obligations and rights. In remarkable words ascribed to Job in the Old Testament, and so shared by the three great monotheistic faiths, Islam, Judaism and Christianity, 'If I have infringed the rights of slave or slave girl . . . what shall I say when he holds assize? Did he not create them in the womb like me?' (Job 31.13–15) It is such insights which lead to the foundational view that 'each human being is valuable in a unique way and worthy of respect irrespective of her personal characteristics or qualities, and that this value is equal for human beings'.[126]

It is a creative and essential exercise to bring into conversation these great religious insights with the work on human fulfilment as equal capabilities sensitive to individual needs. For example, it will encourage Christian anthropology to recognize the human as unique individuality as well as shared humanity, the profundity of difference in and through inclusivity. For Elizabeth Anderson, such sources begin to suggest and require 'a normative vision that can be linked to and employed by contemporary egalitarian movements on behalf of people excluded'[127] from effective participation in global societies.

Running through these developments one is increasingly aware of the importance of *process*, confirming earlier reflections on global and particularly religious change. The latter indicated movement beyond restrictive interpretation of belief as church-going to wider manifestations of the human spirit in continuing search for fulfilment. It is that understanding of dynamic process which is reflected so powerfully in interpreting the human as freedom to pursue fulfilment, as capability to function, rather than simply achievements. What is also important is that such under-standings can be accompanied by new ways of measuring. Human pursuit of flourishing, like the religious, cannot be confined to the economics of material achievements. That continues indispens-able for both, yet now connected to other, more process informed understandings. Significantly, this then links to emerging environ-mental debates with their critique of the unduly restrictive concepts and practices of mainstream economics. These develop-ments creatively interact with theological developments, engag-ing with dialogic interpretations of God, Christ and Church. Engaging with the Other, including as different, while holding on to commitment to the inclusive whole, leads to more dynamic and process informed theology. It stands in sharp contrast to fixing truth into some rigidly abstract conceptual framework 'to the exclusion of that free play of ever-shifting meanings and associa-tions by which a tradition properly unfolds'.[128]

It is that same breadth which also requires that understanding of the human as personal and social fulfilment to be supported and complemented by social arrangements reflecting equivalent eco-nomic and political concerns. For equal capabilities to function as human beings centrally includes opportunity to express self-cho-sen choices as political decision-making, through democratic gov-ernance, and in registering economic choices through market mechanisms. So for Iris Young, freedom of *self-determination* in eco-nomic and political arrangements creatively complements Sens' equality of capability for *self-development*: 'Just social institutions provide conditions for all persons to learn and use satisfying and expansive skills in socially recognized settings, and enable them to play and communicate with others or express their feelings and per-spectives on social life in contexts where others can listen.'[129] So promoting the human through individual and social fulfilment becomes the basis of the attack on marginalization processes.

Such developments connect with renewed and growing recog-nition of human rights and international and national affairs, and, as important, with the human development debate. The latest work of the UNHD Reports, including formative contributions by Sen, acknowledges this critical connection.

The emerging field of human rights has involved recognition of two traditions, the communist bloc's promotion of economic and social rights, and the West's advocacy of civil and political rights. With the collapse of communism in 1989, the two have been creatively brought together in one tradition, thereby allowing, and indeed requiring, constructive interaction between human rights and human development discourses. This, in turn, is acknowledged in the understanding of human development as freedom and capability to pursue self-chosen purposes, linking, as they do, functionings in economic and social fields but also in participatory social arrangements. The linkage between political and social rights is also confirmed by discourses on the nature of human rights. They involve understandings of rights as foundational freedom from interference by others, but also therefore as claims on others to provide support for people to defend substantive freedoms to be and to do. For individual rights to flourish requires supportive social arrangements, just as they require informed individual participation for their flourishing and to prevent authoritarianism.

We are also aware how interdependent humans rights and development are in a global economy. Educating women both affects their contribution to economic life and household dynamics. In India, it has been linked to declining domestic violence against women by two thirds. Expanding capabilities and securing human rights are therefore essential for empowering poor people to reduce marginalization. Civil, political, economic, social and cultural rights are all causally linked and thus can be mutually reinforcing. They generate a *synergy* indispensable for the poor to secure rights and capabilities. So human rights have intrinsic but also instrumental value, linking freedom of participation to freedom from discrimination and poverty. Building capacities in one generation becomes the means for securing economic and social rights in the next. When extended to environmental concerns it points to the feasibility as well as necessity of intergenerational endeavours which these concerns so patently require.

The burgeoning of human rights directives, from foundational 1948 UN Declaration of Human Rights, and regional conventions, including Arab (1983) and African (1988), to recent developments of international tribunals against national abuses of human rights (1993), reflects another emerging component in the requirement for global discourses, traditions, ethics and laws. Globalization trends and problematics make that now both necessary and indispensable for human fulfilment. Human rights developments therefore reflect determination to recognize matters of common concern and collective goals, while acknowledging the importance of diversity of cultures. So the Convention on the Elimination of All Forms of Discrimination Against Women (CEDAW 1979) accepts diversity of gender and wider cultural traditions, but not as discrimination against women. Like Ruether arguing for feminist ethics, we need 'to go beyond particularities on the ground that women's human rights cannot be abandoned because of the post-modern critique of universalism'.[130] Given the centrality of women to marginalization as victims and solutions, this convention is particularly significant.

The supportive role of traditions in human rights' debates is confirmed by the formative contribution of moral discourse, as in the parallel debate on human fulfilment. Human rights essentially express our intrinsic entitlements, including through our claim on others: 'a person's dignity is the source of other persons' duties towards her'.[131] They recognize that certain things ought not be done to people because of the claim of human dignity. Again, as with basic human needs, they are not now based on universalist essentialist views of the human, but on common experiences, which therefore become context-transcending. They therefore provide an important basis for emerging international ethical discourse.

It is into that ethical debate that Christian tradition inserts both historical influence and continuing potential force for good. Emphasizing human life as inviolable, because God-given, it again powerfully informs this discourse, as with human development.

Any consideration of marginalization, and its implications for understanding the human, inevitably therefore has a most powerful normative dimension. An integral part of that dimension is commitment to justice. The methodology used in this essay has required us to begin with the marginalization problematic, located in, and indeed forcefully required by, damaging contemporary contextual change. Like Lebacqz, we therefore accept that 'in order to understand the meaning of justice we need to listen to the experiences of those who are suffering injustice'.[132] Engaging with such injustice is therefore, as with the dynamic development of the human as freedom or capability to pursue fulfilment, a recognition that justice is not an achieved state of affairs. It is rather a 'continuous effort to overcome injustice. Justice is an ongoing *process* to diminish injustice and establish something more just.'[133]

On that basis, building up an understanding of marginalization, and what it does to and for the human, including its responses, does rightly involve conversations with contemporary justice theorists. This essay has therefore explored human capabilities in critical dialogue with utilitarians, libertarians and liberals. References to basic human needs and human rights have drawn heavily on justice theories of feminist political philosophers and theologians, from Iris Young to Karen Lebacqz, and Ann-Cathrin Jarl.

Against that backcloth I have chosen to focus on one strand in justice theory. Given the injustices of the present global economy, what could it mean to develop an understanding of justice which is global in reach yet sensitive to differences, and which also gives high priority to addressing the marginalization problematic? Already, hints have been made in this essay relating to the challenge and possibilities of global ethical discourse. Yet these are quite insufficient, given the dimensions of the challenge. So I propose to develop them in a more substantive direction with reference to John Rawls, as amended by Professor Göran Collste of the University of Linköping.[134]

In *The Law of Peoples* (1999), Rawls applies his *A Theory of Justice* to international relations. The resulting global principles include non-intervention, basic liberties and human rights. Yet he omits his famous and highly relevant *Difference Principle*, that inequalities are only acceptable if in favour of the least advantaged. Given globalization processes and their intimate relationship with marginalization, this odd decision needs to be justified. So he recognizes the growing dimensions of the poor South, demographically, challenging the liberal traditions of the North. We can therefore no longer assume that liberal views of human nature and distributive justice, central to the arguments of this essay, are thus applicable to nations of the South and their peoples.

Yet, as Collste indicates, to argue that Rawls' view of human nature is Western, and therefore not universally acceptable, is highly questionable. For non-Western philosophies and religions have generated insights which resonate with Western. So, as Gewirth notes, 'Although some other cultures stress the communal nature of life more than the Western, it is not clear why this is incommensurable with a view of human beings as moral persons having equal worth. Indeed, this view can be found in many other cultures than the Western.'

Similarly, the commitment to distributive justice is highly relevant to the poor South, because its predicament is partly explained by Western colonialism and imperialism, and by lack of resources and presence of traditions or customs that the living destitute have not chosen. Thus, as Collste argues,

> are not the arguments in favour of the Difference Principle applicable also to other nations than liberal ones? If he thinks not, Rawls seems to embrace a form of moral relativism. The fact that an unequal distribution of welfare in the poorer countries implies far more suffering than an unequal distribution in the richer countries, provides a further argument for including the Difference Principle in a Law of Peoples.

Justice therefore requires that *global inequalities* are only *justifiable if they benefit the poorest.*

It is that significant reformulation of the greatest justice theory of the twentieth century that is highly relevant to the search for ways of engaging global changes and problematics, including marginalization, in the twenty-first century. It illustrates potential resources in justice theories for being integral parts of that task.

Wild Facts of Marginalization: A Statistical Profile

Divisions between and within nations have been recurring features of human history. The emergence of the first towns and cities in the Middle East, India and China, over 2,000 years before the birth of Christ, was quickly associated with spatial segregations between rich and poor. Denunciations by Old Testament prophets witness to both divisions and their connection to the subjugation by powerful of powerless. To those divisions must be added the oppressive invasions and conquests by nations of nations, and by religions, including Judaism, Christianity and Islam.

Modernization processes, as unparalleled accelerations of industrialization and urbanization, added new dimensions to these historic trends. Demographic and wealth-creating explosions from the late eighteenth century were precisely that, explosions of energy cascading across the world with profoundly positive and negative consequences. Their increasing frequency, intensity and interactions created such remarkable synergies as to thrust contextual change into a whole new ball game. What has happened to the world since the 1960s is an astonishing intensification of that scenario. It is in that context that contemporary marginalization processes must be considered. As with every other area of change, it is the wild facts which tell the story most vividly.

Take marginalization processes between nations. Contemporary trends in this historic generation from the 1960s to the present are increasingly alarming. The gap between richest and poorest 20% of the world's peoples grew from a ratio of 30:1 in 1960 to 60:1 in 1990, and then astonishingly, in only five years, to 74:1. What makes these changes more disturbing is that they were accompanied by dramatic increases in wealth-creating of 90% during 1970–89 (as Gross World Product). For the UNHD Reports, main source of these statistics, the 'degree of global inequality is at least as severe as the worst national inequalities' (1999). Those global inequalities are most powerfully epitomized by the wildest of wild facts, that the net worth of the 358 richest individuals in the world equalled the combined income of the poorest 2.3 billion people, 45% of the world population.

It is when these divisions are translated into what it means for children, men and women that they become the most focused challenge to justice. The scandal of this poverty is that the UNHDP estimates to provide the basic human needs of the marginalized requires $40 billion per annum. Combined yearly military spending was $800 billion during 1985–94.

For the Boffs, at the heart of the struggles of liberation theology for the poor against such injustice, this translates into 500 million people starving, 1.6 billion with life expectancy of less than 60 years, 1 billion living in absolute poverty, 1.5 billion with no access to the most basic medical care, 814 million who are illiterate, and 2

billion with no regular dependable water supply.[135] But let me
bring it down to children, the most vulnerable and innocent of the
victims of such change. Of children born live, *13* out of every *1,000*
die in their first year in industrialized countries, against *110* in the
Least Developed Countries (LDCs). Children under five who are
seriously underweight, are 4% of the industrialized world, and
43% of LDCs.

Most importantly and disturbingly, accelerating global marginalization is but the continuation of much longer-term trends
intrinsically part of modern urban-industrialization processes
themselves. For example, differences of production and wealth
between major pre-industrial regions of the eighteenth century
were, by today's standards, remarkably small, indeed, modestly
in favour of what later became known as the Third World, say a
ratio of 1:1.8. In the nineteenth century, the gap between Western
countries and the rest widened, at first slowly, and then with
increasing rapidity. By 1880, per capita income in the developed
world was double that of the Third World, by 1913 treble, and by
1950 fivefold. British and Indian populations had similar per
capita levels of industrialization in 1750. By 1900, India's was
one hundredth of Britain's, 'the lot of those who increase their
numbers without passing through an industrial revolution'.[136] But
it also depends on whether you are allowed to.

Against these disturbing trends, it must be firmly recognized
and applauded that the 1960s onwards witnessed general
improvements globally in certain key areas. Advances in education and health in the developing world have therefore narrowed
the gap with industrialized countries. Between 1970 and 2000, in
developing economies, life expectancy improved from 55 to 65
years (1998), adult literacy from 48% to 77% (1998), infant mortality from 110 per 1,000 live births to 64 (1998), and the primary-
secondary enrolment ratio from 50% to 72%. There were also
important income poverty reductions in some countries, particularly China, moving from 33% of the population in 1978 to 7%
in 1994. India's fell from 54% (1974) to 39% (1994).

Disturbingly, Sub Saharan Africa experienced no improvement
from the lowest base in the world. Twenty-two out of 25 of the
poorest nations are in Africa, and particularly in Sub Saharan
Africa. Some 54% of the population live below the UNDP poverty
line; its population is exploding at 2% per annum (doubling every

22 years), and is not offset by equivalent, or greater if poverty is to be reduced, increases in GNP per capita. It is the only region where poverty is projected to *increase* in the coming decade. Clocks go backward as well as forward in our world. The movement to global integration is not simply about progress at all.

The UNHD Reports have developed the Human Development Index to measure progress in relation to wider interpretations of human capabilities elaborated earlier in this essay. Using indices relating to income, education and health, its 2000 Report is particularly illuminating for the light it throws on inequalities between nations and regions, and some of the likely explanations. Since this measurement system will be developed further in Chapter 6, a brief summary of some of its findings elaborates emerging wild facts in more appropriate detail and related to a broader and more adequate view of human fulfilment.

First, it confirms the wide disparities in human development achievement globally:

- The bottom 22 nations are all in Africa, and particularly Sub Saharan Africa (Sierra Leone, Niger and Burkina Faso are at the bottom of the league table, the USA, Norway and Canada at the top). Canada's HDI value of 0.935 (out of 1.0) is four times Sierra Leone's of 0.252. In other words, Canada has to make up a shortfall of 7% in human development (HD), Sierra Leone 75%.
- Disparity between regions is also significant. Sub Saharan Africa has twice the distance to cover to achieve full human development as Latin America.
- The connection between economic prosperity and HD is neither automatic nor obvious. Countries with the same incomes have very different HDI values. Vietnam and Guinea have similar incomes, yet Vietnam's HDI is 0.67, Guinea's 0.4.
- Countries with similar HDI in 1975 end up with very different values in 1998, and vice versa. South Korea and Jamaica each had 0.68 in 1975; in 1998 Jamaica was 0.74, Korea 0.85. In other words, and most importantly, the *policies pursued by countries, with regard to health, education and income, are major determinants of marginalization and human development.*

With regard to marginalization processes within nations, the story is, as between nations, one of profound inequalities. Equally, it is also a changing picture. In Asia, between 1960 and 1990, inequalities decreased in Hong Kong, India, Malaysia, Singapore and Taiwan, yet worsened in Bangladesh and Thailand. In Latin America, Columbia and Cost Rica they improved, whereas in Argentina, Brazil and Peru they worsened. In wealthy OECD nations, the lowest inequalities were in Scandinavia, the Benelux countries, and what was West Germany. The USA, Ireland and Switzerland had the highest inequalities. There has been some increase in inequalities in Sweden, Japan, Germany and Belgium, with the most serious in the USA and Britain. It is the latter nations which control social disturbances associated with profound inequalities by increasing committals to penal institutions. If the global economy follows the neoliberal route advocated by many Americans, these disturbing consequences are likely to become more widespread.

As with global marginalization processes, within nations inegalitarian trends vary between income, health and educational functions, and between genders and races. For example, in the USA, trends in education and health have been more encouraging than trends in income, even though inequalities in education and health remain significant, unlike in Scandinavia. So, black men in Harlem were less likely to reach the age of 65 than men in Sri Lanka. Health for Hispanics was even worse. Women's health and education were better, but remained worse with regard to earnings. It is this complexity of marginalization processes, as they impact selectively on groups, which is revealed by this complex character of deprivation. For people often experience 'two or more forms of marginalization – such as racial and gender-based injustice – and the results are thus "multiplicative" in nature'.[137] What has emerged, therefore, is the profound connection between, say, health and inequality. That is certainly confirmed by British experience. A recent survey of 700 electoral wards in the North of England revealed death rates four times as high in the poorest 10% as in the richest 10%. If infant mortality rates of babies born in the 'best health' constituencies were applied nationally, 7,500 infants would not have died in the period 1991–95. The conclusion is stark: 'In the developed world it is not the richest countries that have the best health, but the most egalitarian.' [138]

The emergence of an underclass in developed economies, however contested a concept, particularly symbolizes the new global turbulences of marginalization processes in this generation. For these underclasses are 'not just pockets of deprivation within national societies, they are faultlines along which the Third World rubs up against the first'.[139] Britain's underclass therefore reflects the profoundly changing character of the post-1960s, with the collapse of male manual worker jobs and full employment, fragmentation of the old working class, rise of means tested welfare benefits and their erosion of habits of working, saving and honesty, and the resultant alarming growth of workless households from 6.5% (1975) to 19.1% (1994). The underclass therefore represents marginalization from effective participation in mainstream economic, social and political life and concentration into 'settlements of the marginal, the socially problematic and the welfare-dependent,' what Galbraith has called 'centres of terror and despair' in the great industrial cities of America and Britain, 'Hobbesian jungles' where 'wild, adolescent males, now increasingly armed' cause 'universal fear'.[140] For Bauman, they become the poor's response to the global borderless world as 'self-defence-through-aggression'. Yet at exactly the same time, and as part of the same processes, the trend is also to the growth of walled, gated proprietary ghettos of the wealthy, to 'the fortification of localities',[141] now housing 10% of the US population. Their inhabitants are part of the growing number of wealthy who 'Rather than pay taxes to fund decent public schools and adequate social welfare programmes . . . instead pay exorbitant fees for private schooling, security forces, alarm systems and firearms to ensure that the social decay of poverty and inequality does not spill over into and disrupt their country club lives.'[142] It is these ghettos of underclass and wealthy which represent the de-valorization and valorization of globalization processes as they impact on urban life through the segregational consequences of marginalization.[143] It is not surprising that such divided societies should be associated with poverty and inequality, and that this should be reflected in such indices of social dislocation as growing imprisonment and crime. In this, Britain is now following the path of the USA with its 'increasingly repressive state counteracting the effects of violence which results from the increasingly precarious position of the large mass of the population, notably the black'.[144]

Explaining Marginalization: Problem of Inverse Alchemy

Why so much poverty in the midst of such wealth was the age-old question Tawney, Temple and Beveridge sought to answer in the East End of London in 1903. Theirs was but another stage in that journey which began in modern times in the eighteenth century. Then the connection between wealth and poverty was described by Dr Johnson as a 'secret concatenation' which 'links together the just and the mean' for their mutual benefit. The growing size of the domestic market, associated with the division of labour, meant that the rich with much of the population were increasingly dependent on the contributions of many others for their life style. Luxury was therefore seen ultimately to produce much good, or in the words of Mandeville's classic defence of these developments and arguments, the *Fable of the Bees: Private Vices, Public Benefits* (1723). This interpretation was amended by Christian political economists in the early nineteenth century, with their suggestion that poverty and inequality were an inevitable outcome of scarcity, used by a benevolent God to bring the best out of his creation by providing incentives for improvement. These benign explanations are still present today in the theory of the trickle down of wealth for the benefit of the poor, and in the carrot and stick approach to the deprived. Yet then, as now, they were strongly criticized. For Rousseau, this deeply English paradox had to be rejected because, in a zero sum understanding of life, the rich could only become rich at the expense of the poor. More importantly, by 1820, the crude optimism of Johnson and pessimism of Rousseau were replaced by a growing recognition of the complex paradoxical nature of the problematic, whether 'the emerging manufacturing system (was) the solution or merely an expression of a deeper problem'.[145] It is this more nuanced approach reflecting earlier polarized interpretations, but going significantly beyond them in terms of engaging the complex multilayered nature of wealth creation and marginalization, that is developed in the rest of this section.

Given these early informative explanations of wealth and poverty, elaborated with increasing sophistication by the end of the twentieth century, we could be forgiven for assuming, like the economist Samuelson, that 'No new light has been thrown on the reason why poor countries are poor and rich countries are rich.'

That a relationship between wealth and poverty exists is generally accepted. The well-rehearsed arguments concern the nature of that connection. Yet revisit them we must. For an essay on marginalization not to do so would undermine its credibility. Descriptions of problematics must be accompanied by explanations, not least because the third essay (Part 3), on reconnecting Christianity to public life, relies on it. This is but to acknowledge the widely-accepted linkage between definitions, explanations and responses. Policy proposals reflect analysis for good or ill. More importantly, the first essay highlighted the complex, multi-layered, multicausal, interactive processes of contemporary change. The least this suggests is that 'no one has a simple answer' for such contemporary problematics as marginalization, and so 'all proposals of panaceas are in a class with millenarian dreams'.[146] I have therefore reflected these insights by developing three distinct areas or layers of explanation, relating to economic growth, governance and the paradoxical nature of modernization processes. They are all profoundly interconnected.

Economic growth: prerequisite for building capacities

It would be easy to pass over this dimension as a contribution to interpreting and overcoming marginalization. There is too much evidence, as the third area will explore, linking economic processes causally to marginalization. Yet there is also too much evidence indicating economic growth as essential for delivering resources for people's capabilities to function effectively. Economics remain indispensable for meeting the most basic challenge to human functioning, namely starvation, along with resourcing education, healthcare and economic life. It also plays a central role in measuring performances, including in the Human Development Index of the UNHD Reports.

Another criticism of any serious consideration of economic growth is the role played in it by cultural factors, often associated with the West in general and the Protestant work ethic in particular. Yet that linkage, as Chapter 1 illustrates, has been firmly located in a wider context. Unease over what are perceived as other Western phenomena, like modern technology, finance, production and communications, including globalization, similarly should not be constructed into reasons for not facing up to them. Given the nature of change, these cannot be sensibly avoided because clocks cannot be turned back without even greater costs to human lives. Such unease over economic growth probably reaches its sharpest with regard to damage done to the environment by the combination of economic growth and demographic explosion. Yet if the task is to promote sustainable human development, then economic growth is likely to be indispensable. What is not being argued is the case put in the late 1950s by Galbraith and Crosland that increasing production will greatly reduce inequalities, that the universal rising tide of growth will lift all boats. That only neglects the problem of those with no boats, or boats with holes in them, as we shall see.

Beginning in Britain in the late eighteenth century, and becoming a global phenomenon by the late twentieth, modern economic growth has attracted a variety of judgements from wholesale approval to equally emphatic rejection, the latter particularly involving environmental concerns, and current anti-globalization protests. Yet it is important to separate out key *features* relating to economic processes themselves not least because, as this essay has repeatedly recognized, a productive economic life in which all participate in various ways is essential for human fulfilment. Such an isolating is therefore required to pursue this enquiry, even though economic life cannot in reality be disconnected from more malign processes like marginalization. That is but confirmation that we are dealing here with a multifaceted problematic, in relation to which economic growth is one such distinguishable facet.

By the mid nineteenth century, it was becoming clear that Britain was entering a *virtuous cycle* of economic growth. It was composed of a variety of elements, powerfully and mutually reinforcing, linking markets of size and demand allowing divisions of labour, building communications, promoting new technologies, encouraging investment capacity, supporting good government and fostering supportive cultures. Together, they generated greater productivity in producing goods and services, leading to increasing income per capita, and thereby breaking through into ever-increasing patterns of self-sustaining economic growth. Economic knowledge and practice grew fast enough to generate a continuing flow of improvements, most significantly growing faster than population increases. In the past, the latter had regularly outpaced the former, making increasing per capita income impossible. That is still the case in many underdeveloped economies, and unless that is reversed, they are unlikely to break out of poverty and into effective participation in the global market economy. Once again, there is growing recognition that the role of women is central to that breakthrough into the virtuous cycle of economic growth. When they obtain the freedom of capabilities to function for human fulfilment involving education, healthcare and participation in economic life, then that also makes an essential contribution to the nation's economic well-being, leading to higher incomes and lower birth rates, and therefore to the increase of income above population growth.

Clearly, there is an alternative process, a *vicious cycle*, where income per capita does not outstrip population growth. Given the speed and extent of change since the 1960s it has become ever more difficult for the poorest nations to break out of that cycle. Not least because, in an increasingly competitive global economy, the most developed economies are accelerating away from the least developed. They are favoured by emerging patterns of change and economic growth which in turn further exclude the poorest. The sheer size and complexity of demand for heavy investment in infrastructure, economic and social capital, and good governance, including education and training in technological developments, places an increasingly heavy burden on essentially pre-industrial economies. Constrained by technological backwardness, poor fragmented domestic markets, unsupportive cultures, and corrupt, inefficient governments, they are condemned to patterns of low productivity and therefore low per capita incomes; they are relegated to 'a vicious circle of poverty and incapacity'.[147]

It is important to recognize that, in this historic generation of change and marginalization, different nations have successfully moved from vicious to virtuous cycles, illustrating the possibility of such movement, and that there is no one route to economic growth although there are certain common features. For example, in 1960 South Korea's per capita GNP was $230, the same as Ghana's. By 1990, it was ten to twelve times more prosperous, and had become the world's thirteenth largest trading nation, with decreasing population growth. Its male literacy rates were 96% and female 88% (1986). Five million were in secondary education, and 1.3 million in higher. Contrast Somalia, with 18% adult male literacy and 6% female, and 37,000 in secondary education (1986), and with population growth far outpacing economic growth. The dynamic status of women is a key factor in these differences, confirming the 'strong inverse correlation between the adult female literacy rate and the total fertility rate'.[148] That is the size of the task of overcoming marginalization, not least because the balance increasingly favours advanced economies. Yet that does not reduce the sheer significance and feasibility of these processes of economic growth for human well-being, processes so complex that they cannot be imposed, yet which also require the support of advanced economies. That complexity is a recognition that causes of economic growth are exceedingly hard to pin down, more like a set of loosely related events, and yet equally clearly more complex, widespread and recurring than accounted for by mere chance or Western oppression. It is these features of the virtuous cycle of economic growth which have to play a central part in explaining marginalization and how to overcome it.

Indispensability of good governance

There has been renewed interest in and recognition for the essential role of government in overcoming marginalization. From the British government's White Paper, *Eliminating World Poverty* (2000), to the World Bank and IMF, there is now a strong stress on good governance, repeating Adam Smith's much earlier acknowledgment of its central role in modern economies.

The rise of the state through the twentieth century, particularly since 1945, has been associated with the expanding role of government in managing economies, and its interaction with welfare policies, including education and healthcare. The current unscrambling of government and nation state through globalization processes has both confirmed the importance of some of these roles in the face of global challenges to local communities, suitably reformulated, and also the need to become more involved in forms of international and global governance. Facing up to environmental challenges increasingly requires both.

There are a number of particular and important lessons being learned in this field for addressing marginalization. For example, the need to face up to corruption. Easily excused by charges of Western political interference, the corrosive effects of institutionalized corruption as the use of political power for private gain demonstrably destroys economies, undermines public and private morality, ruins environments and corrodes intellectual integrity. It is a cancer which 'diverts resources from the poor to the rich. It increases the cost of running businesses, distorts public expenditure and deters foreign investors.'[149] It is arguably the biggest brake on economic growth and business in Latin America, the Caribbean and Sub Saharan Africa. Conversely, its removal would ratchet up their effectiveness in the war on poverty.

Importantly, such problems are drawing strategic bodies like the IMF and WB to acknowledge that 'politics and economics are interdependent throughout the world's struggling economies'.[150] This crucial connection begins further back than corruption, with the foundational requirement for peace and order. For without that, no progress to human fulfilment is possible. Yet that is precisely the obstacle faced in many developing economies. In the most desperate there is no government: 'We don't even know how to send them a message.'[151] In 100 developing economies, recent domestic and regional conflicts have exacerbated poverty and stagnation. Twenty of the poorest 34 nations are, or have recently been, involved in conflict. Ten of the most indebted cannot qualify for vital debt release programmes because they are in conflict. And Britain is the third largest arms exporter.

It is only on the foundation of peace and order that the constructive relationship between political and economic functions in the modern state in the battle against poverty can then be developed. For there is now much evidence that economic growth is necessary but not sufficient for achieving this end. It also requires the support of government to promote education, healthcare, infrastructures and other investments, including partnership with a strongly encouraged private sector. That has been the way South East Asian economies delivered economic growth and human fulfilment, with and through education and healthcare, the economic, social and political in a profoundly interactive relationship. This is to be preferred to the Indian state of Kerala, with an impressive record of state support for education and healthcare, but poor understanding of economic growth processes, and therefore resulting low incomes. Human rights and development require both income and health/educational promotion.

These achievements then lead to growing recognition of the importance of participatory government, of democratic politics, as integral to the struggle against marginalization. Sen has long argued that the most effective policy against famine is democracy. 'Political freedom in the form of democratic arrangements helps to safeguard economic freedom (especially freedom from extreme starvation) and the freedom to survive (against famine mortality).'[152] On that basis it is possible to proceed to promote the active involvement of the excluded in developing their own futures, their own freedom to be and to do, through democratic politics at local and national levels. Linked to this are a whole series of empowerment programmes, with the poor, and especially women, as central agents. 'Political rights, including freedom of expression and decision, are not only pivotal in inducing social responses to economic needs, they are also central to the conceptualization of economic needs themselves.'[153] What advanced economies are also learning is that majoritarian democracy does not deliver this either. Galbraith's politics of contentment, of majoritarian democracy, effectively marginalizes minority groups, communities and individuals from effective participation in governance. The task is therefore to move from majoritarian to inclusive democracy, as Chapter 6 will explore. It is about removing the *distance* between *us* and *them*, ruler and ruled, a factor decisive in the Irish famine of 1845, and famines in the later twentieth century. It is a recognition that 'The removal of poverty, therefore, requires not just economic growth but also security and empowerment, which implies strengthening the ability of the poor to remove inhibiting factors such as discrimination and inequity.'[154]

The paradox of marginalization: the challenge of inverse alchemy as structural injustice

For Leonardo Boff, the Brundtland Report, *Our Common Future* (1987) was right to focus on the problem of sustainability, and wrong not to link it causally to modern economic growth processes. He does exactly that: 'The real causes of poverty and environmental degradation . . . are the result of precisely the kind of development being practised, one that is highly concentrating and that exploits people and nature's resources. Hence, the more intense this kind of development that benefits some, the greater the dire poverty and deterioration produced for the vast majority.'[155] Yet the value in this judgement is lost because of its naïvety.

Rightly, as another liberation theologian, Fr Gonçalves, observes, the answer does not reflect the complexity of the questions: 'Five years ago there were lots of answers and few questions . . . Today it's the other way around: we've got very few answers and lots of questions.'[156] Now some of these questions have been identified in relation to economic growth and governance. Yet they are not sufficient. For we have repeatedly encountered processes of economic growth and marginalization running side by side, including chronologically, from the late eighteenth century, and gathering pace together from the 1960s. There are too many coincidences, too many interconnections, to leave it there. So two further questions will be pursued in relation to this linkage. First, is there something about modernization processes themselves which generates marginalization? And second, does this lead to the production of structural injustice? These lead, in turn, to two further brief reflections on what it means to handle economic growth and politics in ways which begin to address these problems.

Modernization processes

This is recognition that modernization processes themselves, from industrialization and urbanization to economics and economies, while creating great wealth also contribute to marginalization processes. Four examples illustrate this interpretation:

- In economics: modern mainstream neoclassical economics is based on the recognition that each individual seeks to maximize her utility. It does not work with inter-utility comparisons, and therefore an intentional commitment to equity. According to economists, 'we really cannot say that food for the hungry yields more utility than a third TV set in a rich family's second house'.[157] It also treats land as a factor of production, a property relation not a force of nature. Land is therefore justifiably open to exploitation by the human for economic benefit. This feeds directly into the problem of a world economic system expanding beyond the capacity of the global ecosystem to support it.
- In capitalism: many commentators, from Schumpeter and Habermas to the theologians Preston and Demant, have observed how capitalism, including as the market, has an

inbuilt tendency to invade other areas of human endeavour, from politics and culture, to family life. As a result it may liberate by promoting instrumentality, but it also corrodes by overriding the intrinsic value of life-forms. Therefore the values extrinsic to itself on which it depends would be so damaged in the long term that capitalism and market will collapse.

- In technology: technological developments are so central to the drive of modern economies, and liberation of the human from backbreaking toil yet, in Marx's vivid language, they are also productive of exploitative systems. In 1856, he observed '"In our days everything seems pregnant with its contrary"'. Machinery, blessed with the power of shortening and fructifying people's labour, had indeed starved and overworked them. The sources of wealth, by some *inverse alchemy*, had become sources of want.'[158]
- In globalization: in the old world, the rich needed the poor to make and keep them rich, a kind of inverse of Johnson's secret concatenation. In the new global economy, the rich get richer much more quickly and easily through speculation in new technologically instantaneous financial markets, and as a result are increasingly distanced from the poor. For Bauman 'New fortunes are born, sprout and flourish in the virtual reality, tightly isolated from the old-fashioned rough-and-ready realities of the poor . . . *The new rich do not need the poor any more.*'[159] They are no longer tied, unlike the poor, to the obligations of place.

Although these perspectives on modernization processes come from a variety of sources, the feminist economist Julie Nelson brings them together by connecting gender and environment in a particularly illuminating way. For her, the problem lies in neoclassical economics, and the treatment of women and nature as 'passive exploitable resources'. This is not just 'coincidental, or incidental to neoclassical analysis. Such thinking is part of a broader cultural way of viewing the world, with roots going far back in history.'[160] It is the problem of modernization itself.

Structural oppression

Most commentators acknowledge poverty is not a natural phenomenon, a mystery to be accepted as fate. It is a human construct, a 'product of history and a creation of people'.[161] That is seen at its most obvious in the exploitation of people through war and imperialism. Yet, as with economic growth, the substantive problem of marginalization is much more complex and nuanced. For marginalization is 'systematically reproduced in major economic, political and cultural institutions'[162] in a variety of forms from poverty to racism, sexism, ageism and homophobia. It is the overlapping effects of these diverse forms of oppression which so damage people. It is therefore unhelpful to portray any one as a fundamental determinant from which the others are derived.

We have seen how, by 1820, Johnson's optimism that riches worked to alleviate poverty was replaced by growing concern of whether 'the emerging manufacturing system (was) the solution or merely an expression of a deeper problem'.[163] That deep unease over the profoundly paradoxical character of modern wealth creation has grown and become more analytically organized. It has meant for example, that inquiries into marginalization processes have increasingly focused on structural explanations. As Tawney noted in 1912, 'there is a unity underlying the individual cases of poverty; . . . they are connected with social institutions, specimens of a type, pieces of a system . . .'. When two in every ten is in poverty in Britain today, then their predicament cannot be accounted for by personal or communal defects alone. When three out of six billion are undernourished, then that is even more the case. One is forced to accept that 'the very structure of opportunities' is collapsing. Therefore, 'Both the correct statement of the problem and the range of possible solutions require us to consider the economic and political institutions of the society and not merely the personal situation and character of a scatter of individuals.' So wrote the sociologist C. Wright Mills in his beautifully crafted *The Sociological Imagination*.[164]

It is that structural feature of marginalization, which excludes people from effectively determining their lives, from being significantly free to be and to do, which lies at the heart of why some are rich and so many are so poor. It is about *where* you are located in a whole bundle of oppressions, from class, divisions of

labour, and gender to race, age and sexuality, which so significantly determines one's life choices. For example, 'Race or caste can
be a factor with far-reaching influence on many aspects of day-to-
day living – varying from securing employment and receiving
medical attention to being fairly treated by the police.' The very
different treatment of women and men, and especially boys and
girls, is particularly marked in many parts of the world, especially
in Africa and Asia: 'The observed morbidity and mortality rates
frequently reflect differential female deprivation of extraordinary
proportions.'[165]

Alongside and through these exclusions run the complex interconnections of class and divisions of labour, often in new and
more nuanced mutations in a global economy. Essentially a distinction between decision-makers and implementers, it results in
the alienation of the latter, in the sense of the ability to participate
in decision-making, exacerbated by the increasing appropriation
of rewards by the former. It is a process identified by Adam Smith
at the beginning of this journey, with his deep unease that the
division of labour was at the expense of the quality of life of the
worker. In the contemporary global context it has particularly
disturbing manifestations. So the ratio of rewards going to US
chief executive officers (CEOs) as against the average factory
worker has risen from 44:1 in 1965 to 326:1 in 1997, dramatically
contributing to the widening gulf between rich and poor in
advanced economies. Yet, as Sen observes, it is wrong to tie such
compensation-distribution to contributions alone in modern
complex economies since productivity is clearly the function of a
complete set of one's capabilities as well as actual effort directly
involved. For example, the contribution of education is increasingly influential in economic productivity. Yet since it is so
unequally distributed, that translates into inequity in production,
regardless of the choice you make. In other words, to tie reward to
contribution-distribution simply rewards the capabilities of the
rich for their advantages. 'Inequalities in resource endowments
and inequalities in capabilities are self-reinforcing, and so a
system that ties reward to contribution is likely to induce deepening inequality over time.'[166] It all points to the significance of *processes* of oppression, embodied certainly in the decisions of powerful
individuals like CEOs, but even more in the norms, habits,
symbols and assumptions underlying institutional behaviour, in

other words, in the normal procedures of everyday life. It is revealed, too, in the dominant meanings of a society so easily universalized, and effectively marginalizing those not part of the dominant groups. For them, they are 'always looking at one's self through the eyes of others, of measuring one's soul by the tape of a world that looks on in amused contempt and pity'.[167] That is what it is like to be in a marginalized group.

The critique of such structural inequality requires more than an understanding of distributional justice and freedom. For once the division of labour and class is in place, 'enforced and reproduced by authority and credentially', then the 'redistribution of goods does not appreciably alter the process that produces that distributive pattern'.[168] So, in terms of highly discriminatory trading arrangements, favouring the rich world's agricultural systems to the detriment of the poor world's, then global free trade does not liberate the poor but confirms and extends these already gross divisions. 'In short, the unequal rewards that agents take from the market may have far more to do with unequal substantive opportunities to secure resource endowments than with free choice.'[169] It is a most significant recognition that 'the predominant approaches to justice tend to presuppose and uncritically accept the relations of production that define an economic system'.[170] We are therefore driven beyond Rawls and the global difference principle, to extend our interpretation of justice beyond a fair allocatory system. With Iris Young, we now also focus on 'the more central question of the best way to control the *process* to realize social needs and the full potentialities of human beings'.[171] We are driven into the wider processes of social justice, which begin to address such structural matters.

Now this takes us into two areas, inevitably, once again, the economic and the political. And, because we cannot begin again, we commence with structures given to us.

Pro-poor economic growth

Proposed by the UNDP, in the light of detailed experiences and research, this recognizes that the poor are unlikely to receive a fair share of necessary increasing economic growth if they are not empowered politically and economically. It therefore addresses the lack of that automatic link between economic growth and progress in human rights already identified. This leads to promoting partnerships between public service delivery, particularly in health and education, and private sector growth, to generate more equal and effective human capabilities.

> Indeed, our study (UNHDR 1996) shows that, since 1960, no country has been able to follow a course of lopsided development – where economic growth is not matched by human development or vice versa – for more than a decade without falling into crisis. During the past three decades, every country that was able to combine and sustain rapid growth did so by investing first in schools, skills and health while keeping the income gap from growing too wide.[172]

What such pro-poor economic growth policies therefore involve includes working with the market by:

- encouraging growth in sectors where the poor are concentrated – in agriculture, rural industries, and small-scale urban enterprises;
- expanding programmes with known high impacts on the poor's capabilities – healthcare, education and microfinance;
- eroding gross inequalities, since the greater the inequalities the higher the growth rate needed to reduce poverty.

The test of such policies is the reduction in the absolute number of poor people (for the proportion of the poor can decline even as numbers increase).

Promoting inclusive democracy

As self-determination through empowering poor and other marginalized people and groups, promoting inclusive democracy is therefore a significant movement beyond majoritarian democracy, as recognized earlier. Only within that framework of supportive socio-political arrangements can the self-development of individuals occur. It is recognition that most successful cures for poverty in the end come from within, that 'at bottom, no empowerment is so effective as self-empowerment'.[173] Overcoming that social and economic inequality which 'correlates with relative lack of civic and political voice'[174] certainly involves bringing the marginalized, especially vulnerable groups, into decision-making structures. Yet it also includes recognizing how even modes of expression exclude, therefore requiring development of other modes of discourse, like the narrative form, alongside reasoned argument. The final essay (Part 3) will develop the implications of these reflections with regard to church, theology and Christian political economy.

The three areas of explanation – economic growth, governance and structural inequalities – are essentially overlapping consensuses. They have intentionally not been reduced to systematic discourse. Like Keynes, I am aware that the chief danger to our enquiry, 'apart from laziness and wooliness, is scholasticism, the essence of which is treating what is vague as if it were precise and trying to fit it into an exact logical category'. Dogmatisms abound in plenty in explanatory commentaries on marginalization processes, not least in theology. They are a luxury we cannot afford, given this problematic in this greatly changing and increasingly complex context. Yet patterns have emerged in this investigation. Issues have been identified which need to be part of interpretations of and responses to marginalization. And, because of the continuing acceleration of contemporary change, and the continuing intractabilities of global divisions, we can 'never regard a question as exhausted' (Marx).[175] The task is likely to be ongoing for the foreseeable future.

4

THE GREAT DOUBLE WHAMMY

A Case Study of Marginalization and Religion

Of great books written in the twentieth century, Max Weber's *The Protestant Ethic and the Spirit of Capitalism* has a particular place in my affections, not least because of informative footnotes, often longer than the main text! Published in 1904–5, it examines the origins and nature of the relationship between the emerging forces of capitalism and Protestantism in the sixteenth and seventeenth centuries. What particularly impresses is that the author begins his enquiry by asking, why were there more Protestant than Catholic technical college students and industrial apprentices? In 1900, that was a matter of significance, for Germany's economic growth beginning to outpace Britain's, particularly in the more technologically advanced chemical, engineering and steel industries. A decisive factor in that success was the contribution of superior educational, training and research capacities. From such a contemporary concern, he began to look for its causes, and this took him back to the sixteenth and seventeenth centuries, to the early powerful connection between capitalism and Protestantism.

It is not difficult to see links between Weber's agenda and mine. Chapters 1 and 3 recognize the significant contribution made by wider cultural factors, including religion and ethics, to economic growth. It is that relationship between Christianity, ethics and economics which will play a foundational role in reconnecting Christianity to contemporary public life in Chapter 6. Perhaps more importantly we both begin with a problematic of critical contemporary concern.

In my case, this enquiry began with the primary question, can the urban church survive? The decline of mainstream churches in Britain and Europe is substantial and disturbing, and set against the background of increasing urbanization. Even more so, it is located in the context of dramatic change, particularly since the 1960s, operating at local but also increasingly at global levels, and affecting every area of life, including religion. These features figure largely in explanations of church decline, in terms of secularization theory and its modifications, with modernization processes in general and class in particular occupying dominant positions. The latter includes the greater resistance to the routines of churchgoing life found in more deprived people and communities. Both factors, modernization and class, feature prominently in the study of marginalization in Chapter 3.

Once again, however, we need to return to the problematic itself as experienced by people and communities. Our detailed work in Manchester allows and requires precisely that our continued engagement with urban church survival focuses more and more on the connection between marginalized communities and churches. For local churches in potentially terminal decline in the Diocese of Manchester are also significantly located in communities enduring endemic marginalization. That is what I mean by the double whammy of marginalization and religion.

Of course, it was not easy to explain a double whammy to the Swedes. You may remember John Major's general election campaign in 1992, concentrating on the Labour Party's failure to come clean about the full cost of its public expenditure programmes and the likely taxation required to fund them. It was his splendid categorizing of them as a double whammy which caught the public's attention.[176] What I am arguing is that the double whammy of double whammies is that combination of increasing marginalization of peoples, nations and environments, and increasing marginalization of our understandings of God and church from that marginalized context. For the disproportionate presence of marginalized churches in marginalized communities allows and requires Christianity to engage both sides of that same coin. By promoting more effective churches in more effective communities, it would be able to engage the multilayered nature of marginalization processes. And that becomes the paradigm for the broader and greater task of reconnecting Christianity to the life of peoples and societies in a global context. The third essay (Part 3) is a contribution to that end. This brief chapter should therefore be seen as an addendum to the larger Chapter 3 on marginalization, in much the same way that Chapter 2 on religious change concludes the first essay on contemporary change. Both illustrate the nature and importance of connections between change, marginalization and Christianity. They provide an essential empirical basis for the task of reconnecting faith and society.

This case study of marginalized churches and communities in Manchester is also a reminder of the continuing importance of a location within such a large enquiry. Technological transformation of time and space is identified in Chapter 1. It requires, among other things, necessary qualifying of the traditional emphasis on the importance of place for human living, including religious associations. Yet that impact of globalization surely calls for a reformulation of our understanding of location rather than its rejection or retention as unchanging model.

Ackroyd's review of Duffy's story of the village of Morebath through the great religious changes of the sixteenth century reminds us of the continuing 'genius of place' which 'survives within this narrative . . . and proves the assertion that the great forces of the world can best be understood in terms of their local effects'.[177] The value of this Manchester case study is that it embodies and illustrates aspects of these wider forces of change and marginalization, including as they relate to Christianity, and as elaborated in previous chapters. What it does not do, which is therefore an agenda for further research, is provide detailed local studies of particular communities and churches. Tim Jenkins' ethnographic study of the Kingswood Whit Walk is a splendid model of how this could be done to great effect.[178] This, in turn, links to the importance of *narrative* alongside critical social theory. Already alluded to in the discussion of inclusive democracy, it is further elaborated in the reformulation of praxis in Chapter 5.

Four further matters continue to locate the case study in wider contexts confirming and developing its representative character.

First, the study brings together two questions facing Christianity and religion traditionally regarded as in conflict. On the one hand, the tradition of Western Christianity, evolving through secular post-enlightenment and plural contexts, has been driven to formulate and answer the question, can the modern person believe? The religious problem therefore becomes the non-believer. On the other hand, the Christian tradition of poor nations of the South, particularly as liberation theology in Latin America, has been driven to formulate and answer a quite different question, how can the poor be liberated from all that oppresses them? The religious problem therefore becomes the non-person, the marginalized. The two questions and traditions have been regarded as fundamentally opposed, particularly by liberation theology. Yet the Manchester experience brings the two into creative relationship as marginalized communities disconnected from Christian tradition and churchgoing. Interestingly, Gutiérrez also makes that connection when he observes that 'an authentic, deep sense of God is not only not opposed to a sensitivity to the poor and their social world, but is ultimately lived only in those persons and that world'.[179] That takes us into the significance of believing without belonging, elaborated as common or folk religion, and other mutations of religion identified in Chapter 2. It is a reminder that, although the case study focuses on Christianity as churchgoing, there is another dimension of religious life which has traditionally been espoused by the more deprived.

Second, the consideration of churches facing particular difficulties in the most deprived communities of Manchester creates an additional problem of sheer survival in often strategic communities. For divisions between rich and poor, and problems for society that creates, are increasingly replicated in churches. It has been identified as 'the urgent problem of what has been called "the two churches, a growing separation between the Church of the rich and the Church of the poor" '.[180] It is a challenge experienced across denominations. A Methodist leader in Manchester has observed, 'We share the anxiety you express over the disparity between the relatively prosperous churches of South Manchester and the struggling ones in the North of the City. We share concern over the real possibility of a growing disconnection between the more prosperous churches and the least prosperous.' The model of church as bias for inclusivity, developed in Chapter 5, is partly a response to this problem.

Third, the case study needs to be located in relation to two developing traditions of engagement with marginalization. On the secular side, there is a long history of government involvement in urban affairs, particularly deprived communities. Recent outbursts of energy have included the important *Urban and Rural White Papers* (2000), *National Strategy for Neighbourhood Renewal Action Plan* (2001), and *Indices of Multiple Deprivation* (2000). Local Strategic Partnerships are particularly important because they seek to foster collaboration between local government and the private and voluntary sectors to co-ordinate public interventions in deprived communities. The Diocese of Manchester employs a Partnership Officer to promote local church involvement in such partnerships, including the regeneration schemes of such significance for deprived communities. On the churches' side, there is also a long tradition of organized involvement in deprived urban communities from the late nineteenth century. Once again, there has been a recent upsurge in activity springing from the seminal *Faith in the City* initiative (1985), including the follow-up reports, *Living Faith in the City* (1990) and *Staying in the City* (1995), and the powerful Church Urban Fund, whose millions have levered in many more millions of partnership funding to resource local church projects in marginalized communities. The National Children's Home report *The Cities* (1997) also stands in this tradition, as does the work of individuals like Graham Ward's *Cities of God* (2000), and Andrew Davey's *Urban Christianity and Global Order* (2001). The latter leads significantly into the connection between British urban ministry and the emerging global Anglican Communion's Urban Network. Alongside these initiatives, the Diocese of Manchester has also been progressing its strategic involvement in the problem of its urban churches. Its initial report, *Changing Church and Society: Developing a Strategy for Mission in the Urban Priority Areas of the Diocese of Manchester* (1998), has led to a second stage of activity based on the report *Becoming One Body: Beyond Changing Church and Society* (2001). This case study emerges out of research undertaken for the latter.

Finally, once again the issue of the measurement of deprivation arises particularly in relation to local church life. The Indices of Multiple Deprivation have delivered detailed high-quality statistical profiles of local communities across the country. Corresponding local church information is much less detailed and reliable, but beginning to emerge. Both face the problem identified by Hobsbawm that: 'All statistics are answers to specific and extremely narrow questions, and if they are used to answer other questions . . . they must be treated with extreme caution.'[181] In addition, the case study suffers from the limitation of working only with churchgoing statistics, therefore omitting all reference to more diffuse but equally significant characteristics of religiosity identified in Chapter 2. The latter may be of particular importance in deprived communities, certainly historically and probably in the contemporary context as well.[182] Yet despite these qualifications, basic churchgoing statistics continue to be important for measuring basic organizational activity. They are also significant because of the recognized consequences of church membership for voluntary contributions to community life, and the likely dependence of common and folk religion on it for survival. These implications for church life are further elaborated in Chapter 5.

The challenge of marginalization in Manchester diocese, a conurbation of over two million people, is revealed particularly in two sets of information relating to communities and churches facing most difficulty. It is therefore demonstrably a multilayered phenomenon, linking secular and religious processes in one complex reality.

Communities in the diocese facing most difficulties

New information has emerged which helps define and describe such communities. The government's Indices of Multiple Deprivation (IMD) are statistically robust, up to date, and based on over thirty indices. They include measurements of income, employment, health, education and access to other basic services. Significantly, these therefore provide connections with the capability functionings of the UN's Human Development Index used to identify global inequalities. Deprivation in Manchester is integrally part of global marginalization processes. For the purposes of this case study, the IMD identify the most deprived communities at local electoral ward level throughout England. Information generated is also used as a determinant for allocating urban resources, and is becoming an important part of diocesan pastoral information and planning. What the indices reveal is profoundly disturbing and provocative.

Of the 167 electoral wards in the diocese, 61 (36%) are numbered in the most deprived 10% in England. The consequences of such marginalization for the whole sub-regional society, its children, men and women are profoundly predictable, from early deaths to underweight and underperforming children. Yet what is not always as predictable about today's deprivation is its location. For the figures contain amazing surprises. What is the most deprived local ward in England? Well, it's not in Ken Leech's beloved East End of London. It's not in the inner-city communities of Newcastle, Birmingham or Liverpool. It's not in inner-city Manchester, in Hulme, Moss Side or Ardwick. All predictable, all attracting the attention of government ministers, social activists and theologians. All morally obvious, all actually wrong. The poorest ward in England is in the 'garden city' of Wythenshawe, on the southern outskirts of Manchester, bordering the great international airport, and the lush pastures of Cheshire and Chester diocese. Wythenshawe, great satellite town, designed by Barry Parker who with Unwin created Letchwood, therefore stands in the tradition of the garden cities of Ebenezer Howard, and the outburst of New Towns, again in the astonishing post-1945 generation. For Hall, it is 'truly England's third Garden City', and 'Despite its modern shabbiness, it still retains the unmistakable feel of a garden city layout.' It still, for him, as the fruit of two generations of urban planners, has the form of 'a secular Last Judgement: the virtuous poor would be assisted to go directly via the settlement house or the municiple housing project to the garden-city heaven'.[183] But it hasn't quite worked out like that, like all such dreams.

The evidence of 36% of wards being in the most deprived 10% nationally supports the judgement that the Diocese of Manchester does not simply share the problems of any major conurbation, but also has a disproportionate share of the most deprived areas in the country. Significantly, they are predominantly focused in the city of Manchester, with 27 wards, but also in the city of Salford (9), and in the satellite towns of Rochdale (8), Bolton (7) and Oldham (7).

Some 104 parishes lie entirely or mainly within these most deprived wards. They are found across 16 of the 22 deaneries which constitute the diocese. The deaneries of Ardwick, Hulme, North Manchester and Salford each have more than 10 parishes entirely or predominantly within the most deprived 10% of wards. Bolton, Oldham, Rochdale and Withington each have up to 10 parishes. Ashton, Bury, Eccles, Farnworth, Heaton, Heywood and Middleton, Stretford and Walmsley each have up to 5. That's a lot of the diocese. That's about the 'collapse of the structure of opportunities' which C. Wright Mills used earlier in this essay to explain why some are rich and so many are poor.

Churches facing most difficulties in the diocese

In the face of the major decline of the diocese, described in Chapter 2, and of all the mainstream Christian denominations, it is not surprising that the diocese now has a number of churches facing acute difficulties, increasingly raising the question of sheer survival. (In passing, I am constantly amazed how church leaders, committees and local Christians essentially totally avoid the questions presented by ecclesiastical death. If you cease to exist, what's the point of reforming liturgies, theological education, spirituality, and social witness? In other words, what we face in marginalization language is the equivalent of imminent death by starvation for some, and for others, the reduction of their capabilities to function as fulfilled human beings below such a level as to put meaningful existence beyond their reach. Manchester has a disturbing number of churches in both categories.)

Initially, we have defined churches facing acute difficulties when they meet either or both of these two criteria:

- Churches with an average Sunday attendance (all ages) of 25 or less. The problem here is death by attrition, of often elderly congregations literally dying one by one. This is compounded by the even smaller number who are active members (often less than 10 out of a congregation of 20), who do all the routine jobs to keep a church in existence. What they therefore rarely possess is any remaining energy to develop the necessary involvement of the church in the local community, to promote that outreach which leads to a return flow of new members to build up the local church to the minimum necessary for effective existence.
- Churches with an electoral roll of less than 51. This indicates that churches with a smaller fringe membership to draw on are likely to have greater difficulties in developing the essential out-reach of the church than churches with larger electoral rolls. The rapid reduction of baptisms, confirmations and marriages is symptomatic of a church increasingly irrelevant to what people regard as essential for the pursuit of human well-being. For terminal decline is likely to involve two complementary

processes reflecting the linkage between core church membership and surrounding penumbra of believers not belonging. On
the one hand, it suggests that if numbers of core members drop
below a basic minimum – 51 out of, say, a parish of 5,000–10,000
surely indicates that, especially when less then 25 attend with
any regularity – then the wider penumbra begins to erode,
accelerating as a more unbelieving younger generation reaches
adulthood. On the other hand, the core itself is also dependent
on that outer membership and wider penumbra of believing not
belonging. If that begins to erode then again the consequences
for the core are profoundly disturbing in terms of sheer survival
in the medium to long term. It is recognition that 'religious institutions cannot flourish without the passive acceptance of larger
numbers in the population and that the future of religions in
Europe will depend very largely on the complex relations
between the two'.[184]

Now 42 churches meet one or both of these criteria. Most qualify
on the basis of low electoral rolls, but 18 fall into both categories.
They are concentrated by far in the Manchester archdeaconry (30),
the principal location, again by far, of the most marginalized communities. Yet they are also present in the Bolton (3) and Rochdale
(9) archdeaconries, again reflecting the broader spread of the most
deprived localities. Only in 7 of the 22 deaneries are there no such
churches. In other words, churches facing most difficulties spread
across the diocese, impacting on most areas. Yet within that
general coverage, 66% fall within the most deprived wards. This
does not detract from the fact that there are a considerable number
of churches in the most deprived 10% of communities which are
well attended. Deprivation, and its links with churches facing
most difficulty, live side by side with wealthier communities and
churches with reasonable attendances. That is precisely what
marginalization processes describe.

The costs of such marginalization, as our report *Becoming One
Body* acknowledges, are stark: 'The gap between deprived and
better-off communities has consequences for the quality of life in
general, and for crime and disorder in particular. Equally, a
separation between struggling and better-off churches does not
improve the ability of the whole Church to be a force for change.'
The report therefore concludes, 'If the Church is to be credible in

addressing inequalities in our society and world, it must first put its own house in order. This means balancing our concern for the Diocese as a whole with an equal concern for its least advantaged churches and communities – in other words, we must learn to identify priorities within the whole.'

It is to that agenda, of how to address that double whammy of marginalized societies and churches, that the final essay turns. It does so in the light of the first two essays. For they have illustrated the connection between the two forms of marginalization, and therefore the real possibility that in addressing the contribution of Christianity to overcoming marginalization that may also have constructive implications for addressing marginalization as a whole. And that is because it is part of the wider task of engaging the multilayered processes of marginalization.

PART 3

RECONNECTING CHRISTIANITY AND SOCIETY: THE THIRD ESSAY

5

PERFORMATIVE CHRISTIANITY

Demarginalizing Theology and Church:
Reflections on Religious Theory
and Organization

In the light of the first two essays, we can now address marginalization processes with the purpose of so eroding them as to
generate a more inclusive society and world. That has been the
vocation of many in our world from the beginnings of urban-
industrial societies. None has succeeded in the global sense,
though some nations have achieved more than others, including
Scandinavia and South East Asia. Certainly, vocal critics of capitalism and globalization, whether religious, political or both, have no
better answers to this great problematic. It is easy to preach good
news to the poor and condemn their rich oppressors, whether
people or systems. It is immensely more difficult to deliver. This
essay is therefore a modest, selective enterprise, setting out insights
to further dialogue with others, rather than attempting definitive
answers. It is about work in progress, describing my own working
agenda approaching retirement, but also reflecting the awesome
complexity of addressing this historic marginalization problematic
which continues to evade the best endeavours of people and institutions more competent than anything I can say or do. But that
does not matter. This divine imperative obliges all Christians,
people and nations to share this agenda, from whatever perspective, and with whatever skills they happen to have. This is my
offering of where I am up to in that task.

This essay is divided into two chapters exploring what reconnecting Christianity to marginalization processes could mean. Chapter 5 attempts this with regard to theology and church as essentially the reformulation of theory and organization in our greatly changing context. Chapter 6 engages in the task of reformulating the tradition of Christian political economy, of relating Christianity to political economy as a central force in global change and marginalization.

Of course, the idea of reconnecting such matters is open to obvious challenge because in both areas, or chapters, there are existing connections, and sometimes strong ones. I therefore use it principally to illustrate my own task of reconnecting society and Christianity, including reformulating theology, church and political economy. Both chapters constitute one unfolding essay, characterized by recurring and connecting themes. For example, reflections on church and interfaith in Chapter 5 reappear in a form appropriately different for Chapter 6, as examples of religious economics. That is a reminder that although religion is predominantly interpreted through Christianity, signs will emerge of the possibilities, rapidly becoming indispensable, of *interfaith* conversations, ethics, and practical programmes.

What is especially important is that all this work, given the findings of the first two essays, is *problematic* based and focused. It is therefore *practical* in character, particularly interpreted as *praxis*, as the interaction of practice and theory. Reflections on theology and church, as two sides of the same coin, therefore interpret them as a profoundly *performative* reality. It is in this sense that these reflections are offered as of wider significance for other disciplines and organizations seeking to reconnect to emerging changing contexts and their global problematics. It is my belief that what can appear to be internal religious conversation is transformed by the problematic addressed and what this requires of all disciplines and organizations. Discoveries in religious-based approaches will therefore resonate with findings of others, to their mutual learning advantage. For example, the conclusions of this essay can be summarized as recognizing the importance of being *problematic focused, contextually located, interdisciplinary and performative in essence*, and *tradition based*. These inform all the reflections on theology as theory, church as organization and Christian political economy. But intimations for mutual learning are even more focused. For example, it becomes evident that churches can and should be interpreted as of profound empirical importance for the shared task of restoring communities. As verifiable locations for altruism and voluntarism they become necessary partners for effective regeneration. They are also thereby central to the re-engaging of economics and ethics. This becomes even more the case when the essential layer of empowering marginalized communities and churches is addressed and facilitated. Rethinking praxis-based theory and organizational life similarly has obvious implications for other disciplines and institutions. They become especially geared to engaging marginalization when informed by what I have come to describe as a *bias for inclusivity*, the reconciling of positive discrimination with and for inclusion, and embodied in appropriate measurement systems. Again, this is a replaying of a recurring theme of difference and commonality. It becomes, for example, a critique of emerging styles of common good and global ethics, and a promoter of the preferred alternative of *differentiated solidarity*. In the end, it is all about the necessary reformulation of traditions in the light of the demands of global change, elaborated through such problematics as marginalization. That is the obligation placed on Christianity as theology and church. It is equally an obligation placed on other religions and disciplines like economics.

Marginalization and the Reformulation of the Theological Task: Reflections on Mutating Theory

Engaging contemporary change, as it bears on marginalization processes, elicits two major responses by religion in general and Christianity in particular. The first is essentially a refocusing on orthodoxy, from the rise of religious fundamentalism, affecting all the great faiths, to more subtle, complex and sophisticated restatements of faith, including in Christianity, from the neo-orthodoxy of Hauerwas in the USA and Banner in the UK to the radical orthodoxy of Milbank, Ward and Pickstock in Britain. The second is the way of reformulating tradition in the light of greatly changing contexts. Again, this has a continuous history throughout the modern age and across denominations and nations, from the liberal catholicism of the Anglican Charles Gore in Britain and the progressive orthodoxy of the Baptist Walter Rauschenbusch in

the USA in the late nineteenth century, to the restatement of the
task in our plural post-modern context by MacIntyre. His description of tradition as 'an historically extended, socially embodied
argument', confirmed by Thiemann's interpretation of 'an ongoing conversation about the nature of the Christian faith and life', is
particularly creative and is used in this essay. Similarly, Castells
confirms the secular importance of tradition in the formation of
identity in the global context:

> This is why identities are so important, and ultimately so
> powerful in this ever-changing power structure – because they
> build interests, values and projects around experience, and
> refuse to dissolve by establishing a specific connection between
> nature, history, geography and culture. Identities anchor power
> in some areas of social structure, and build from there their
> resistance or their offensives in the informational struggle
> about cultural codes constructing behaviour and, thus, new
> institutions.[185]

All recognize that the survival of tradition and identity, clearly in
major difficulties in such rapidly changing contexts, requires
major adaptation. It is the task of reformulating tradition in changing contexts to better engage those contexts. It is about changing
religion in and for changing contexts. It is what Davie refers to as
the mutation of memory, so formative in traditions and identities.
This exercise, therefore, is an exemplar of what other disciplines
are or should be engaged in, and also a clear statement of where I
am coming from in this interdisciplinary project. As an exercise in
Christian social thought and practice, as Christian social ethics, it
should be recognized and affirmed as a legitimate and necessary
contribution to contemporary debate.

Engaging marginalization, in and through such change, and by
reformulating the theological task itself, has led me to address
three particular issues, regarding the nature of praxis, a bias for
inclusivity, and public theology.

Theology as praxis: a critical reinterpretation.

The challenge of marginalization processes to peoples, environment and religion is the historic and contemporary problematic

which these essays address. It is an agenda of such complexity and intransigence as to be almost, at times, beyond human understanding. That is only compounded by location in context of changes unparalleled in history, and informing marginalization processes as both cause and effect, explanations and solutions. Addressing that whole problematic now requires interpreting the theological task as the centrality of praxis, but reformulated in terms of its constitution and connections to theological reflection.

Take the centrality of praxis for theological task. In my last book, *Public Theology for Changing Times*, my editor persuaded me not to begin with the changing context of Britain since the 1960s, but to open the argument with theological reflections on the nature of God, Christ and Church. She defended this change of order because, in an increasingly plural context of post-industrial and post-modern society, it was crucial to let people see where I was coming from theologically in terms of affirming identity through elaborated faith stories and communities. It would thereby become a spirited response to critics, like radical orthodoxy and biblical evangelicalism, who charge traditionally liberal mainstream Christian social ethics and social responsibility with promoting essentially practical atheism – that is, promoting practices and theories which are the same as everyone else's, embodying nothing distinctively Christian. These essays do not follow that pattern. They begin with an examination of change and marginalization processes, including their relationship to religious change and marginalized churches. They are consequently problematic-based, an indispensable foundation of theology as praxis, of theology as performative discipline. Let me unpack these central concepts.

Take theology as praxis. Praxis is an important Marxist tradition, bringing together practice and theory into one performative understanding. For Jaggar, 'As Marx uses it, praxis consists in conscious physical labor directed to transforming the material world so it will satisfy human needs. For Marx it is praxis rather than pure rational thought which is the essential human activity.'[186] It is this interpretation which deeply informs liberation theology, which takes marginalization most seriously of all contemporary theologies. It argues persuasively that the first task of theology facing such a problematic is not theological at all. It is rather praxis, and that consists of two interacting commitments. On the one hand, it involves practical solidarity *with* the poor in their struggles *against* the oppression of poverty and *for* freedom to pursue human fulfilment. On the other hand, it requires developing explanations of such poverty and oppression, and particularly resorting to Marxist theories, including the dependency theory. Only then does the second stage require theological reflection on that praxis, using the Bible and Christian tradition, appropriately reformulated in the light of that interaction with praxis. Other liberation theologies have adopted a broadly similar approach, including feminist theology, with its foundation in the experiences of women. Yet commitment to praxis as a basis for reformulating Christian theory has a much longer and broader pedigree than liberation theologies imply. These have been elaborated by Forrester in his *Truthful Action: Explorations in Practical Theology*. So he links it to Aristotle's practical wisdom, or phronesis, as the fruit of reflection on experience, and then into medieval nominalist philosophies, and Duns Scotus' view of theology as practical science concerned with God's activity as well as our practice. Both conflict with Aquinas and the neo-Thomism of radical orthodoxy with their emphasis, following Aristotle's prioritizing, on contemplation and pure theory above practice. In contemporary social sciences, praxis is an interpretation of theory developed through such tools as reflective practitioner, emphasizing ongoing dialogue between theory and practice. It certainly resonates with Polanyi's 'tacit knowledge', and the economist Arrow's 'learning by doing'.[187] Taken altogether, they have contributed, as illustrated in textbooks of practical and pastoral theology by Ballard and Pritchard, and Holland and Herriot, to new rigour in methodology, relevance in practice, broadening the scope of the subject beyond 'the narrowly ecclesial to encompass the whole field of practice', and pioneering ways of 'relating theology, social analysis and practice which is mutually fruitful and does not fall into either the trap of idealism or the barrenness of materialism'.[188]

Take theology as therefore performative discipline. This follows on logically from interpreting theology as praxis. It recognizes Christianity, in Gore's language, as initially and primarily a way of life, that what Christ 'offers to men is not first a doctrine about God . . . to be apprehended by the intellect, and afterwards, it may be, applied to life. It is the opposite. It is a life which He teaches, a way of living to which He points men.'[189] For Elaine Graham today, identifying theology as a performative discipline is because 'if theological values have any substance, they will exist in primary form as bodily practices, clinical, liturgical, kerygmatic, prophetic, and only derivatively as doctrines and concepts'.[190] Such interpretations become even more appropriate, indeed essential, for theology engaging marginalization. Then it is about performance, in terms of eroding those processes, and that requires measurement for effectiveness. Consideration of the Human Development Index in Chapter 6 deals with that obligation. It is but a following of the biblical injunction '"By their fruits shall ye know them" remembering that political justice and wisdom must be one of the fruits by which any system of thought is to be judged.'[191]

Yet recognizing theology as praxis, and therefore as performative discipline, requires significant reformulation of these traditional ways of interpreting them, if they are to engage the marginalization problematic of the first two essays, with all their implications for thought and practice. That reformulation needs to be undertaken in two areas: first, interpreting praxis as solidarity with the marginalized in a variety of forms must interact with broader more diverse interdisciplinary programmes, with which, indeed, it should become more closely identified. Liberation theology has traditionally been too restrictive in its interpretation on both counts. A multilayered, multicausal phenomenon like marginalization demands such a reinterpretation through extension. Second, it also requires recognition that theological reflection does not *follow* praxis, but is in *a process of continual interaction with it*. That reinterpretation results from reflection on contemporary change processes, and the role of religions in them. These modifications of praxis theory are so important that they require further elaboration.

First, take the need to recast by extension the components of praxis for the theological task. The first two essays have set out the complex nature of contemporary change and marginalization processes. That in turn requires much broader interpretations of analysis in praxis, including greater willingness to engage far more seriously with a greater variety of disciplines. In the case of marginalization, these will necessarily include economics, economic political and social history, philosophy and sociology. Such commitment to an interdisciplinary task is based on the principle that none are value-free, yet all have important insights to contribute to more adequate interpretations of marginalization. They now include the environmental sciences, but again interpreted within broader commitments to dialogue with all life-forms. For Boff, this is 'a new way of engaging in dialogue with all beings and their relationships'.[192]

A serious charge against liberation theology is that it does not sufficiently acknowledge this interdisciplinary commitment. Essentially, it is too theological, imposing theological and moral categories on other disciplines. From the first essay, it can be seen that in a plural world, and particularly in the West where churches face major decline, prioritizing theology above other disciplines is empirically inaccurate and contrary to the dialogic principle which the contemporary context and nature of God and Christ so require. For example, it has been argued that liberation theology is primarily interested in 'the moral dimension of the economic system', and therefore failed 'to present a rational, empirical analysis directed to specific institutional problems and economic principles'.[193]

The early Christian socialists, led by F. D. Maurice, exhibited a similar weakness. Their primary commitment to the Fatherhood of God as requiring the brotherhood of man was embodied in the promotion of producer *co-operatives* and conversely their rejection of *competition* as 'a lie'. The problem is that the opposite of competition, in the discipline of economics, is not co-operation but monopoly. In other words, Christian socialism, and now liberation theology, have attempted to substitute theological and moral categories for socio-economic ones. For South African liberation theologian and economist, Moll, its use of Marxist dependency theory particularly illustrates this profoundly deficient understanding of the interdisciplinary task.[194] For it gave no reasons for choosing this theory above other conflicting Marxist theories. More importantly, it did not therefore engage with other non-Marxist theories. For example, it revealed little understanding of economic growth, its achievements and theories. Without such full engagement in the interdisciplinary task, as a warning to liberation theology, then as Shakespeare observed with regard to radical orthodoxy, the result will be 'the further self-marginalization of theology into a ghetto world where few will care to converse with it – and not simply because they are fallen secularists'.[195] In the process of addressing marginalization, it is essential that the way it is done does not further marginalize Christianity from the public realm of such problematics.

As important, the essential involvement in praxis of solidarity with the marginalized, which liberation theology has done so much to foster, equally requires major broadening. For example, there have been important developments in understanding how voices of the marginalized can be heard *and* empowered (the two are inextricably linked as 'giving a voice to . . .'). Here I use the work of Leonie Sandercock, Australian urban planner, in conjunction with Iris Young, American political philosopher. Sandercock recognizes that local communities, and especially the marginalized, have 'grounded experiential, intuitive contextual knowledges which are often more manifested in stories, songs, visual images and speech than in typical planning sources'.[196] On that communal basis we can then see the significance of Young's recognition that one of the most important reasons why the marginalized are excluded from society is the preference of decision-makers for reasoned argument rather than modes of communication used by the disadvantaged. In other words, 'A norm of "articulateness" devalues the speech of those who make claims and give reasons, but not in a linear fashion that makes logical connections explicit. A norm of dispassionateness dismisses and devalues embodied forms of expression, emotions and figurative expressions.'[197] This major problem applies equally to marginalized churches as to marginalized communities. Churches face particular difficulties in Manchester partly because they are excluded by chosen discourses and systems of ecclesiastical decision-makers. Empowering voiceless people, communities and churches consequently involves recognizing alternative ways of expressing experiences and preferences as an intimate and indispensable part of being free to be and to do, to pursue one's self-chosen purposes. Young therefore identifies three alternative modes of communication:

1 *Greeting or public acknowledgement.* A simple, basic way of acknowledging the Other, the beginning of a process of communication, its condition rather than goal. It could be particularly useful in initiating grass roots interfaith relationships.
2 *Affirmative use of rhetoric.* Pro-rational argument denigrates emotional language by promoting 'universalistic, dispassionate

culturally and stylistically neutral arguments that focus the mind on their evidence and logical connections, rather than move the heart or engage the imagination'.[198] In contrast, rhetoric will recognize the legitimacy of the emotional tone, the use of figures of speech, metaphors, and humour, the use of visual aids, and calling attention to histories and idioms of the audience. This contrasts with Habermas' tendency to purify language as rational communicative reason.

3 *Narrative as situated knowledge* to foster understanding among people with very different experiences. Telling stories can help marginalized groups express themselves and the wrongs they suffer, thereby contributing to their consciousness-raising, 'the knowledge-producing power of stories in context.' Narratives achieve this, not least, by informing the ignorant of what marginalization actually means for people's lives. I think, in this connection, of the social novels of the Christian socialist Charles Kingsley in the middle of the nineteenth century, who with Gaskell and Dickens did so much to raise middle-class consciousness to the condition of the poor, a crucial stimulant to later nineteenth-century reform. It is a particularly useful tool, too, in interfaith situations. Through storytelling, 'outsiders may come to understand why the insiders value what they value and why they have the priorities they have'.[199]

Yet, as Young recognizes, you can't generalize from stories. They must never be substituted for reasoned argument. They must complement it. To listen to all, and especially the marginalized, is not to avoid distinctions between good and bad. Nor is it to avoid the hard, rigorous analysis of the social sciences. Barbara Harrison rightly recognizes that what causes oppression demands the Christian response of hard interdisciplinary work: 'Knowledge is a prerequisite for relevant ethical work. Christian social ethics must be continually informed by the surrounding reality through the social sciences.'[200] But it is now joined by a variety of modes of communicating voices of the marginalized. That is something many argue for as narrative theology, and few achieve. Again, it provides an agenda for further work, complementing earlier recognition of the need for ethnographic studies of marginalized churches in their marginalized communities. Reformulated theology as praxis now includes all that.

But it also includes one more essential modification in terms of the changed relationship between praxis and theological reflection. Much experience now suggests that the theological task, like political philosophy's development of justice theory, begins with major contemporary problematics, in my case, marginalization. That is addressed through praxis, as reformulated above. Liberation theology has then traditionally seen theological reflection on that praxis as a second act or stage in the theological process. I am now clear that the theological task rather promotes the *interaction between praxis and theological reflection as one stage and process*. That process is essentially a continuing dialectic between the two bodies of knowledge. There is no resulting synthesis because the continual interactive process is the synthesis. It becomes 'an endless cycle of interactions between our faith and our life and work; between what we believe, what we experience and what we decide to do. Faith colours life and affects our work. Life and work bring with them new experiences which affect our faith. For much of the time these interactions are unselfconscious. For some of the time they are not.'[201] It is this interpretation of theological task as ongoing *process* of interaction between praxis and theological reflection which is particularly important, not least because it resonates, for example, with the emergence of a process interpretation of human capabilities in the second essay on marginalization. It is powerfully resonant, too, with liberation theology's development of the theological task as hermeneutic circle, of action leading to reflection, leading to action, and so on. It focuses on a *process* by 'which we ascend to higher levels of understanding and more appropriate and faithful practice through a *constantly moving process* of radical questioning'.[202]

The nature and significance of that interactive process has been elaborated in my *Public Theology for Changing Times*, tracing the process from the late eighteenth-century, formative early stages of modernity, to the present. So it evolves through initial interaction between the *secular age of voluntarism*, of commitment to activities of enterprising individuals, companies and voluntary bodies, operating in a free market with minimal state interference, and the *theological age of atonement*, of life seen as journeys of individual souls through the vale of tears of earthly existence to eternal home, of life therefore as time of trial, of testing, generating precisely those virtues of hard work, thrift and sobriety so supportive of enterprise and voluntarism. It then moves into the late nineteenth century until the later twentieth century, as interaction between the *secular age of the state*, as local and central government, increasingly intruding into more and more areas of human living, as mass markets, media and urban populations, and the *theological age of incarnation*, regarding our journey as through God's world, co-operating with Him by promoting signs of His Kingdom on earth, an interaction embodied in the work of William Temple, supreme expositor of incarnational theology and promoter of the welfare state. Finally, from the dramatic changes of the 1960s, we begin to move into a new epoch, with the interaction between the *secular age of partnerships*, a recognition that in an increasingly post-industrial and post-modern context, no one discipline can explain such complexity, and no one sector, private, public or voluntary, can engage it effectively. Such plurality rather demands partnerships between disciplines and sectors. Interacting with that is the *theological age of reconciliation*, of entering into such partnerships by seeking to find ways of holding together such diversities and bearing the cost which that involves, ultimately focused in and through the cross of the cosmic Christ. All these interactions are essentially two-way streets, of secular informing theological, and vice versa. For Hammar interpreting Tracy it suggests a 'mutually critical correlation between the interpretation of Christian tradition and the contemporary situation', implying that 'the social sciences can put critical questions to the Christian interpretation of faith and vice versa'.[203] Indeed, the interaction itself develops an existence of its own. For the great Jewish philosopher Martin Büber the relationship between the *I* and the *Thou* becomes so substantial as to become the *in-between*, what Matsuoka refers to as an *interstitial zone*, where speakers and hearers do not come together in the culture of each other but in such a zone, the result of 'both interlocutors interacting with each other'.[204] It is through such interactive processes, as they bear on each other, including through an interstitial zone, which describes the nature of change processes in modernity. It leads to changing religion in and through changing contexts. And, in addition, it contributes to developing a more inclusive or deliberative democracy. By recognizing different contributions of a variety of groups, 'it maximises the social knowledge expressed in discussion, and furthers practical wisdom . . . A public that makes use of all such knowledge in its *differentiated plurality* is most likely to make just and wise decisions.'[205]

Now it is this broadening of analysis in praxis, and interacting praxis and theological reflection, which should increasingly inform our pastoral practice. That is, it is by measurable results of this process of engagement with marginalization that theology and Christianity will be held to account. Reflections in Chapter 6 on a Human Development Index illustrate this requirement in detail. What it means, of course, is that such an enlarged and reformulated understanding of praxis and theological reflection can now be more sensibly used for testing religious adequacy. For the preference of liberation theology for orthopraxis over orthodoxy was always too simple and unreflective of the complex nature of the theological task in relation to marginalization. I can therefore subscribe to Graham's interpretation of theology as 'a performative discipline' but not in such a way that 'the criterion of authenticity is deemed to be orthopraxis . . . rather than orthodoxy'.[206] Like Marx's *Theses on Feuerbach* in 1845, it is rather a recognition that 'The philosophers have only interpreted the world, in various ways; the point is to change it.'[207] But that is about interacting praxis and theological reflection, as orthopraxis and orthodoxy, in the development of Christian theology or theory.

Theology as the bias for inclusivity

The brevity of this section belies its significance for the emerging thesis of this book. I will go so far as to say that if something like this regulative principle is not developed then marginalization in church and society will not be seriously eroded. Protestations of politicians, economists and church leaders assuming otherwise are hardly worth the paper they are written on. Yet the bias for inclusivity is equally a critique of much radical posturing. Preferential options for the poor, the great slogan of liberation theology, often gives the impression that a bias to the poor, as poor society and church, will solve everything. It won't. To ignore the possibilities and likelihood of economic growth is as imbalanced as ignoring structural inequalities. A bias for inclusivity seeks to encompass both.

Something like this principle is important for additional reasons.

First, it connects us to the central place the poor now occupy in global secular and religious debates. The work of the UNDP and Sen will not go away but will grow in stature and political-economic significance. Similarly, by far the majority of Christians in this global context are poor. International ecclesiastical arenas like the WCC and Anglican Lambeth Conference will be increasingly influenced by their interests. Boff is right to declare 'Never in the history of Christianity have the poor become so central.'[208] Second, this concern links the two questions which have dominated the churches of the North – can modern people believe? – and the churches of the South – can the poor be liberated from the oppression of poverty? The double whammy of marginalized communities and churches brings them together as two sides of the same coin of marginalization. A bias for inclusivity is emerging as a guiding principle for the Diocese of Manchester facing this double question. Reflections on the body of Christ as an exemplar of church *and* society confirm that connection. Third, elaborating the principle in church and society takes us further into the issue of inclusive or deliberative democracy, and the role played by positive discrimination in empowering the marginalized. Again, this connects back to the discussion of the role of narrative in praxis, and forward to the consideration of political economy in Chapter 6. Fourth, the development of this principle with reference to the body of Christ clearly links to the following consideration of the church, and to its normative importance for informing theory and practice, for example in determining measurement systems, as the Inequality Adjusted Human Development Index in Chapter 6.

Given the great problematic of the double whammy of marginalization processes, interactions between secular and theological programmes must be increasingly informed by a bias for inclusivity. For being committed, as divine imperative, to the *whole body politic* and the *whole body of Christ* surely now requires unequivocal commitment to inclusive global society and church. Conversely, it leads to rejecting those processes that increasingly dispense with the most marginalized people, communities and environments, and with churches and Christians facing most difficulties. It is therefore about putting people, creation and hence God back at the centre of our concerns and strategies. And that will require concern for the whole, for all people and creation, for all parts of society and church.

Now to put that inclusive concern into practice is driving more commentators, in church and society, to recognize that the nature and extent of the marginalization we now face requires developing a preference for the marginalized. For Hicks, whose *Inequality and Christian Ethics* is the best book in this field, 'The kind of "preference" that is called for, by God and consequently by human actors on personal and policy levels, is that which promotes the full inclusion of all people within society.'[209] In secular discourse, it is Sen's combination of the aggregate principle of utilitarianism, which maximizes the sum total of all utilities irrespective of distribution, and the Rawlsian distributional difference principle, which requires maximizing 'the advantage of the worst off, no matter how this may affect the advantages of all others'. It is therefore his justified claim that 'I have not argued for a specific formula to "settle" this question, and have concentrated instead on acknowledging the force and legitimacy of both aggregative and distributive concerns.'[210]

What I have done is to attempt such a formula combining concerns for the whole and for the marginalized. For the divine task therefore becomes to strive to bring back the marginalized into full participation in church and society. That becomes the challenge: being so committed to the whole, that we are driven to therefore pay particular attention to the needs and hopes of the most vulnerable. In other words, for Hicks: 'in order for God's love to be universal, God's care is not equal. Rather, it is extended according to "need".'[211]

Now it is that powerful paradox which must inform and challenge our future work on church and society. If it is not grasped and embodied in life then grave marginalization will continue to invade and corrode the lives of all people and the environment. For the obligation to be biased to the marginalized is clear and decisive given evidence of damage caused by increasing marginalization and endemic poverty in today's global society. And churches are increasingly recognizing that. Accordingly, the historic work of the Latin American Roman Catholic Bishops on the *preferential option for the poor*, begun at Medellin in 1968 and continued at Puebla in 1979, was gradually extended to incorporate other marginalized groups, including black people and women. Yet that dimension of God's love, the biblically based preference for the vulnerable as widows, orphans, sick, children and poor, has to be reconciled with the dimension of God's love as universal. It concerns a preferential option for the marginalized moving from an excluding view of society and church to an inclusive one. For the Papal *Instruction on Christian Freedom and Liberty* (1986): 'The special option for the poor, far from being a sin of particularism or sectarianism, manifests the universality of the Church's being and mission. The option excludes no one.' It is a bias which is therefore 'not an arbitrary bias or a denial of the universality of God's love. At the intellectual level, it ensures that the experience of the poor and powerless is taken into account. It encourages *"moral inclusiveness"* by insisting on full participation of all in the life and decision-making of the community. And it promotes *"religious inclusiveness"* by affirming both God's universal love and his preferential care.'[212]

For Christian theory, this formative argument draws on Pauline teaching on the church enlarged into a model for secular polities. At first sight the seminal image of church as body of Christ appears to make the rather commonplace assertion that an effectively functioning whole relies on contributions of its different parts. Yet, as Forrester observes, Paul takes 'an idea common in the culture of his day and reshapes it *radically* to make it serve a new purpose'. For the image was commonly used 'to suggest that some parts were superior to others, that some were made to rule and others to obey'. For Paul, as for members of the body of Christ, 'Diversity of gifts and functions does not lead to diversity of worth, esteem or status.'[213] He rather affirms difference in terms of individual gifts and needs, including capabilities, but all equally and fully members of one body, with the vulnerable particularly acknowledged because 'those parts of the body that seem weaker are indispensable' (1 Cor. 12.22). And, most important of all, it is increasingly seen as a model for human living equally applicable in society as well as church, powerfully relevant to the complementary task of addressing the double whammy of marginalized communities and churches. It becomes recognition that 'Humans are intended to live in community with one another, a form of living that is modeled, albeit imperfectly, by the Christian church.' It is an interpretation of 'Congregational life in a modest way serving as models of ecclesial polity that prefigure renewed community.'[214]

It is therefore that regulative principle of bias for inclusivity which should now inform our practical theology for engaging the double whammy of marginalization processes. And that is more politically feasible because its concern for the whole is reflected in concern for the marginalized. For it requires formulating strategies and practices, as Hicks rightly observes, in 'as universal terms as possible while having the disproportionate effect of promoting the well-being of the most disadvantaged'. It leads to targeting within and for inclusivity.[215] Pro-poor economic growth and democratic policies precisely reflect this principle.

It is the deliberations of political philosophy which develop these concerns in ways applicable to church as well as society. For example, both are committed to greater democracy and participation, yet both are beginning to recognize (secular opinion more than religious) the marginalizing character of majoritarian democracy, the 'temptation towards coercion in a context of moral pluralism'.[216] Including marginalized groups in the bodies politic and religious is therefore likely to involve targeting for inclusion. Yet targeting is unlikely to be effective in the long term unless preceded by the empowerment of the marginalized: 'Effective targeting follows from empowerment, not the other way round. . . . The poor have to be organized to advance their interests – to stand a chance of being heard and taken seriously.'[217] There is little point in wasting resources on 42 churches in major difficulties in Manchester unless preceded or accompanied by other forms of empowerment, including, for example, use of other forms of communication and deliberation in addition to reasoned arguments. This then takes us into another paradox, that empowering the marginalized is likely to include discriminatory action in relation to such marginalized groups as the poor, black people, women and churches. It acknowledges that 'A politics of difference argues . . . that equality as the participation and inclusion of all groups sometimes requires different treatment for oppressed or disadvantaged groups.' Yet that contradicts the principle of liberal equality and non-discrimination. It is as though whatever we do, we permit discrimination. Yet it is likely that unless differential treatment occurs we will not mitigate the influence of the current bias and blindness of institutions and decision-makers at all levels, and the endemic marginalization accumulated over the last two hundred years. It is in this context, that 'the goal of achieving greater justice legitimates preferential treatment'. It is that *differentiated solidarity* which is therefore being pursued in order to establish more inclusive communities where positive discrimination will no longer be required.[218] It is a necessary variation on the theme of bias for inclusivity.

Theology in post-christian public arenas: reworking public theology

Forrester, with characteristic skill, acknowledges it is easier to begin by saying what public theology is not. For example, it is not the 'in-house chatter' of an increasingly inward looking Church. Nor is it therefore expressed in technical theological language which fails to connect with people and interests outside the charmed circle of ecclesiastical life. Nor is it tied to a continuing established Church. In an acceleratingly secular and plural society, with churches also marginalized through massive decline, that position becomes increasingly untenable. Recent disestablishment of the Swedish Church should be a model for the churches of England and Scotland, not least because the Archbishop of Sweden confirmed the result had been greater public interest in hearing church opinion on contemporary issues.

So what is that public voice of theology? For Forrester, it is essentially 'talk about God, which claims to point to publicly accessible truth, to contribute to public discussion by witnessing to a truth which is relevant to what is going on in the world and to the pressing issues facing people and societies today'.[219] It therefore takes public squares seriously, for example by addressing such global problematics as marginalization. Yet it is inevitably ecclesial, rooted in the Church primarily, yet with essential roots also in the academy. Without the Church, as foremost embodiment of Christian tradition, it would be likely to dwindle into insignificance in an increasingly secular academia. Equally, however, unless the Church promotes public theology able to engage the public square, not least because it recognizes the disciplines of so doing, including working with other disciplines and interests, then the Church will become even more marginalized. Facing such marginalization processes, Church and public theology need each other. It is argued in these essays that both also have recognizable and significant contributions to make to engage in such contemporary problematics.

Justification for such a claim for the value of public theology is twofold. First, in terms of toleration, this requires public recognition (not agreement) of the legitimacy of those insights which constitute Christian identity and also depends on its involvement in society. Internal Christian beliefs about God and Christ affirm and demand acknowledgement of human dignity, and are inextricably part of debates and struggles for human rights and needs. The universal horizons of this narrative do not permit the extraction of "the story of Jesus" to serve as the legitimation-myth of a small community in its self-imposed exile from the world.'[220] Forrester's interpretation of Christian presence in the contemporary secular arena, as *fragments* embedded in Christian beliefs and traditions, is compatible with this justification for public theology. Indeed, it is the most satisfactory because it requires recognizing the public importance of Christian insights, their connection to church and tradition, and yet the need for appropriate expression in a public secular plural square.

Second, complementing arguments intrinsic to Christian belief and tradition are more utilitarian reasons for public theology today. The Christian churches have well over a billion members, millions of churches, leaders and other resources. With other religions, they become major sources for good as well as harm. To simply highlight the latter is as fatuous as rejecting global economy, technology and demography because of the harm they do. As we will see in the next section, there are now strong empirically based arguments illustrating the importance of churchgoing for preserving and promoting altruism and voluntary service in community life and wider society. If virtuous public life becomes more central to facing global questions, for example by rejecting public corruption, as Chapter 3 identifies, then churchgoing as a substantial source of character formation and public service is likely to increase in significance.

Developing the argument for public theology requires paying particular attention to two issues, equally relevant to any theory or religion seeking public embodiment. On the one hand, there is the question of *how* to express understandings and beliefs in the public square given the impact of plural post-industrial and postmodern contexts of competing narratives, including other faiths. This problem is exacerbated for Christian churches in Europe facing rapid marginalization, and so no longer able to claim such a voice by right. On the other hand, there is a question raised of the traditional commitment of churches and theologians to the concept of the *common good*, now seriously undermined by growing acknowledgment of the significance of difference and plurality. Essentially, both questions are concerned with how to negotiate public expressions of religious identity in a globalizing and modernizing world. This agenda has already begun to be pursued with regard to the reformulation of tradition required by changing contexts in order to better inform them. This is a reminder that the focus on more procedural matters should not detract from the task of developing the content of public theology. So considerations of such process issues like methodology as praxis equally play a part in formulating the substance of public involvements, including in Christianity's case, its development as a bias for inclusivity. Chapter 6 addresses this quite directly and substantially by elaborating a tradition of Christian political economy for such a problematic. They all contribute to 'fleshing out' public theology as 'faith seeking to understand the relation between Christian convictions and the broader social and cultural context within which the Christian community lives'.[221] Promoting public theology involves developing such connections.

For recognizing connections between the secular and theological in the contemporary arena has informed these three essays. That linkage has historically been the case throughout the modern era. The emerging global context and challenge of marginalization clearly continues to require it, not least because of the latter's relationship to religious decline in the West. Developing this argument through such connections consequently contributes to the construction of a public theology for emerging global economy and other challenges. It is to share in Forrester's important conviction that 'theology may have a modest but constructive and questioning contribution to make both to the theoretical discussions which undergird policy and to policy-making itself'.[222] Yet learning from processes of contemporary change and marginalization, and from the interaction of secular disciplines and theology, suggests the nature of the theological contribution to such public concerns and debates will itself therefore require continual reformulation. That it will need to persist as a public theology is also equally clear. The nature of contemporary change and marginalization in an increasingly global context will at least require a theology both commensurate to the size of those tasks and reflecting their complexity. Central to this reformulation of a public theology will be the issue of how to express such religious informed convictions in increasingly plural public contexts in terms of rethinking process and common good.

Reformulating procedures for theology making public statements

This is an indispensable issue for public theologians, not least because of Rawls' objection, as leading political philosopher of the twentieth century, to such religious interventions. Involvement of religions in promoting conflict justifies this stance. Yet the historic and contemporary involvement of Christianity in such critically important concerns as human rights and development suggests this objection can be addressed satisfactorily if certain procedures are followed. In identifying them, I have used the American theologian Thiemann's three criteria for evaluating religious contributions to the public sphere.[223] In other words, it is not whether religious arguments qualify for such a public role, but what kind of arguments qualify. Again, in elaborating these criteria, their relevance for other religions, philosophies, and political and economic theories, will become evident. The criteria are as follows.

First, the religious contribution must be *broadly accessible* to and in the public arena. This requires theology to translate its understandings into publicly accessible discourse. Arguments must therefore be open to public examination. This rules out church speaking to church as public theology, just as it does being so distinctively Christian that nobody else can engage with it. This particularly applies to academic theology and indeed all other disciplines. Following this criterion, the story of the good Samaritan becomes a great narrative of altruism, immediately connecting to similar debates in economics and politics. Interestingly, the requirement of translatability may well increasingly rule out theistic language. Christians, and particularly church leaders, assume this is still acceptable. Yet Gill's important research now suggests that 'given the choice, a large and increasing section of the British population avoids using theistic language and does not hold theistic beliefs'. The rapid decline in churchgoing, particularly among young people, is likely to make use of theistic language 'increasingly strange to many people in the future'.[224] This confirms my reawakening to the central importance of *ethical discourse* in general, and *to Christian social ethics* in particular. Ways of developing this skill, with regard to this criterion, are discussed next as part of replacing the common good in our discourse, including through reformulated middle axioms.

Second, the criterion of *mutual respect* will remain central to public debate since disagreements in increasingly plural contexts will be inevitable, though not necessarily always incommensurable. This certainly involves rejecting coercion in the public sphere, and being willing to live peaceably when disagreements are unresolved. In addition, making truth claims, the right of all citizens and organizations, including religions, should not be accompanied by denunciation of others for making their claims. This links to the earlier reflections on marginalization and capability functioning, recognizing the individual as free agent, with capability to be and to do. For mutual respect is more than tolerance because it recognizes the moral agency of those from whom you differ. It therefore involves your freedom of speech, including a condition of 'similar freedom for others and which prohibits activities that wrongfully harm others'.[225] This criterion leads to promoting the value of a wide range of understandings and claims in public discourse, including as more inclusive, deliberative democracy. Such dialogue calls 'for initiatives that will permit encounter and close relationship with all those who are collaborating in the construction of society, so that they may discover their complementarity and convergence'.[226]

The third criterion relates to *moral integrity* and *space for dissent*. On the one hand, it requires consistency of speech and action. Consequently, as the US Roman Catholic Bishops recognized in their statement *Economic Justice For All*, 'All the moral principles that govern the just operation of any economic endeavour apply to the Church . . . indeed the Church should be exemplary.'[227] (They are now learning this principle applies also to the sexual behaviour of their ordained members.) It is also a timely reminder to churches in Britain that a bias for inclusivity must shape their lives as well as society's. On the other hand, it means that the Other as opponent, and particularly as minority, continues to have basic rights, even when disagreements are profound and unresolved. 'To dehumanize one's opponents in the process of dissent is to undermine the moral integrity of the very conscience that motivates these actions.'[228] This applies equally to globalization protesters as to its advocates.

Rejecting the concept of the common good, the second issue for the process of developing public theology

The common good has figured large in public theologies and the work of public theologians, from the Roman Catholic Bishops of England and Wales' statement on *The Common Good* (1996) and the Anglican report *Faith in the City* (1985) to the work of Ronald Preston. It has recently reappeared as a suitably global ethic in the work of the American theologian, Stackhouse. For him it takes the form of 'the neo-Kantian promise of a cosmopolitan state where all particular loyalties are overcome in a non-confessional public theology based on universal right'.[229] McCann and Neuhaus have similarly developed a natural law basis for American public decisions as a way of keeping all on board,[230] but with the likely result of silencing others by claiming a kind of natural law objectivity.

Running contrary to this important tradition of moral discourse is the influential argument that our plural context is now dominated by competing narratives, increasingly irreconcilable. It spells the end of all grand narratives, and the rise, for its most able expositor, MacIntyre, of 'rival and incommensurable moral premises'.[231]

Yet both common good and incommensurable diversities are unable to provide adequate bases for public theology for our global context, the former because it cannot cope with diversity, the latter because it cannot promote collaboration of differences. Essentially, therefore, both are unable to engage differences constructively, if for very different reasons. And that is the task in an inevitably and irreversibly plural world, given the common threat of global problematics. The three procedural criteria for a public theology are precisely about that, how different religions and secular theories can participate in public debate. And for Sen, human fulfilment is about recognizing the different capabilities for the functioning of each individual faced by the common threat, say, of starvation, bad health and illiteracy.

As the gap between richest and poorest continues to grow, with damaging consequences for life itself for the latter, the pressure of moral arguments for justice will be to put aside particular claims of, say, gender and race and unite behind proposals for universal basic human needs. Yet to extend that argument into one for the global common good, in the way Stackhouse does, means that both fail to recognize that 'an urge to unity and mutual identification does indeed have exclusionary implications'. For the pressure is to collapse 'the temporal difference inherent in language and experience into a totality that can be comprehended in one view. This ideal of community denies the ontological difference within and between subjects.'[232]

It is Young who helps sort out these problems in her discussion of how we can move towards deliberative or inclusive democracy. For the problem arises when this involves privileging unity as a common good of all, as prerequisite for, or goal of, such democracy. As prerequisite, this assumes a core of shared values, which in a plural multi-cultural society cannot be done. And, as a goal of democracy, it requires putting aside your interests for the common good, yet with the likelihood that that will express the views of dominant groups. Both exclude differences by overriding them. The task therefore is to find ways of working together on *particular problems*, say, by identifying what Rawls usefully describes as *overlapping consensuses*.[233] It is not about putting aside differences, but rather addressing each global problematic by co-ordinating interests, theories and religions. Each partnership is therefore essentially *provisional*, suggesting and developing a model of 'differentiated solidarity'.[234]

It is with regard to this interpretation of difference and inclusion, and the feasibility of connecting them without collapsing one into the other, that Christian social ethics can make a useful contribution. For Ronald Preston's continued advocacy of the common good, irrespective of changing plural context, is probably unsustainable. Yet his development of middle axioms should not share the same fate, because they offer a process for arriving at moral judgements that respect the competing pressures a differentiated solidarity identifies and reconciles, and also comply with Thiemann's three criteria. For middle axioms have traditionally offered an intermediate level of moral guidelines between general moral principles arising from a Christian system of belief (or from any other faith or theory bases) and detailed policy recommendations in a particular context. They consequently provide a sense of direction for facing up to a chosen problematic in a particular time and place thereby ensuring their provisional character. Even more usefully, emerging as intimate parts of the seminal development of ecumenical Christian social ethics, enabling different traditions, denominations and cultures to collaborate on particular problems, they can now be extended to provide the same facility for the collaboration of faiths and other belief systems. In this connection, I have been interested to see how a theological research student from South East Asia found them to be an appropriate tool for engaging economic problems in a multicultural context, with Christianity very much in a minority position. In a quite different context of post-revolutionary South Africa, they also appear to provide a useful tool for public theology in a period of reconstruction. This represents a significant development for a liberation theology bitterly opposed, in the past, to all such 'Western' consensual tools.[235] Whatever the use, they offer, when their recognized deficiencies are addressed, a potential tool of some importance for promoting a public theology for a differentiated solidarity.

Marginalization and Reformulating a Connecting Church: Reflections on Institutional Change

In the same way that a context characterized by complexity and plurality has pointed to the importance of dialogic or connexional theology, so a key theme of a church equally committed to engaging that context is also likely to be characterized by making connections both to marginalization processes and to other churches and faiths. Both are required by the end of Christendom, the first by the continuing decline and marginalization of the churches in Europe, the second by an increasingly global context full of different faiths and none. In other words, there is no going back to the dominant and dominating Church of Christendom. We have no choice but to go forward and that presents churches with possibly their greatest challenge yet. Reflecting on marginalization processes, including as they deeply affect churches, does, I believe, generate creative and exciting discoveries and possibilities. This section of this final essay sets out some of these findings – essentially, perspectives on what it could mean to be church in a marginalized global context. It becomes a central part of the answer to the original research question, can the urban church survive. In this sense, I have been surprised that reflections on theology and church, subjects seemingly so 'internal' to Christianity, should generate such strong connections with matters of serious concern in wider debates. For example, material on churchgoing and altruism/voluntarism is of serious relevance to what is needed for community regeneration, and for reconnecting economics and ethics in Chapter 6.

Reflection on what it should mean to be church in our context takes us firmly into the sub-discipline of ecclesiology. The following research material relates particularly to Church in its institutional form. David Jenkins reminded me of its importance when we worked for the William Temple Foundation in the late 1970s. Much of our work was with secular institutions but this drove him to recognize the importance of therefore also taking the Church seriously as an institution. Of course, reinterpreting the Church is a much broader task than that. Other parts of this chapter have contributed to such an agenda, including reflections on the bias for inclusivity as the body of Christ and how the Church can participate in public debate. What follows complements this material by focusing on two areas. The first directly addresses the double whammy by bringing together the promotion of more effective churches and more effective communities, in terms of what that means for being church. The second addresses globalization and plurality, by extending church as intrafaith, as ecumenical, to church as interfaith, as truly *oikonomia*, to the whole inhabited world. Both reflections are written from an understanding of church fully incarnated in the contemporary context. The theological debate is over what this means for the *identity* of the church. For unless the church has some clarity about what it means to be Church as against what it means to be other institutions, then it is likely to be overwhelmed by other participants in the global marketplace. Involvement in the plural context of a post-industrial and post-modern society like Britain today only confirms that need for such clarity. It has driven many to renewed concern for narratives and traditions in the formation of faith stories and communities. Our work in Manchester has confirmed these findings. We recognize that we have to build more effective churches, and that will involve being clearer about our *identity* as worship, nurture and mission. Backed by *resources*, like buildings, clergy, laity and finance, and engaged in *outreach* to the local community, the participation of such Christian institutional identity in partnerships to build more effective communities becomes much more feasible.

This importance of building identities for such social involvement has been confirmed by research used in these reflections. Gill's work on churchgoing and community building is particularly informative.[236] He has illustrated how regular churchgoing results in greater involvement in voluntary activities and altruism. Interestingly, he connects the formation of such virtuous character to patterns and ethos of worship. There is wide support for that claim, including in Christian social ethics. Preston argued this, as does Forrester: 'The cult is the nourishing heart of Christian practice . . . Enactment of the liturgy . . . is the place where the Church is most fully church.'[237] My findings enlarge that. They suggest the heart of Christian identity is worship *and* service. It is the two together which must form the basis of Christian character formation for engagement with marginalization and other contemporary global problematics. The WCC has rightly worked with such an understanding of ecclesiology.

> The being and mission of the Church, therefore, are at stake in witness through proclamation and concrete actions for justice, peace and integrity of creation. This is a defining mark of *koinonia* and central to our understanding of ecclesiology. The urgency of these issues makes it manifest that our theological reflection on the proper unity of Christ's church is inevitably related to ethics.[238]

Being church therefore becomes worship and service, thereby engaging marginalization and also taking us into interfaith *oikonomia*. It is an understanding of church in conflict with the idealizing and romanticizing of a thereby essentially exclusionary church by Hauerwas and radical orthodoxy. Like Graham, 'I would refute the neo-Barthianism of Hauerwas and the postmodern Christendom of Milbank, simply because, as well as being insufficiently dialogical in theological terms, these models are sociological fictions and fantasies which bear no resemblance to the lived experience of Church and culture in Britain today.'[239] Working with Gill's empirical research keeps our feet firmly on the ground of church as hymn-singing and meals on wheels. Yet a distinctive Christian identity remains central to that ordinariness. Like Fergusson, I am therefore arguing that 'The Church should seek to maintain its homogeneity as a moral community while acknowledging its stake in the peaceful maintenance of a pluralist society. It should expect to meet both the hostility and hospitality of alternative moral arguments since it offers a distinctive vision but one which is not lacking in connection with other convictions and aspirations.'[240] Being church is about an identity which includes dialogue and outreach through worship and service as its distinctive heart. Making connections with other 'convictions and aspirations' to address common problematics becomes an intimate part of its ministry and mission.

Being church as more effective churches in more effective communities

Reformulating the church now involves facing up to marginalization in general, and therefore as marginalized churches in marginalized communities. Addressing the double whammy in a global context of change, suggests an institutional reformulating of the local church in three directions:

- as multilayered (using Castells' work on flows);
- as bottom-up empowerment (using Young's work on oppression);
- as churchgoing in and for community (using Gill's research).

Rediscovering church as multilayered

Locality continues central to human endeavour. It is where people live and die, and have or do not have, capabilities to flourish. Yet these essays have revealed major changes requiring the reformulation of these commitments. For example, given the transformation of time and space by new communication technologies, Castells is right to focus on the new space of flows as well as the traditional emphasis on flows between spaces. This links to the recognition, in Chapter 2, of the Church's problem of being too tied to local church buildings and their organizations. Later reflections on human fulfilment develop this understanding of *process*, of flows, as does the interpretation of theology as a continual interaction of religious beliefs and secular insights.

All this suggests not the replacement but the reformulation of the local. This leads to much more multilayered interpretations of the emerging church, including as a geographical and non-geographical community, with people now belonging to both.

Take the church as local geographical community. This rightly still attracts major support, reflecting the continued necessity for human living of warm communities. The rise and attraction of Pentecostal churches amid the threatening urban growth of Latin America is a contemporary expression of Methodist communities in the shock cities of industrial Britain in the nineteenth century. Local churches continue to be places where identity is formed, norms created and service to others generated. Mawson's account of the famous Bromley-by-Bow church in a deprived community tells the story of how such a church can and does provide a location for regenerating church and community: 'our major impact has been to start a wider process, stimulating a sense of value and belonging in a local context, celebrating its richness rather than concentrating endlessly upon its many problems'.[241]

Yet now complementing that historic understanding of church is an emerging interpretation of church as networking, embodying Castells' space of flows image. It is recognition of the need to provide ways of being and doing together which geographical communities are either unable or unwilling to offer. For Tiller, this requires relating to networks of people, not necessarily based locally,[242] who share common interests. Information technologies powerfully support such networking. Interestingly, Chris Baker's survey of New Towns indicated only 20% of church leaders prepared to adopt such emerging associational forms. The work of Church Action on Poverty and Christian Aid, linking local churches in deprived communities in England to the Philippines, through a whole series of initiatives, demonstrates how this form of church can engage even global realities.[243]

But then comes the new wild card, flowing across both forms of church and also separate from them. Linked to post-industrial and post-modern plurality, the emergence of the individual and choice heralds for Giddens and Beck a new reflexivity. 'In the individualized society the individual must therefore learn, on pain of permanent disadvantage, to conceive of himself or herself as the centre of action, as the planning officer with respect to his/her own biography, abilities, orientations, relationships and so on.'[244] It is this individual reflexivity which emerges as pick-and-mix religion, as common religion, as New Age religion, as a trend to occasional rather than weekly church attendance, and as an integral part of networking churches to meet particular interests. Church training and support for ministry is still tied to the first model. It has not imagined this third model. Yet it will have to.

Empowering church as bottom-up

There is striking convergence of church and secular opinion on the significance of local empowerment of church and community as indispensable for overcoming marginalization. It is a lesson which government, business and church leaders continue to ignore, or pay token lip service to. In contrast, British urban church practitioners Green, Mawson and Pearce begin with people's common experiences of change, powerlessness, hope and despair which is allowed then to shape the content and structure of the church.[245] Globally, Michael Taylor tells the story from the Horn of Africa, of Christian Aid's experience with pastoral nomads. It was their local skills and understanding which developed the water pumps, which continue to form the basis of their lives. Taylor rightly acknowledges that such participation 'guards against the assumption that outsiders know best, even if an outsider's perspective can be useful. It accepts that people, whether rich or poor, are as wise as anyone about what is best for them and how to bring it about. Participation respects their ability and assumes that everyone has a contribution to make.'[246]

Secular opinion in the human development field supports Taylor's judgement. Crucially, the World Bank/World Development Report (1999–2000) now argues for an empowerment process 'that enables community-based groups to define their own goals and options . . . and to assume responsibility for actions to achieve those goals'.[247] That important conclusion is based on a wealth of experience in marginalized communities in the rich North and poor South. So the DAWN projects working with poor women in India stress that 'there can be no good development if people come from above or from other areas to tell the local population how they will, can or should manage a better economy'.[248] In the USA, shelters for battered women do not just meet a client's needs, but seek 'to empower her to define and meet her own needs, as well as to bring her to some political awareness of the sources of her suffering'.[249]

Importantly, such church and secular opinion are united in rejecting top-down strategies which still dominate government, church and business practice. Regenerating marginalized communities will not be achieved by such processes, indeed they could be made worse. So, in terms of urban planning, Young identifies it as 'a semiprivate process involving a triangle of capitalist developers, city bureaucrats, and elected city officials'. It is the assumptions and interests of these groups that set the parameters of decisions, 'rarely publicly discussed . . . emphasizing big, flashy, visible projects'. Empirical research suggests that 'land use decisionmaking biased in these ways contributes to increasing inequalities'.[250] The task is to change that.

Churchgoing in and for the community

This is essentially recognition of the supremely important task of building up local churches. Reversing church decline makes this essential. It is also relevant, indeed necessary, for the complementary task of building up local communities. The two, I contest, must become inextricably one strategy, the foundation for addressing the double whammy of marginalized churches in marginalized communities. It will therefore naturally prioritize bottom-up empowerment of local church and community. Yet it will also draw deeply on internal dynamics of church life, on ordinary routines of worship and service. These reflect actual experiences of churches and not utopian visions of some theological schools, from neo-orthodoxy and radical orthodoxy to liberation theology. It is an interpretation of church life supported by the empirical research of Gill into *Churchgoing and Christian Ethics*, and by accounts of particular and routine church experience. That is why it is much more hopeful, because it is realistic. What emerges from all this evidence provides powerful support for *connecting* the promotion of more effective local churches to the promotion of more effective local communities for their *mutual benefit*. As an intimate part of the emerging multifaceted strategy of this essay, the church in Manchester's future may well depend on it, as well as the wider task of reconnecting church to contemporary context.

A story from inner-city Hull illustrates this understanding of church, for Manchester's problems are shared across all urban areas. With the arrival of a new minister, a church facing closure began to develop a policy of partnerships with its local communities and the private, public and voluntary bodies involved in them. It generated a series of practical initiatives, from a Sunday Club for the mentally ill, a centre for the unemployed, and a Shelter for the Homeless, to a travellers' club providing a safe place for children. Yet as clergy and key laity recognized, 'Underpinning this approach was the realisation that the local church had to grow numerically to avoid continuing decline and, also, no less importantly to become an effective partner in community regeneration.'[251] That was achieved through renewal of the community but also of the church, with the latter growing from 8 to 35 in only a short period.

What should impress is the ordinariness of such representative initiatives, of stories repeated across the country. When joined with empirical findings from social science research, the cumulative effect becomes most telling. This additional evidence is drawn from Gill's secular survey analysis, with additional supportive evidence from Jenkins' local ethnographic studies.

First, Gill's work is based on the European Value Systems Study Group, BBC, British Household Panel Survey, and British Social Attitudes surveys. From this varied material, he identifies the significance of churchgoing for beliefs, values and participation in voluntary activities of communities. His findings therefore contradict traditional arguments of sociologists that 'the beliefs and behaviour of churchgoers are little different from nonchurchgoers' and consequently *lack social* significance. The evidence rather suggests that 'beliefs of churchgoers are more distinctive than has often been realised by theologians, by sociologists, or even by the public at large.' It is not simply beliefs which differ, but attitudes and participation in voluntary work. For example:

- Churchgoers have 'significantly greater concern about standards than nonchurchgoers'. This links to US surveys which connect churchgoing with low crime levels. These findings speak directly to issues of public morality and order, at the heart of marginalization problems.
- Churchgoers are more likely to be involved in voluntary service in and for the community: 'a surprisingly high proportion of

voluntary workers do go to church and churchgoers are far more likely than other people to become voluntary workers'. It is typically 'an unspoken part of churchgoing culture'.

• In terms of attitudes and motivation, a central part of the discussion on economics and ethics in Chapter 6, churchgoers are more benevolent and altruistic: so weekly churchgoers take the needs of the poor overseas more seriously than do other people, and, equally relevant to these essays, they are more likely to be involved in environmental issues.

In terms of the need to promote more inclusive outreaching churches, Gill also refers to US surveys suggesting that non-literalists, non-fundamentalists, are more likely to be active in voluntary service. Contemporary trends to more fundamentalist Christianity in Catholic and Protestant churches are therefore particularly disturbing for those wishing to promote the interaction of church and community, for they give priority to internal matters: 'a greater proportion of their organizational activities catered to their own members . . . maintaining the social fabric of the church, or are thinly-disguised missionary enterprises'. Another cautionary note is that despite substantial links between churchgoing and voluntarism, no caring group is likely to collapse if the religious withdraw, though 'all would be seriously affected'.

Second, Gill also illustrates the formative influence of regular corporate worship on such caring attitudes and practices. Interestingly and refreshingly, he looks at hymn-singing, covering the great themes of Christian doctrine, irrespective of denominational loyalty. 'It may not be too surprising, then, that regular churchgoers who sing hymns together with other worshippers week by week and over many years are likely to assimilate these distinctive features.' The additional use of sermons and eucharists combine to 'a re-ordering of lives to God *but also* a re-ordering of lives to other people, a re-ordering of human lives to animal lives as well as to the wider environment'.[252] It all contributes to 'a specifically religious justifying reason for acting morally'.[253] And so, as Cronin rightly observes, we are then into the relationship between Christianity and human rights and development, into the heart of marginalization processes themselves.

Third, it is the overlap and connection between churchgoing and community life which is central to the arguments of this essay.

We have already observed the development of that relationship as the attitudes and volunteering of churchgoers. That is particularly important for building up more effective communities. It is confirmed, too, by Gill recognizing that: 'churches today may well be distinctive, but they will still overlap at many points with "secular" communities',[254] not least because their members are positioned within that society. Jenkins' detailed study of Kingswood confirms this. Congregations may have distinctive lifestyles, in terms of moral character and virtues, but

> In every case, the congregation knew the non-church-going population as neighbours or kin. Furthermore, although the chapels appear to be well bounded groups, cut off from the rest of society, in fact the picture is more complicated. Just as the values to which chapel members subscribe are of far wider currency, so there is a wider penumbra to participation in chapel life. A large number of people have some sort of relationship to a chapel other than membership.[255]

Chapters 2 and 4 have indicated the problems of the declining penumbra in relation to core membership.

These reflections are focused on reversing that decline by reconnecting churchgoing and the wider community. The feasibility of that task has been illustrated by the Hull story as representative of many other such strategic initiatives. Research by Gill and Jenkins illustrates the empirical basis provided by existing churchgoing which such strategic initiatives should capitalize on. That is what is meant by promoting more effective churches in more effective communities. It becomes a foundational contribution to reversing the double whammy.

Being church as enlarging ecumenical

Globalization has been acknowledged by most commentators as a dominant feature of the contemporary context. Intimately associated with modernization processes, it combines to exhibit strong linkages with them. Engaging these forces drives the church to redefine itself as renewed ecumenical journeying into emerging interfaith.

Take the *ecumenical Church*. An increasingly global context will require and strengthen relationships between different Christian denominations. It will also underline the strategic importance of worldwide intra-denominational links, like Roman, Lutheran and Anglican communions. Significantly, these global churches bring together North and South, developed and developing economies. What is also likely is that the tired top-down original ecumenical dream of organic unity will be complemented, and it is hoped overtaken, as the common good is, by moves to recognize the complementary contributions of different denominations through partnerships agreements. It becomes the ecclesiastical equivalent of promoting inclusivity through affirming difference. The Porvoo Agreement between the Anglican Churches of Britain and Nordic and Baltic Lutheran Churches may have prototype significance in terms of pursuing the ecumenical through partnerships between different churches based on recognizing each other's ministries and sacraments.

Take *ecumenical into interfaith*. The challenge of globalization problematics to churches is much more seminal. For they are beginning to push the Church to connect its essential reformulation of what it means to be ecumenical to now include movement from intra-faith dialogue and partnerships to interfaith dialogue and partnerships. Küng is at his best when he now requires of the Christian churches and other religions that widest view of being ecumenical as to the whole inhabited world, a truly global *oikonomia*:

> We live in a world in which humankind is threatened by what S. Huntington has called a 'clash of civilizations', for example between Muslim or Confucian civilization and Western civilization. However, we are threatened not so much by a new world war as by every possible conflict between two countries or within one country, in a city, even a street or school. My response to this challenge is: *There will be no peace between civilizations without a peace between the religions! And there will be no peace between the religions without a dialogue between the religions.*[256]

Facing global problematics of seemingly intractable complexity and obduracy, and increasingly impinging on all our lives, sometimes in devastating ways, partnerships alone can effectively address these agendas. And, at the heart of that there must be the ecumenical agenda of intra linking to interfaith dialogue and activity. And that is a profoundly local, national and international agenda for us all. And we are still at the tokenism stage, and given the speed and extent of change, may have little time to move beyond that.

Yet even this modest enquiry has identified constructive possibilities for averting such disaster. For example, Thiemann's three criteria for Christian involvement in democratic plural public arenas are relevant to all religions. Chapter 6 extends this potential into joint work on religious contributions to economics. Earlier reflections on theological method as interaction with the Other have also revealed creative possibilities for interfaith dialogue. The theologian Schreiter's work on inter-cultural hermeneutics takes this further forward.[257] His concern is how to speak and understand across diverse cultural boundaries where a common world is not shared. Successful communication therefore occurs when the speaker feels her speech has lodged with the hearer in ways recognizable to the speaker. Appropriate communication also does not violate the hearer's cultural codes. These, and other criteria developed by Schreiter, are interesting additions to Thiemann's, generating them into a more global context.

Other perspectives from this enquiry equally contribute to the interfaith task. First is the promotion of local collaboration by faith communities with government in community regeneration programmes. There is growing recognition, including by government, that faith communities are well placed to promote more effective communities, because of local networks and experience with capacity-building. The appointment of a Partnership Officer by Manchester diocese is precisely to promote such involvement by churches in local partnerships, including by encouraging other faith involvement.

Second, there is growing recognition of the potential of interfaith collaboration in addressing global marginalization processes. The 1998 World Faiths Development Dialogue is likely to become important in this regard. Bringing together nine religious leaders and the World Bank on poverty and development, the initial meeting was chaired by the Archbishop of Canterbury and the President of the Bank. It is now resourced by Professor Michael Taylor. Already it has led to interfaith work in Tanzania on health, and on food security in Ethiopia. United by commitment to justice and a better deal for the poor, its work pursues problem-based agreements rather than general overarching consensus. Again, there is recognition that faith communities have particular skills and experiences of poverty to bring to such joint working. Equally, they have to be able 'to respect the concerns of those who are trying to combat poverty from a technical and economic perspective'.[258]

Third, many of us were attracted by Küng's pioneering project to develop an interfaith-based global ethic. Yet in methodology and style it is now too close to Stackhouse and McCann's cosmopolitan social ethics overriding confessional claims. The preferred way emerging from these essays is more concerned to develop overlapping consensuses from the different traditions on particular problematics. It is therefore the interfaith version of the *differentiated solidarity* identified in the similar earlier critique of the common good.

Fourth, Boff has an intriguing suggestion which extends the new emerging *oikonomia* of *interfaith* dialogue and activity to include an *inter-earth* dimension, what he describes as 'a truly ecumenical challenge is opening up: to inaugurate a new covenant with the Earth'.[259] It is a powerful global reformulation of the original Noachian covenant between God and Noah after the flood: 'I set my bow in the clouds to serve as a sign of the covenant between me and the earth' (Gen. 9.15–16). The *oikonomia* must come truly to the whole inhabited world of all God's creation.

6

ENGAGING MARGINALIZATION BY RECONNECTING ECONOMICS, ETHICS AND RELIGION

Reflections for a Reformulated Tradition of Christian Political Economy

There has never existed an economic system that has success-fully managed to provide for the well being of all people in a meaningful participatory, non-alienating and non-oppressive way. (Ann-Cathrin Jarl)[260]

The great Christian task is to contribute to reversing this judge-ment by establishing such a global sustainable economy for all. That means overcoming marginalization. And because Christian-ity can and must be integral to that process, it offers and requires ways of reconnecting faith and society. It is a significant and necessary complement to the strategy of overcoming the double whammy by promoting more effective churches in more effective communities. For economy and economics lie at the heart of con-temporary globalization and therefore marginalization processes. Poverty, with all that means in terms of damaged human capabil-ity to be and to do, to pursue one's self-chosen purposes, is inti-mately connected to the lack of economic resources. From famine to undernourishment, from illiteracy to preventable ill-health and early death, the story repeatedly centres on deprivation of economic entitlements. Economy and economics are 'at the heart of much human misery'.[261]

That linkage between economics, contemporary society and Christianity was identified and capitalized on at the beginning of modernization processes by the new tradition of Christian political economy. So Richard Whately, in accepting nomination for the Drummond chair of political economy at Oxford in 1830, the first in economics in the world, observed how 'Religious truth . . . appears to me to be intimately connected, at this time especially' with political economy. 'For it seems to me that before long, political economists, of some sort or other, must govern the world.'[262] That judgement was confirmed by the greatest economist of the twentieth century, J. M. Keynes, when he observed how 'the ideas of economists and political philosophers, both when they are right and when they are wrong, are more powerful than is commonly understood. Indeed, the world is ruled by little else.'[263] And it was Malthus, a founder of the tradition of Christian political economy, successor to Adam Smith who, like Keynes, linked the economic task with addressing the marginalization problematic. In a letter to the great secular economist Ricardo, in 1817, Malthus declared: 'The causes of the wealth and poverty of nations – the grand object of all enquiries in Political Economy.'[264] No wonder Keynes preferred Malthus to Ricardo, the preference for ethical over engineering economics, as we shall soon see. And it is central to this enquiry, not least because we need to acknowledge that many theologians have been obstacles to its effective pursuit, thereby also contributing to marginalization processes themselves. For many theologians pronouncing on the economy are either economically illiterate or perverse. Correcting that fatal deceit can only be attempted modestly by me, including by making more accessible material from the Swedish project on ethical reflection on economic theory. Bringing together economists, philosophers and theologians, including those from the Universities of Uppsala, Linköping and Stockholm, it epitomizes the contemporary interdisciplinary programme.

Its work is badly needed. We have already observed how liberation theology, inspiring in its focus on marginalization, is deficient in its understanding of economics and the interdisciplinary task. Western theologians like Meeks and the radical orthodoxy school, share in liberation theology's rejection of modern economies and economics.[265] Like Bishop Watson, opponent of Malthus in the late eighteenth century, they refuse to accept *scarcity* as the basis of the modern discipline of economics. Instead they proclaim *plenitude*, based on a God of plenty, as their response to the biblical injunction 'be fruitful and multiply'. For them, 'The economy that underpins God's new order is centred on "abundance and extraordinary generosity" epitomized in the gracious self-giving of God in Christ.'[266] Christians are therefore called to participate in that divine economy by their way of life, including through sharing in the Eucharist, where 'resources are neither scarce nor subject to competition. . . . [and] Distribution is made subject only to the condition of one's baptism . . . [therefore]. There need be no poor among us.'[267] It is a view of church as social ethic, as alternative economy, as 'the basis for a political economy that will flow out of God's original plenitude and not be grounded in an inevitable scarcity'.[268] It interprets the relationship between faith and economy by subordinating economics to theology. It is a rash claim that ignores the figures of church decline in Chapter 2, and the requirement to be interdisciplinary from the study of contemporary change and marginalization in Chapters 1 and 3. Leading exponent Long is right to admit '*absurd* as it sounds', for he then goes on to demand 'theologians must maintain the priority of their language over that of the economists; just as the church must maintain its priority over the market'.[269] It is essentially the re-imposition of a new Christendom, rejection of any dialogue with economics, an absurdly inflated ecclesiology, 'romanticizing the Church to a dangerous degree,' and which refuses to receive truth from others.[270] It has no contact at all with actual churches and communities of the double whammy, or with actual economics and economies. No wonder Preston, as theologian and economist, was driven to despair by a century of such theological outpourings, for 'Many have paid no attention to economics but argued a priori from a doctrinal basis. Others have resorted to writers who wrote as if they had studied economics but in fact relied on theories of their own, or relied on those who did so, but never came to grips with economic theory.'[271]

What we can't do, of course, is to start again either by rejecting the basic work of economics over two centuries or modernization processes themselves. Like the reforming economist Sen, the

Christian radicals Cobb and Daly, and many feminist economists, we have to engage critically with what exists. For Young, we need to recognize that 'A model of a transformed society must begin from the material structures that are given to us at this time in history.'[272] All agree that the task is to identify and promote overlapping consensuses between disciplines and experiences to develop inclusive economies and so overcome marginalization. My contribution to that end includes a reintroduction and reformulation of the tradition of Christian political economy. It will thereby become a keystone in reconnecting Christianity and society. The multilayered and multifaceted nature of this task involves at least two objectives.

On the one hand, it requires *reconnecting Christianity and economy* by recognizing the integrity of the disciplines of theology and economics. Like the papal teaching of the social encyclicals, this involves accepting economics as a relatively autonomous discipline, with its 'own laws, its own ways and means, its own techniques and organization'.[273] It equally requires acknowledging theology as an independent legitimate discipline, with its methodologies and beliefs, particularly in God, Christ and church.[274] The two disciplines are then brought together in normative social theory as Christian political economy. It is that definition which then also links to the original tradition of Christian political economy, in the early nineteenth century, through the work of Malthus, Sumner, Copleston and Whately. This in turn was linked to the earlier contribution of Tucker and Berkeley in the eighteenth century. The latter, like his successors, was deeply criticized for taking economics seriously, but as he splendidly commented 'to feed the hungry and cloth(e) the naked by promoting an honest industry, will perhaps be deemed no improper employment for a clergyman who still thinks himself a member of the commonwealth'.[275] In this early tradition, it was Malthus who mediated most between economics and Christianity, rejecting theologies which did not enter into serious dialogue with economics, and economics which did not enter into serious dialogue with ethics in general and Christianity in particular.

On the other hand, the process of reformulating the tradition of Christian political economy, as the concept itself suggests, also involves *reconnecting politics and economics* reflecting again the origins of modern economics as political economy, locating itself

in the broader framework of political life and culture. That wider
concern now needs to embrace ecology, since, as Boff observes, 'It
is because of this overlapping of human being and nature that we
must include the ecological dimension in the notion of social and
planetary democracy.'[276]

Reformulating the tradition of Christian political economy as a
central response to the marginalization problematic has at least
four important parts. Since they form the beginnings of a personal
research journey, I can only sketch their outlines.

1 Identifying, reinforcing and enlarging the connection between
  economics and ethics. This is the embodiment of Christian
  political economy as *interdisciplinary exercise.*
2 Recognizing the need to develop such connections into ways of
  measuring marginalization and steps taken to reduce it. This
  will explore several systems, including Hicks' Inequality
  Adjusted Human Development Index. This is the embodiment
  of Christian political economy as *performative discipline.*
3 Identifying ways in which Christianity and other faiths can
  express religious insights in practical economics. This is the
  embodiment of Christian political economy as *distinctively
  religious economics.*
4 Learning from those movements of Christian social thought
  and practice throughout the history of modernity, which have
  rejected the constructive relationship of mainstream Christian
  social ethics with mainstream economics. I have called this
  important recurring movement the *heteroclitical tradition.* It is the
  embodiment of Christian political economy *in economic* heresies
  as reflection of the continuing need for the reformulation of mainstream tradition in dialogue with other heterodoxical traditions.

All four tasks constitute the reformulation of the tradition of
Christian political economy. They are recognition that 'no dominant culture (or theology or economics) ever in reality includes all
human practice'.[277]

Christian Political Economy as Reconnecting Economics and
Ethics

> . . . the case for bringing economics closer to ethics does not rest
> on this being an easy thing to do. The case lies, instead, on the

rewards of the exercise. I have argued that the rewards can be expected to be rather large. (Amartya Sen)[278]

Amen to that. Developing an argument for the relationship between economics and ethics is both central to understanding and overcoming marginalization and therefore to the reformulation of Christian political economy. Fortunately, it can draw on the persistence of a tradition which has promoted precisely that objective, from Adam Smith as founder of modern economics to Amartya Sen today. Yet the criticisms of such endeavours have also been strong, again from the beginnings of modern economics, but particularly in the last 100 years as the dominant neoclassical tradition of economics has sought to establish itself as a value-free science. It is that tradition which has therefore to be engaged in constructive dialogue. Without that conversation, anything which calls itself Christian political economy will lack credibility. Without the broadening of neoclassical economics by reinforcing an ethical dimension, it too will be found wanting at the bar of history. The stakes of marginalization, including environment, are so high.

There is also an important tradition, particularly embedded in British culture, which has continued to be very critical of modern economics and economies. Essentially, it has charged economics with being 'disinfested of intrusive moral imperatives'.[279] Beginning with the Lakeland poets' bitter rejection of Malthus' work, continuing through Carlyle, Ruskin and Morris, and then reaffirmed by critical contemporary contributions by Raymond Williams and E. P. Thompson, this tradition sought among other things, to remoralize economics and economic life. The theological school of radical orthodoxy and the anti-globalization movement are among its contemporary manifestations. I suppose their attitude was rather splendidly summarized by Walter Bagehot's claim, in the later nineteenth century, that 'no real Englishman in his secret soul was ever sorry for the death of a political economist; he is much more likely to be sorry for his life!'[280] Yet joking aside, this great argument represents 'One of the enduring fault lines in British cultural debate',[281] the conflict between the romantic Coleridge and the utilitarian Bentham, between heart and head. For Toynbee, towards the end of the nineteenth century, it epitomized 'the bitter argument between economists and human beings'.[282] But it was Coleridge, writing at the beginnings of industrialization and urbanization, as 'self-appointed spokesman for human beings',[283] who best captures the spirit of protest against modernization. Like Wordsworth, initially enthusiastic supporter of the French Revolution, and soon to become equally enthusiastic conservative in church and state, his revolt against the spirit of the age, and particularly Malthus, was profoundly more 'a matter of feeling than argument'.[284] So he declared 'It is this accursed practice of ever considering *only* what seems *expedient* for the occasion, disjoined from all principle or enlarged systems of action, of never listening to the true and unerring impulses of our better nature, which has led the colder-hearted men to the study of political economy.'[285]

While understanding the reasons for such criticism, this essay pursues a broader and more constructive interpretation of modern economics by recognizing a continuing tradition *within it* which has quite explicitly recognized the importance of ethics both within modern economics and in a dialogic relationship with it. So for Adam Smith, political economy was clearly related to the wider field of moral philosophy, a complex connection which the Germans and their focus on *Das Adam Smith Problem* quite misunderstood. For Smith clearly saw economy 'as part of the whole of human activity', and he investigated it historically and empirically.[286] As important for this argument, he located all his work in a broad moral framework. Most people begin with Smith's *Wealth of Nations* (1776), the founding text of modern economics. Yet they would be wiser to start higher up the stream, with his *Theory of Moral Sentiments* (1759), and its reflections on sympathy, written while Professor of Moral Philosophy at Glasgow University, and complementary side of the coin to the *Wealth of Nations*. The great enquiry into why some countries were wealthy, and therefore how they could be emulated for the benefit of all, was as much a moral as economic exercise. Central to the marginalization debate, as problematic-based and interacting economics and ethics, therefore, is Smith's assertion in the *Wealth of Nations* that 'No society can surely be flourishing and happy, of which the far greater part of members are poor and miserable. It is but equity, besides, that they who feed, cloath and lodge the whole body of the people, should have such a share of the produce of their own labour as to be themselves tolerably well fed, cloathed and lodged.'[287]

Malthus, Smith's successor, was even clearer that 'the science of political economy bears a nearer resemblance to the science of morals and politics than to that of mathematics'.[288] His task was to promote the moralizing of political economy, a concern acknowledged by discerning contemporaries like Whewell, who located Malthus in 'the ethical school of political economy'.[289]

That interpretation is recognized by the founder of contemporary neoclassical economics, Alfred Marshall, at the end of the nineteenth century, reinforced by his commitment to develop ethical economics including as a contribution to what he called 'the study of the causes of poverty'.[290] (Unfortunately, he allowed the discipline to determine the task not the problem.) His pupil, J. M. Keynes, carried on that tradition, re-rooted as problematic-based, with his focus on mass unemployment. Its finest contemporary expression is in the work of Amartya Sen and his concern for human development. Keynes has best summed up this whole movement as 'profoundly in the English tradition of humane science'.[291] For the contemporary Manchester economist, Steedman, all its exponents emphasize 'freedom, initiative and creativity in their accounts of the market system. It is just false to say that all economic liberalism is centred on utility maximisation.'[292]

The problem, of course, is that contemporary economics is more likely to be dominated by a narrower concern for utility maximization than by a broad tradition of humane science. Neoclassical economics, essentially the mainstream tradition of economics, has therefore evolved as a discipline increasingly disconnected from its ethical roots. Its positive technical character has come to overshadow its normative dimensions. For Sen, this 'serious distancing between economics and ethics' generates one of the 'major deficiencies of contemporary economic theory'.[293] That concern is shared by many, including feminists: 'The way that feminist economists reconnect to ethics and morals is a new development in economic theory.'[294] And Sen is a member of the Editorial Board of the journal *Feminist Economics*.

Others, in contrast, welcome the trend to bring economics closer to physics and further adrift from ethics. So Walras, another key figure in the development of neoclassical economics, saw the task as 'to do for economics what Newton had done two centuries earlier for celestial mechanics'.[295] For Milton Friedman, another major contemporary economist, and influence on Mrs Thatcher, it is that development of the tradition into value-free science which takes strong precedence over Marshall's ethical concerns. In his words, economists now 'curtsy to Marshall, but we walk with Walras'.[296] The commitment is to make economics the most theoretical and rigorous of the social sciences.

In its essentials, the mainstream tradition of neoclassical economics focuses on scarcity. Textbooks like Lipsey's therefore define economics as 'the study of the use of scarce resources to satisfy unlimited human wants'.[297] It is the combination of infinite competing wants and finite resources that produces scarcity as the fundamental economic problem and assumption. Economic resources therefore go where most valued, as indicated by the price system at the heart of the market mechanism. For economist and lay theologian Denys Munby, 'Economising only arises in a world where things are scarce, and choice has to be made. In heaven no problem of scarcity arises, and in hell no possibility of choice exists; economics is a science dealing with the conditions of human life in this world.'[298] For Robbins, influential economics teacher of Preston at the London School of Economics, it becomes 'The Science which studies human behaviour as a relationship between ends and scarce means which have alternative uses.' The basic economic task becomes the allocation of such scarce resources to meet people's wants. It centres on what and how to produce and for whom. Now it is that development of economics as science which then leads Robbins to argue that 'it does not seem logically possible to associate the two studies (economics and ethics) in any form but mere juxtaposition', an extreme view, but now quite fashionable.[299]

What we are therefore confronting is essentially two traditions in economics, what Sen has usefully described as *engineering* and *ethical* economics.[300] Interestingly this connects to the early Christian political economists' distinction between the positive strand in economics (as the technical study of means generating economic laws, and therefore more value-free) and the normative dimension (the study of what kind of economic system you want). For Whately, theology could contribute to the second, in terms of justice, but would learn about the first from the discipline of economics.

Unfortunately, as Sen recognizes, engineering economics has

increasingly dominated the discipline of neoclassical economics. As 'fundamentally a positive social science',[301] it becomes for Milton Friedman therefore 'independent of every value proposition or of every ethical position. Its utility is not to describe "what ought to be the case" but "what is the case" . . . In short, positive economics is, or can be, an "objective" science in precisely the same sense as any of the physical sciences.'[302] It is a tradition stretching from Ricardo in the early nineteenth century, through Jevons, Walras and Robbins to Friedman today. Yet even here, at the heart of engineering economics, values play a formative, if more hidden role. For example, economic theories imply presuppositions about human nature, particularly the understanding of rational economic man. The commitment to efficiency similarly reflects the intrusion of values into economic decision-making. (Both economic man and efficiency will be explored shortly.) Values also emerge when economists make policy recommendations, for example given 'the choice between economic alternatives, then "X" should be chosen'. As Collste has observed the normative dimension of engineering economics as neoliberal economics was particularly influential in the 1980s, with the move from social welfare state valuing equality, to neoliberal minimal state emphasizing private values. 'Thus the theory has contributed to what can be called "the economising" of the Zeitgeist. "Everything must have a price! . . .". The more the social consciousness is influenced by the economic paradigm, the more the sectors of society will be submitted to economic measurement.'[303] And that 'economizing' spirit of the age was associated with accelerating inequalities, and explanations of marginalization discussed in Chapter 3. And it is a significant influence in the global market economy of Chapter 1.

The nature of the task for Christian political economy is now beginning to emerge. As Sen observes, it will certainly involve encouraging the *reconnecting of ethical and engineering economics*, and that will necessarily include critical dialogue with engineering economics not least in terms of its ethical presuppositions. It will certainly not be a matter of jettisoning engineering economics, including its basis in scarcity. It has made significant contributions to our understanding of economics, including economic growth processes. Like Cobb and Daly, with their strong environmentally sensitive critique of neoclassical economics, Sen's engagement with it from the heart of the discipline, and Jarl, feminist economist, promoting the ethical dimension of economics does not mean rejecting the core of contemporary economics, including market mechanisms as the most efficient way of allocating scarce resources. The task is therefore significantly the reformulation of tradition, not its replacement, 'on the basis of a paradigm that both clarifies the excellence of its past work and sets it in a larger context'. In other words we need not 'junk' its axioms. 'Many of them can continue to function, only with more recognition of their limits. The change will involve correction and expansion, a more empirical and historical attitude.'[304]

Now it is that commitment to *correction* and *expansion* that I have repeatedly encountered in the literature. The task of Christian political economy is to encourage such ethical *broadening* of neo-classical economics, and particularly through interdisciplinary dialogue. That involves taking the discipline of economics seriously, including engineering economics, by developing it in relation to such problematics as marginalization. What now follows are reflections on how this is being attempted with regard to three key areas of neoclassical economics: on economic man in terms of human nature and behaviour; efficiency in relation to debates about production and distribution; and the role of governance. Each generates opportunities for ethical conversation with mainstream economics in terms of identifying limitations and observing how such economic discourse can then promote the development of an economics to combat marginalization. Engaging marginalization is therefore not simply about reconnecting Christianity to the public realm. That, in turn, requires reconnecting ethics and economics. And that has to be a central task in reformulating Christian political economy.

'Economic man': platform for reformulating tradition

Any attempt to engage neoclassical economics has to begin with the foundation of its economic theorizing, with its view of human behaviour for addressing scarcity. The concept was introduced by J. S. Mill, father of economic man, consolidator of classical economics. For him, *homo economicus* was 'a being who invariably does that by which he may obtain the greatest amount of necessaries, conveniences and luxuries, with the smallest quantity of labour and physical self-denial with which they can be obtained in the existing state of knowledge'.[305] The contemporary theory is based on the assumption that people are rational. They make rational calculations on how best to use resources to better themselves. When faced with choices, an individual decides between them on the basis of what yields greater personal satisfaction in terms of their utility. People, in other words, choose to get the best possible satisfaction of their own preferences. They seek to maximize their utility. It is a profoundly individual-based understanding of the human, informed by self-interest, expressing its preferences through prices in the market.

This theorizing about human behaviour therefore generates models in which 'we abstract from the rich detail of human behaviour and focus only on behavior that is relevant for coping with scarcity'.[306] It is therefore focused on economic behaviour, and economists are very aware of its restrictive nature. Many critics, particularly theologians, do not realize that 'the view of human behaviour as rational and self-interested is an abstraction, a theoretical construction that is accentuating certain aspects of human behaviour that are used especially for economic decisions'.[307]

Working with that basic description and justification, four issues can be raised which then begin the process of broadening the ethical agenda.

First, it intentionally does not address the wider issues of political economy, of the human as citizen economist. Collste usefully highlights this limitation by recognizing that economically 'the person always chooses the alternative which gives him/her the greatest personal satisfaction (economics, psychological, etc), even if the choice is contrary to the common good'.[308] It is recognition that self-interest relates primarily to behaviour in the market. A poem of Stephen Leacock says it all:

Adam, Adam, Adam Smith,
Listen what I charge you with!
Didn't you say,
In the class one day,
that selfishness was bound to pay?
Of all the doctrines that was the Pith,
Wasn't it, wasn't it, wasn't it, Smith?[309]

But, as Smith acknowledges, other values like equity and justice then apply to wider society. So it is argued: 'motivation for mutually beneficial exchange does not need anything more than what Smith called "self-love"'. Such exchange was vital for economic analysis and resourcing human welfare. But in dealing with other problems – those of distribution and equity and of rule-following for generating productive efficiency – Smith emphasized broader motivations: 'humanity, generosity and public spirit are the qualities most useful to others'.[310]

Yet Sen also recognizes that the self-interested behaviour of economic man itself ignored wider relevant aspects of human nature, including the freedom to be and to do as human rights. So the assumption of neoclassical economics 'that preference satisfaction and nothing else is good could be accused of missing the points of agency, liberty and rights and dignity'.[311]

Second, that understanding of self-interest, keystone of economic man operating in the market, again is both necessary yet insufficient for engaging wider empirical realities. So Stigler is right to recognize that 'self-interest dominates the majority of men'.[312] Yet accepting rational self-interest as legitimate ethical motivation does not mean that it is anything but a narrow account of human behaviour, even though William Temple observed how life could be so ordered that 'self-interest prompts what justice demands'.[313] Yet even rational behaviour, as Butler acknowledged in the eighteenth century, 'may as well be directed towards the well-being of others as towards one's own well-being'.[314] This is but the recognition that we act from different values, including altruism, in the desires for food and sex, and to help others in need. It is at this point that Christian and religious opinion rightly has much to say. For we have seen how Gill's work on churchgoing identifies faith communities as locations for character formation, particularly promoting altruism as attitudes to voluntary service. The economic implications of altruism are explored later in this chapter. The danger, at this point of the discussion, is that theologians can rarely see beyond altruism, and that is of little help in engaging with neoclassical economics. So it is Sen who once again brings us back to economic behaviour, and explains how, even here, self-interest alone is an insufficient basis for explaining it. So with regard to the dynamic economies of South East Asia, and especially Japan, he observes that 'there is strong empirical evidence to suggest that systematic departures from self-interested behaviour in the direction of duty, loyalty and goodwill, have played a substantial part in industrial success'.[315]

Third, the focus of neoclassical economics on the individual is certainly highly relevant to a post-industrial and post-modern context, yet equally fails to account for how the individual is part of a complex social co-operative project, particularly in modern economies. Research into game theory, like the prisoners' dilemma, illustrates this significance of other-regarding motives in decision-making required by at least self-interest. By this objective each of us would better achieve our respective goals by collaborating than if all of us had pursued our individual self-goals.[316] It is strong confirmation of the sociology of knowledge that 'Moral notions are socially generated and – even when this is not realised by the participants themselves – rely upon specific communities for their support.'[317]

Fourth, the concept of economic man is now rightly recognized as problematic. Its masculine assumptions lead feminist econo-mists to explore how it emerged out of nineteenth-century contexts as a particular social construct, reflecting 'androcentric, Eurocentric and bourgeois assumptions that have been virtually culture-wide across the culture of science'.[318] Emphasizing the human as rationality, self-interest and individualism, it ignores the role of the 'other-interested, emotional and social'.[319] This expanding interpretation then allows an important connection to be made with the environment, as the broadening of the human into ecology.

Given such constructive and critical connections, it soon becomes evident that there are a number of overlapping consen-suses working through the reformulation of economic man. So Cobb and Daly operate with a view of person-in-community, still recognizing individuality, and so still in serious touch with neo-classical economics, accepting that 'many principles of classical and neoclassical economics, with proper historical qualifications, will function in an economy based on the different model of homo economicus as *person-in-community*'. Yet they also thereby recog-nize 'that the well-being of a community as a whole is constitutive of each person's welfare'.[320] Feminist economists similarly engage with neoclassical models but critically enlarge and reformulate them. They suggest the Imperfectly Rational Somewhat Economi-cal Person, 'a much more likely person situated in many different social relations'.[321] The economist, Arrow, also accepts ethical enlargement as more empirically accurate modelling: 'by opening an economic formalism for ethical considerations, it can also become realistic in a strictly empirical sense'.[322] It is an exercise in expanding 'the understanding of the characteristics belonging to economic man'[323] into a profound ethical reformulation.

Efficiency and equity: developing efficient ethical economics

The conflict of efficiency and justice, and the trade-offs we are required to make between them, are a perennial part of the ethical and economic task. It is raised particularly sharply in economics where it causes much misunderstanding, because many fail to recognize the nature and role of efficiency in neoclassical economics. Again, it was J. S. Mill who suggested an early distinction between production and distribution as a way of addressing these questions; they take us to the heart of the marginalization problematic.

For Mill, effective production followed the laws of the market, and efficiency was the primary economic principle which determined that. The distribution of goods and services again follows the principles of market economics *but* could also be informed by wider societal concerns, reflected classically in the principle of justice. So governments could allocate market resources through taxation and welfare systems as a necessary corrective to market inequalities. How to manage trade-offs between efficiency and justice therefore requires facing up to not what is good but what is better than what. It is out of these debates that valuable findings are emerging relating to the possibilities of efficient ethical economics for addressing marginalization, including environment.

With regard to production, there is considerable agreement on the effectiveness of the market mechanism: papal social teaching summarizes this opinion: 'the free market is the most efficient instrument for utilizing resources and effectively responding to human needs'.[324] Understanding this premise is particularly important because it involves accepting that the market economy is not designed to bring about just or equal outcomes but rather the most efficient. The value of efficiency is therefore central to neoclassical economics, reflecting the importance of *avoiding* the waste of scarce resources by *maximizing* their use. Even in relation to these definitions, questions are rightly raised with regard to those resources not measured by the price mechanism (much of women's and voluntary work, and environment, though all are being addressed by economists), and by the influence of the unequal initial distribution of resources before entering the market which connect to unequal outcomes. Both limitations are important for interpreting global economy and marginalization.

With regard to distribution, neoclassical economics ties this to contribution, payment being commensurate with the net contribution of the factors of production, land, labour and capital. Achieving higher rewards therefore requires improving the quality of your factor. Unless society through government interferes in this distribution then the results are likely to be efficient but at the cost of equity. Sen develops a useful critical agenda for such neoclassical economics.

First, he indicates how your productivity (and therefore contribution and reward) is the function of the complete set of your capabilities, as well as actual effort in production. Consequently, inequality in educational provisions will lead to inequality in productive effort regardless of choices made in the market. It is therefore wrong to tie distribution to contribution since this simply rewards 'the capabilities-rich for their advantages'.[325] In complex modern economies, societies past and present are repositories of knowledge and skills that dictate productivity levels. This is to recognize the contributions of families, health and education to production.

Second, he acknowledges how competitive market theory is controlled by income distributions resulting from decisions at the economic margins. This is reflected in the basic tool of welfare economics, the Pareto Optimality principle, which accepts improvement for some providing none are penalized. Again, as Sen observes, this principle still applies even 'with some people in extreme misery and others rolling in luxury'. Accordingly, an economy can be optimal in this sense as long as the miserable cannot be made better off without cutting into the luxury of the rich. Pareto optimality can, like '"Caesar's spirit", "come hot from hell"'.[326]

As a result of such criticisms the possibility emerges for an empirically based ethical economics which is also more efficient. For example, UNHDR surveys are now regularly suggesting that 'successful long-term economic growth is strongly linked to egalitarian public policies related to income, education and healthcare'.[327] So the UNHDR 1999 highlighted the crucial role of economic productivity and growth but within the wider framework of the human development of all citizens. This linking of production and distribution as two sides of the same coin of pro-poor economic growth is of profound importance for a Christian political economy. It is also increasingly recognized by other international organizations like the World Bank (2000–2001) whose studies found that 'the responsiveness of income poverty to growth increases significantly as inequality is lowered', and so more equal societies can grow faster. Therefore, for example, 'greater gender equity, and equity in general endowments and assets, has a double impact on poverty reduction because in more egalitarian societies the impact of growth rate is greater and the growth rate will itself prove to be higher'. It is the conclusion of these arguments which is then most striking, that *'justice is good for the economy'*.[328] It is therefore acknowledged, learning from the experience of the South East Asian economies, that we are dealing not as much with consequences of economic reforms, but economic consequences of social reform. For Sen, 'The market economy flourishes on the foundation of such development.'[329]

Integrally now part of such efficient ethical economics is the concern for sustainability, powerfully argued by the Brundtland Report, *Our Common Future* (1987). It is recognition that development is not just about human but also environmental development. So economic growth becomes not just pro-poor but also pro-environment, 'a process of change in which the exploitation of resources, the orientation of investments, the paths of technological development and institutional change, are in accordance with current and future needs'.[330] This then connects to the question raised in Chapters 1 and 3 with regard to the optimal scale of the economic system in relation to the wider ecosystem, and the effectiveness or otherwise of developing ways to internalize and distribute between generations external environmental costs through the market mechanism. It is the combination of such pro-poor and pro-environment economics which addresses marginalization, illustrating the efficiency of ethical economics, and confirming the judgement that 'There is therefore no real dividing line between economics and ethics; they merge together.'[331]

Economics and governance: reclaiming political economy

The neoclassical view of the state is intentionally minimalist: 'the less the state intervenes in the market, the better'. Arising as reaction to mercantilism's corporate interference in trade and business in the early eighteenth century, classical and then neoclassical economics developed a view of the free market treating such intervention with outright hostility. Reappearing as Thatcherism and Reagonomics in the 1980s, it deeply informs neoliberal dimensions of the global economy. Essentially, it argues that 'The optimal efficiency of the economic system presupposes that individuals have the opportunity to compete on a market without any restrictions. Behind this view lies the assumption of "the invisible hand", i.e. the idea developed by Adam Smith that if different actors compete on the market and act solely out of egoistic motives, the result of the competition will lead to the greatest social utility.'[332] This does not imply that government has no role in economic life; it has certain key but confined functions, from maintaining law and order to ensuring competition. It is a role accepted from Adam Smith to the present. This understanding of minimal state complements and underwrites the neoclassical commitment to the individual. Yet at precisely this point, revealed in the earlier exploration of the UNDP and Sen's interpretation of human capabilities as both individuality and social, engaging with marginalization requires reformulating what it means to be human and consequently what it means to promote inclusive societies. In this way, the neoclassical understanding of governance is pushed into wider frameworks. The arguments which support such developments emerge from engagement with the economics of marginalization, although they clearly lead to repositioning politics in relation to economics. They are strongly linked to earlier arguments in the book.

First, Sen's work on famines[333] has demonstrated how they occur under authoritarian regimes. The presence of democracy, with its civil and political liberties, creates an accountability of government to people which has ruled out the likelihood of famines.

Second, UNDP research has repeatedly indicated the close relationship between economic performance and good government, with politics working in partnership with business to promote economic growth. When that is directed into pro-poor and pro-environment economic growth then more egalitarian consequences benefit the poor and society as a whole. So, 'A longitudinal UNDP study . . . compared the economic development of the industrialized countries between 1870 and 1970. It showed Sweden and Japan, two countries with extensive social intervention, were two of the most successful ones in economical terms.'[334] This commitment to targeted active government is closely associated with the importance of opposition to institutional corruption, and the promotion of peace, identified in Chapter 3. It also links to earlier recognitions that empowering marginalized groups, like women, is crucial for their inclusion in society and more effective functioning of the economy.[335]

Third, there are important overlapping consensuses of theological and secular opinion suggesting that eroding marginalization and promoting more inclusive economies and societies is increasingly associated not just with democratic governance, but now with the transition from majoritarian democracy, with its tendency to exclude minorities, to inclusive democracy. Here I am thinking of the work of Sen as economist, Young as political philosopher, and Boff as liberation theologian. For example, the latter argues for 'an extended and enriched democracy' incorporating environment.[336] But it is Young's research which creatively reformulates this trend into a *'differentiated solidarity'*.[337] This allows her to widen participation by empowering marginalized groups in political decision-making through positive discrimination strategies, including broadening communication beyond reasoned argument by the use of narrative. Recognizing shared needs and rights, but equally difference, should be seen as necessary political expression and accompaniment of Sen's connection of general human rights and development to the different capabilities required to properly function as human beings. And it all becomes the embodiment of theological understandings of the body of Christ as a bias for inclusivity.

Fourth, overlapping consensuses also occur between Collste's earlier adaptation of Rawls' difference principle, targeting justice on behalf of the marginalized but now extended to the Law of the Peoples, and Young's development of the principle of differentiated solidarity on a global scale. This then becomes significant for rejecting a universal global ethic and government while accepting the need for political collaboration globally in ways which acknowledge the integrity and necessity of local participation, including civil society. It is affirmation that 'Coupled with arguments for global governance, this conception of the self-determination of peoples produces a vision of local and cultural autonomy in the context of global regulatory regimes', each addressing key global problematics like environment and security.[338] The challenge to existing international bodies like the IMF, WB and WTO therefore becomes their development into open democratic governance but also into the inclusive democracy of differentiated solidarity, empowering poorer nations for their effective involvement in such global governance.

It is these cumulative developments to democratic governance, arising out of basic commitment to develop the capabilities of each person to function in her society and world, to be free and to do, which brings together commitment to ethical economics and inclusive governance. It therefore reclaims the multifaceted concept of political economy as a way of engaging contemporary marginalization. It is what we will promote as the central part of reformulated Christian political economy.

Christian Political Economy as Measuring Marginalization: Developing Performative Disciplines

The overall task of developing Christian political economy includes bringing closer together moral and economic discussions. How we do this has involved critical conversations between ethics and neoclassical economics. Yet much more needs to be done. For if we begin with the marginalization problematic, then that will also require connecting economics and ethics in very practical ways. Developing appropriate methods of measuring marginalization, and the effectiveness of measures to reduce it, must be central to any such endeavour. It is embodying Christian political economy concerns in practical measurement systems, an exercise in applied ethics and theology as performative discipline. If governments providing resources to combat marginalization use impact statements to see if their money is spent effectively, then theology committed to praxis informed by a bias for inclusivity will need to do likewise.

Yet this necessary focus on measuring marginalization runs into the problems identified in Chapters 2, 3 and 4 as a growing tendency to rely on measuring quantifiable achievements, from church to economic growth, and how this is informed by viewing the human as economic man. That restricted understanding has been challenged by recognizing key contributions to economic welfare which extend beyond income measurements and link to an interpretation of human capabilities and the complexity and dynamic nature of realities.

Measuring marginalization has to reflect all these findings. It has to record measurable achievements, say in reducing illiteracy, acknowledging with the chief executive of Coca Cola that 'what gets measured gets done'.[339] Yet it will also take account of more elusive realities like capabilities to function, the freedom to be and to do, accepting with Paula Rayman that 'we measure what we value'. Like the UNDP, it becomes an agenda 'to put people back at the centre of development',[340] surely an agenda for Christian political economy.

Developing ways of measuring the marginalization identified in the second essay will therefore have the following features. It will be:

- Multilayered, and so able to encompass different strands of marginalization, and reflecting the complexity of contemporary change. For example, it will engage with the centrality of resources as income, in distributional terms within nations as well as more traditional aggregative scoring between nations. But it will also work with capabilities in education and health, and moving further to include civil and political liberties, and environmental concerns.
- Global, in that it will need to be able to assess 'the state of human development across the globe'.[341]
- Provisional, reflecting inadequacies of existing data. For example, 66 developing economies have produced no recent information on income poverty (US$1 a day, 1993). Yet it also accepts we are dealing with 'provisional definitions of the society yet to be constructed, as evolving principles reshaped by the continuing encounter with an evolving society' and global debate.[342] Villa-Vicencio's comments here link to the middle axiom methodology in Chapter 5, and wider acknowledgement of the process character of change, religion, marginalization and the human.

Such a multilayered global measurement system is best based on the UN Human Development Index (HDI), tracked through annual UNHD Reports, extended to include their material from the Gender-related Development Index (GDI) and civil and political rights. Alongside this should run Hicks' Inequality Adjusted HDI, (IAHDI), adapted to identify inequality of distribution of capabilities within nations, and therefore taking us into the centre of marginalization processes. Finally, we need to add environmental impact measurements as used by Cobb and Daly. Work on church marginalization measurement was begun in Chapters 2 and 4, and needs to be linked to these systems. I will briefly elaborate the latter with sources, illustrating how they embody the measurement principles identified.

Primarily, the basic HDI was developed by annual UNHD Reports from 1990 to indicate how countries are achieving decent standards of living for their people. It is therefore global in reach, despite limitations in data coverage. Essentially, it measures average achievements in each country in three basic areas of human development, following Sen's key capabilities to function:

- A decent standard of living measured by GDP per capita (total production of a nation divided by number of people). This measurement arose around the Second World War as a classic indication of the economic wealth and growth of a country. Yet by 1971, it was regarded as a too narrow and one-dimensional measurement of economic-social performance. For example, it excluded the contribution of the informal sector (of major significance in developing economies and women's work), and of environmental impacts. Yet despite limitations, it rightly remains indispensable for our measurement system because of the centrality of economic performance for sustaining and enhancing human life, and because economic welfare and GNP generally advance together. Ready availability of statistics in this field stand in sharp contrast to the following indices, a clear indication of distorted ethical priorities: 'Why should trade balance data be available soon after the end of every month, while data on child malnutrition or school enrolments often take years to produce – years that excluded children may never recover?'[343] Correcting that situation is a clear priority for Christian political economy.

- A long and healthy life, relating to problems of preventable morbidity and mortality, often linked to birth and early age survival, but increasingly focusing on life expectancy at birth.
- Good knowledge, again relating to the proportion of people in primary, secondary and tertiary education, but increasingly focusing on adult literacy, including years spent in formal education.

The HDI is a composite index of these three variables, generating a value range from 0 to 1. It therefore reveals the distance a country has to go to reach the norm of 1. Accordingly, it also allows inter-country comparisons. The HDI 2000 therefore revealed a state of human development (HD), based on 174 countries, of:

- 46 in the highest category (HD of 0.80 or more). Canada, Norway and the USA led the field.
- 93 in the medium (HD of 0.50–0.79).
- 35 in the lowest (HD less than 0.50). The bottom 22 were all in Africa, particularly Sub Saharan Africa.

More detail can be found in Chapter 3.

However, we need to add further measurement systems identified in the UNHD Reports.

First, the Gender-related Development Index (GDI), which measures achievement in the same three variables as the HDI, but as inequalities in achievement between men and women. Given the critical importance of the development of women for overcoming marginalization, the GDI must play a central role in our measurement system. What it reveals, for example, is that, in comparison with the HDI ranking, the GDI shows Ireland falling 12 places, Saudi Arabia 33, but Poland rising 13.

Second, because governance, including civil and political liberties, has figured so prominently in this enquiry, identifying progress in such human rights must also be central to our measurement system. The UNHD reports acknowledge this, attempting to introduce it in 1991–92, but failed to continue because evidence was too impressionistic. The 2002 Report, *Deepening Democracy in a Fragmented World*, has returned to this theme. This remains a major challenge to UNHD Reports and Christian political economy.

Hicks has done valuable work in developing the HDI to take account of inequalities within nations, an essential progression for effective engagement with marginalization processes.[344] In other words, in income measurement, per capita levels of aggregate production of a nation do not reveal income distribution within the nation. He has therefore set distributional information alongside the aggregate information of the HDI, using the same three functioning areas. This allows us to combine aggregate and distributional information. In Hicks' words, 'I extend the project from predominantly aggregative indicators to include distributional measures as well',[345] using the Gini coefficient tool from the discipline of economics to enable comparison across goods. By combining such data in each of the three areas, the resulting IAHDI allows us to identify inequality of performance within and between nations, including with reference to racial and gender-based groups. For example, in the USA, 'when inequality and income-based productivity are factored together, "well-being growth" in the Kennedy–Johnson era far exceeded that in the Reagan era'. It was a similar story in Britain, with the 1980s revealing significantly poorer performance than in previous decades.[346]

One further measurement is required in relation to environmental concerns. This follows the Brundtland Report principle (1987) that economic growth should meet 'the needs of the present without compromising the ability of future generations to meet their own needs'.[347] Much work has been done in this field, for example in Sweden.[348] I will illustrate its feasibility with reference to Cobb and Daly's Index of Sustainable Economic Welfare (ISEW). This accepts the need to run environmental alongside social and economic indicators. Although they acknowledge with regard to environmental indices, 'a great deal of arbitrariness in even the best effort to account for depletion of "natural capital" ', the ISEW covers such critically important areas as: costing damage done to water quality (water pollution), air pollution costs (including acid rain, emissions, etc.), noise pollution costs, loss of wetlands, damage to farmland (erosion, urbanization, compaction of land through over-fertiliser use), the depletion of non-renewable resources, and the cost of dumping waste products into the environment (CFCs, CO_2, radioactive storage). On this basis, the ISEW is used to measure the 'true health of our economy over the past 36 years'. It reveals a growth rate considerably below the GDP rate, with progress made in reducing air pollution, but most significantly, regression in the total index linked to growing inequalities in the 1980s. In terms of measures to combat environmental damage, the message is similar to that which connects pro-poor economic growth, reducing inequalities, and overall performance, 'that the choice of policies by the government can indeed have a positive effect on economic welfare even if they do not increase physical output'.[349]

In other words, developing an effective marginalization measurement system suggests that 'A global policy regime is just to the degree that it promotes the harmonization of capabilities to achieve functionings at a level that is sufficient, universally attainable and sustainable.' Yet the multifaceted nature of the system suggested is but the early stages of a *process* and not a final moral pronouncement; it is 'a place to begin a conversation about policy', with a variety of disciplines and voices, North and South.[350] And a reformulated Christian political economy must be part of that conversation.

Christian Political Economy as Embodying Faith Convictions: the Role of Religious Economics

Developing Christian political economy, particularly in dialogue with economics and other faiths, must recognize the potential in religious traditions for enlarging the economic project, especially with regard to critical engagement with marginalization processes. It should acknowledge that Judaeo-Christian–Islamic traditions have incorporated important experiences of economic life, and continue to do so. I will justify these claims with reference to the campaign for debt remission led by the Christian-inspired Jubilee 2000 coalition, and Muslim interest-free banking. Since the first is well known to Christian opinion. I will pay more attention to the latter.

In terms of resonating with themes emerging from these three essays, this particular discrete contribution to Christian political economy is intriguingly insightful.

First, the examples highlight the central role of finance in emerging global contexts. We have observed how financial markets, through new communication technologies and deregulation, are becoming almost a law to themselves, disconnected from real economies and governments. As accumulated debt, especially of Low Income Countries, finance has also become a major factor in marginalization processes. Addressing such matters therefore recognizes that religious traditions must engage with core economic realities of today's changing global context.

Second, cancelling the unpayable debt of the poorest nations, and providing low-cost credit for their local empowerment programmes, illustrate religious awareness of some principal causes and solutions of marginalization.

Third, the examples illustrate how religious traditions incorporate historically and contemporarily important experiences of and for economic life. Although references are made to Jewish, Christian and Islamic traditions, this essay focuses on Christian political economy albeit with interfaith and interdisciplinary work now a formative part of that Christian identity. As part of that enlarged identity, the movement against international debt embodies the theological principal of a bias for inclusivity and is explicitly rooted in Old and New Testament teaching. It therefore reflects the concern for a distinctively Christian contribution to economic life which radical orthodoxy and others argue for so strongly. The legitimacy of that concern is therefore acknowledged and elaborated in this section on Christian political economy, yet in such practical detail not found in these other theological schools. The critique of that concern is argued by the fact that it must be only one of four parts of Christian political economy. It is one way only in which theology and economic praxis can and do interact as a two-way street. This consequently confirms and broadens our understanding of theology as a performative discipline.

Lastly, the inclusion of an example from another faith, Islam, shows how this dimension of Christian political economy occurs in other religious traditions. This provides opportunity for interfaith dialogue and practical collaboration at all levels of global society, and especially in local projects. It certainly allows the church to reformulate itself as a gradually extending ecumenics, to the whole created order.

Jubilee 2000: debt relief as altruism and enlightened self-interest

As partnership with other faiths and NGOs, the campaign of Jubilee 2000 for releasing the poorest nations from the oppressive burden of unpayable debt is a classic example of the way religious beliefs can interact with economic realities and change them for the better.

So, on the one hand, it focuses on proclaiming the Lord's Jubilee year of 2000, and its hoped-for deliverance of people from the slavery of marginalization through debt. For so it was recounted in the Old Testament, 'And you shall hallow the fiftieth year, and proclaim liberty throughout the land to all its inhabitants; it shall be a Jubilee for you.' (Lev. 25:10). And, in the New Testament, Jesus, in his first address in the synagogue interprets his ministry through that jubilee, 'The Spirit of the Lord is upon me, because he has anointed me to preach good news to the poor. He has sent me to proclaim release to the captives and recovering of sight to the blind, to set at liberty those who are oppressed, to proclaim the acceptable year of the Lord.' (Luke 4.18–19). It was this biblical message which inspired Wilberforce and other Christians in their historic movement to liberate black slaves in the early nineteenth century, and then Jubilee 2000's campaign at the end of the twentieth century. They are fine illustrations of Gill's research, in Chapter 5, showing how regular churchgoing informs characters of voluntary giving and altruism.

On the other hand, the inspiration of Christian tradition and faith experience today, was to therefore respond to the marginal-ization problematic of the poorest nations' debt. Because it has become unpayable, they struggle to simply pay the interest, and that is at immense cost to their economies, people and environment, and, conversely, to the great benefit of the richest nation creditors. In 1999, according to the IMF/WB, the 41 Heavily Indebted Poor Countries (HIPC), four-fifths in Sub Saharan Africa, owed $127 billion. The agreed task was to find ways of faster debt relief, to free fiscal resources to allow these nations to improve human development. Their need was desperate, with 40% of people income poor, 34% of children under five suffering malnutrition, and 43% of adults illiterate. Yet one of the poorest, Zambia, spends 40% of its yearly budget on debt servicing, allowing 6.7% for basic social services.[351] To free even a modest proportion of that 40% would enhance millions of people's basic capabilities to survive and move into more fulfilled lives.

Now it is the interaction between Christian tradition and the global economic problematic which generated Jubilee 2000, a coalition which has 'forced Third World debt to the top of the international agenda, and in doing so it helped to bring the interest of the poorest people to the front of economic debate'.[352] Remarkably, 24 million signed its petition, complemented by the great grass-roots demonstration at the Birmingham G8 Summit in 1998. As a result of such pressure, bodies like the IMF/WB are now committed to relieve up to 70% of the $127 billion debt of the HIPCs, a moving illustration of how religious altruism combined with enlightened self-interest, can achieve substantial economic change.

Muslim interest-free banking: alternative to usury-based economic development

One of the most decisive religious responses to economic life in general, and neoclassical economics in particular, is the rejection of usury or interest in financial transactions. As Muslim interest-free banking (MIFB), it represents the re-emergence in the 1970s of a tradition which played a prominent part in Judaic, Christian and Islamic religious economics at least up to the late middle ages. Because of this representative history, it is worth exploring it in more detail as an exemplar of embodying distinctive religious insights in contemporary economic life, of effective ways of engaging marginalization, and of interdisciplinary dialogue.

The theological origins of the rejection of usury are well known, and shared across the three great monotheistic faiths, yet with different elaborations and some shared interpretations.[353]

Jewish tradition was law-based, running through the Torah, and exemplified by the deuteronomic obligation 'You shall not lend upon interest to your brother' (Deut. 23.19f.).[354] Its concern was to protect community life, and particularly the poor, from the divisive oppression of debt. And, because it restricted this require-ment to the religious community, it reinforced its identity in the midst of hostile religions, traditions and tribes (strongly resonat-ing with the recent Islamic resurgence). It was therefore a two-tier system: no usury charged to members of the religious community, yet lending at interest to outsiders was legitimate. It was a bias to poor brother at the expense of the Other. In the great twelfth-century Code of Maimonides, 'it is written unto the heathen thou shalt lend upon interest'. By the twentieth century, in terms of Jewish tradition and state, 'The prohibition on interest has lost all practical significance in business transactions, and is now relegated to the realm of friendly and charitable loans.'[355]

Christian tradition shared the Old Testament foundations of the critique of usury, but in the New Testament embodied its universalist and inclusivist strands in blanket condemnation of usury, following the injunction of Luke: 'Lend expecting nothing in return.' (Luke 6.35). Medieval Catholic teaching, strongly influenced by rediscovery of Aristotelian thinking, itself through Islamic sources, continued that rejection of interest, but sought ways to readjust to commercial expansion by legitimating charging for productive loans, at the lender's risk, and not therefore infringing the belief in the barrenness of money. These religious attempts to control economic activities fell into disrepute from the sixteenth century onwards in Europe: 'religious dogma ceased to represent an analysis of existing society'; its place was therefore taken by the new discipline of economics, which did.[356]

Islamic tradition's early condemnation of usury, *riba*, was based on teachings of the Qur'an and the Shari'ah, the divine law governing private and public life. Usury was regarded as exploitation of the poor, contrary to the integrity of the religious community, in conflict with *ummah*. By the early modern period, 'Like Christianity Islam forbade usury; and like Christianity it managed to forget this economically inconvenient doctrine when it needed to.'[357] But, unlike Western Judaism and Christianity, Islam experienced a revival, again in the astonishing post-1960s generation, and manifested, for example, in developing distinctive Islamic teaching on economics. And MIFB is part of that strategic development, reflecting the search for identity in the midst of threats of globalization, post-modernity, and plurality. It is therefore 'the only religion at present engaged in a serious attempt to practically apply its moral and ethical teaching with regard to the concept of usurious lending within the context of the market-place, i.e. a global free-market economy'.[358]

Incorporating the religious condemnation of *riba* into the banking system reflects Islamic understanding of a community concerned to protect the poor and foster productive partnerships. The money deposited in banks is lent to clients, say to build a factory. In return, the industrialist pays a specified percentage of the profits for a designated period, which is passed on to its depositors by the bank. Losses are similarly shared. Trade-oriented activities therefore replace credit activities and interest: 'interest-bearing loans are replaced by profit-seeking investments'.[359] Such banking can closely relate to micro credit schemes (essentially provision of low-cost credit at local level), and again follows the principle of the provision of loans in money or in kind (say, cattle), with agreed proportions of profit shared with the bank. In poorer Islamic societies in the South, this can be a particularly important form of credit, respecting local religious beliefs, and involving communities in decision-making. The role of the Islamic Development Bank, more agency than bank, provides loans, often in partnership with other agencies, including the WB, to support local projects for long-term development. The major MIFBs in the North, including now in Europe, emerged in the 1970s: in 1977, the International Association of Islamic Banks was formed to promote interest-free banking through partnership schemes; in 1975, the Dubai Islamic Bank was founded, the Kuwait Finance House in 1977, and the Saudi Bank in London in 1981. These operate parallel to traditional Western banking systems, but standing as a financial paradigm for facing up to marginalization from an Islamic perspective, a reminder that 'Social goals are understood to form an inseparable element of the Islamic banking system that cannot be dispensed with or neglected.'[360]

It is such Islamic banking methodology which could have a 'major role in the development of the Third World', in the struggle against marginalization, but also in actually addressing the modern economic system itself from the perspective of a distinctive religious tradition. It suggests for one commentator, that 'A puritan and scripturalist world religion does not seem necessarily doomed to erosion by modern conditions. It may on the contrary be favoured by them.'[361]

Both Jubilee 2000 and MIFB illustrate the feasibility of embodying distinctive insights, drawn from religious tradition, in global economic life, albeit in restricted areas. Yet given the power of both Christianity and Islam in the poor South, their potential for contributing to engagement with marginalization is great. For example, both lead directly into the burgeoning field of microcredit and then into microenterprises, linking with such success stories as the Grameen Bank and the UNDP Special Unit for Microfinance. They exemplify that potential for partnerships against marginalization which Clare Short, the UK Secretary of

State for International Development, advocated in her address to the Church of England's General Synod: we need to construct 'a worldwide alliance of people of faith and moral purpose to ensure that we commit ourselves to the elimination of extreme poverty from the world' during this new century.[362] For such micro schemes provide both skills and resources for self-development, and thereby, through empowering local people, also contribute to self-determination; and increasingly they are geared to women, at the centre of struggles against marginalization. Young is right to recognize that 'Currently some of the most creative social movement activities in the world involve people seeking equitable development of their local economies in demanding transnational attention to matters of democracy and distributive justice.'[363] That takes us back into the emerging debates, so recognized in these essays, about gender inclusivity in economics and politics, into arguments for differentiated solidarity. That is why these two examples of religious economics are of such potential importance. They are about the practice of political economy, informed by a bias for inclusivity. And because they are so religiously inspired and embodied by religious people in society, they therefore become a central part of this reformulation of the tradition of Christian political economy.

Christian Political Economy: the Role of Heresy in Reformulating Tradition

A context increasingly dominated by globalization and pluralism invariably provokes insurgency. Whether as an anti-globalization movement, religious fundamentalism or political-ethnic tribalism, people and communities are struggling to define and protect identities. It is easy for dominant mainstream traditions, like the global market economy, neoclassical economics and orthodox Christianity to ignore such threats to the cohesion of their comprehensive theories and institutions. Yet the complexity of contemporary change and context will inevitably challenge and require traditions to change. That will be particularly the case if they wish to influence such change for the better. Learning from the changing context is an essential part of such mutation of tradition. Listening to the Other is indispensable to that process whether as interdisciplinary or interfaith engagement. Yet the task of reformulating the tradition of Christian political economy requires moving even wider, into dialogue with heresies, in this case theological economics. Writing the three essays in this book has driven me to this conclusion.

The stories I want to tell to illustrate strengths and limitations of such heresies have emerged from my research and teaching in Christian social ethics. I have called them the *heteroclitical tradition*. This describes how these stories of modern Christian social thought and practice all deviate from established norms of mainstream economics and economies. They could therefore be seen as economic heresies, contrary to orthodox doctrine.[364] I will briefly tell the stories, and then identify lessons to be learned for reformulating Christian political economy and wider traditions. Our context and its global problematics like marginalization are likely to require such reformulations. Central to that task, I have now come to see, is making connections. Overcoming the marginalization of peoples, environment and Christianity requires no less.

Over the years I have become aware of recurrent episodes in modern Christian social ethics, running from the late eighteenth century to the present, which I have provisionally titled the heteroclitical tradition. Essentially, it seeks to connect Christianity and economics by using one economic feature in a particular period to embody Christian beliefs and values within the contemporary economic situation. The examples all relate to struggles against marginalization, not least because they all coincide with periods of significant economic unrest. None has become mainstream economics or theology. Yet they have all excited theological and economic interest, and exercised considerable influence within their contexts. Indeed, they should be regarded as heresies in the positive and critical sense, for example as used by James Cone in his black theology and Rosemary Ruether in her feminist theology.[365] By this I mean serious alternatives to dominant mainstream traditions in theology and economics which deserve serious attention but never the recognition given to mainstream practices. All therefore represent alternative scenarios to dominant traditions, yet because of their imbalanced concentration on very particular, indeed singular, problems or possibilities, they never translate into feasible alternatives. In that sense they represent the impracticality of the utopian. In identifying these stories of the heteroclitical, I have found support in Galbraith's delightful

Short History of Financial Euphoria,[366] from seventeenth-century Dutch bulb speculation and the eighteenth-century English South Sea Bubble, to US junk bonds of the late twentieth century. A brief recitation of these heteroclitical stories will indicate the breadth and insightfulness of this tradition.

- Beginning in the late eighteenth and early nineteenth centuries, with the emergence of urban-industrial societies and modern Christian social ethics and economics, we find the story of the conflict between Malthus and the romantics, led by Southey, Wordsworth and Coleridge, in collaboration with the utopians Godwin, Condorcet and Owen. The latter worked with belief in progress to perfection, involving radical restructuring of institutions, including economic, so freeing people to become fully human. Malthus and the Christian political economists rejected that utopian abundance and perfection because it ignored the constraints of finitude and sin, that man '(n)either is, or ever will be, in a state, when he may safely throw down the ladder by which he has risen to this eminence'.[367] There will always be struggle, but yet also possibility of improvement, but never perfection. So Malthus recognized the value of social-economic experiments like Owen's New Lanark Mills, but not as universal panaceas.
- F. D. Maurice and the early Christian socialists concentrated on producer co-operatives around 1850. Arising from Maurice's belief that the Fatherhood of God required the brotherhood of man, the little producer co-operatives sought to reject the belief that competition, despite being central to classical economics, was seen as contrary to God's purposes of fellowship among human beings. They therefore reflected Maurice's belief in the primacy of the ethical, rooted in theology, but not in conversation with economics. For if it had been, he would have realized that monopoly, not co-operation, is the opposite of competition. The experiment in theological economics soon failed because it overlooked the human frailties of managers and workers, and basic economic laws of production.
- Stewart Headlam, leader of the radical Christian socialist Guild of St Matthew (1877), promoted the Single Tax in the 1880s to take land into public ownership. Like many radicals in the 1880s in the USA and Britain, Headlam advocated Henry George's Single Tax as the answer to problems of industrialization

and urbanization. Land ownership in Britain was certainly a problem, with 80% in 1873 being owned by fewer than 7,000 people. Speculation exacerbated urban land problems for rapidly growing populations. Yet George believed that '*all* the ills of the economy followed from the commodification of land and could be eliminated by its abolition'.[368] But here too was a recognition of land as trust, and as sustainable.

- Conrad Noel and Maurice Reckitt advocated, through the Church Socialist League (1906), Guild Socialism in the 1900s as a form of workers' control. This involved sorting out society's problems by reorganizing industries on medieval craft guild bases, controlled by members (workers).

- V. A. Demant, Maurice Reckitt and the Christendom Group promoted Major Douglas' Social Credit scheme in the 1930s to inject demand into the economy. This was deeply opposed by economists like Denys Munby and Ronald Preston for its grave economic flaws, for example the problem of increasing money supply and high inflation. For Munby, reviewing Demant's work, 'learning, wisdom and prophetic insight afford no guarantee that error will be eliminated, where technical knowledge is lacking'.[369]

- Liberation theology used the Marxist-Leninist dependency theory in the 1970s and 1980s, attributing Third World poverty to Western capitalism. For Gutiérrez, even though he later modified his views, 'The dynamics of the capitalist economy lead to the establishment of a centre and a periphery, simultaneously generating progress and growing wealth for the few and social imbalances, political tensions and poverty for the many.'[370] The reliance on one theory, contested by Marxist and mainstream economists alike, illustrates the problem of undue reliance on a particular tool, and that primarily sociological, for engaging complex political economy matters.

- David Jenkins and others attacked the neoliberal free market as an assault on market economies in the late 1990s. For Ronald Preston, this represented a serious flaw because it failed to separate the adequacy of the market as the most efficient allocative mechanism on offer from its neoliberal ideological misuse.[371] The latter is open to such strong criticism, the market mechanism much less so. The radical theologians fail to make this distinction sufficiently.

- Radical orthodoxy promotes today late medieval neo-Thomist economics. Essentially the work of Long,[372] this includes strong criticism of mainstream Christian social ethics, but develops an inadequate alternative economy based on the medieval economics of just price and wage, and rejection of usury.

There are important links between some of these episodes. For example, the first and last converge as romantic rejection of modernization processes. Interestingly, all were ignorant of economics, and some have provoked important criticisms by economists, including Christians. Here I think of Malthus' critique of Godwin, Munby of Demant, Moll of Liberation theology's dependency theory, and Preston of Jenkins. Because of their concentration on particular insights and their attempts to embody them in their contexts, they are all stories of failure. Adherence to them is likely to bring Christian social ethics into disrepute and contribute to further marginalization from public arenas and debates. More importantly, they have never effectively addressed marginalization processes pre-eminently because of their mono-causal analysis, focusing, say on producer co-operatives, or land, workers' control, credit, and dependency theory. To identify such complex realities as marginalization processes with such single causes leads inevitably to simplistic unachievable solutions. That imbalanced approach is only compounded by almost pathological rejection of industrialization, urbanization, capitalism, market economies and now globalization.

Yet the value of each story is its inclusion of an insight of renewed importance in the contemporary context. For example, Godwin's advocacy of justice, Maurice of co-operatives and microenterprises, Headlam and the intrinsic value of land, guild socialism and employee participation schemes, Major Douglas and microcredit programmes, liberation theology and the critique of oppression in economics and politics, David Jenkins and the critique of neoliberal global ideology, and radical orthodoxy's valuing of interest-free finance.

Their significance is even greater. For they remind us of the importance of critical engagement with mainstream economic and theological traditions, of 'Questioning the ostensibly unquestionable premises of our way of life.'[373]

But yet again, it is how the critique is formulated and argued, in dialogue with other disciplines and experiences which determines its viability. That commitment to interdisciplinary collaboration is now prerequisite for effective involvement in complex contemporary problematics. A reformulated Christian political economy is committed to such dialogic relationships; witness the critical engagement with neoclassical economics, measurement systems, religious economics, and theological-economic heresies. The latter reminds us of the value of building up 'a timely reservoir of reforming proposals' in critical interaction with the mainstream tradition of economics.[374] It is that multilayered character of a reformulated Christian political economy which represents the possibility of more effectively reconnecting Christianity to such a problematic as marginalization. It is in that sense that I for once agree with radical orthodoxy, that 'The theological task is the proliferation of a complex space.'[375]

The heteroclitical tradition has one more lesson to teach us. For it stands as a reminder of the importance of alternatives to mainstream traditions in economics and theology. So it warns these traditions that unless they adapt to changing contexts and problematics, they are unlikely to survive. Indeed, they would not deserve to. So far, capitalism and mainstream economics have endured because of their willingness and ability to reformulate their traditions in the light of greatly changing contexts. That is about mutating memories and traditions. The sheer awesome power and complexity of great global problematics, including marginalization and the environment, located in the emerging context of such rapid change, will be a supreme test of that ability.

Yet this challenge to reformulate tradition applies as much to Christianity as to neoclassical economics and market economies. For MacIntyre has reminded us that a tradition is likely to face 'epistemological crisis' when it is 'inadequate for engagement with a changing context'.[376] The rapid decline of the churches in Europe and increasing irrelevance of Christianity to the public square suggests such a crisis now exists, epitomized by the double whammy. This final essay has sought to reconnect Christianity and society by reformulating Christian tradition in response to the challenge of changing contexts and global problematics. For example, it has begun to reconstruct Christian political economy as an 'enlarged narrative'.[377] The result goes way beyond the original tradition and its contemporary manifestations, by drawing on other Christian and ethical traditions, and by engaging in critical conversation with different disciplines, experiences and faiths. In this sense, it rejects any view that the Church is the social ethic, 'a closed community with its distinctive economics'. It portrays rather a Church that is 'located in this world and has distinctive sources for ethical reflection and practice'.[378] What is emerging from these essays is therefore a profoundly dialogic interpretation of Church, theology and Christian political economy. To reproduce or maintain a tradition which essentially excludes the Other would fly in the face of all the evidence and ethical insights emerging from this enquiry.

Faith as making connections

It is as though the answer is in the problem. For in addressing the marginalization problematic, which so separates peoples, environment and religion from each other, the way forward surely becomes a process of reconnecting peoples, environment and religion. The more I have entered into this enquiry, the more I have been driven to use words like linkages and connections. *Making connections*[379] is what I am left with at the end of these essays. For given the analysis of changing contexts and marginalization, the journey has required reconnecting politics and economics, and then Christianity, in a new tradition of Christian political economy, of linking engineering and ethical economics in a critical broadening of neoclassical economics, of linking praxis and theological reflection in an interactive way, of extending the Church into interfaith, of projecting theology into the public square, of developing human capabilities into functionings, reflected in appropriate interlinking measurement systems, of a bias for the marginalized which is also for inclusivity, of the foundational connection of difference and commonality as differentiated solidarity. If I look at all that, it is as though the Christian task becomes participation in the making of a great patchwork quilt, weaving all these different insights and experiences into a whole, a rich tapestry of immense variety.[380]

It is that theme of making connections which then takes us into the environment and the nature of God. For linkages between political economy and the human are increasingly extending into the ecosystem. Responding to that becomes the task of an even more enlarged narrative. It is as though for Boff, a 'new paradigm . . . is coming to birth – that of connectedness'. And that, as he rightly concludes, takes us into understandings of God, Christ and Church as profoundly and irretrievably dialogic. Indeed, it is as though 'The logic of the universe is dialogical; everything interacts with everything'. The Greeks expressed this as *perichoresis*, meaning circularity and the inclusion of all relationships and beings. Strikingly, in Christian tradition, it points to the relationship of 'mutual presence and interpenetration between God and the universe or between the three Divine Persons among themselves and with all creation'.[381]

So it is that dialogic or perichoretic logic, linking divine and ecological realities, which takes us into contemporary change, into the great marginalization problematic, and therefore into the reconnecting of Christianity with that total context.

NOTES

Introduction How I Changed My Mind: Problematics and Processes

1. C. Brown, *The Death of Christian Britain: Understanding Secularisation 1800–2000*, Routledge, 2001.

2. R. Gill, *Churchgoing and Christian Ethics*, Cambridge University Press, 1999.

3. This is a well-documented procedure. For example, Tim Jenkins, *Religion in English Everyday Life: An Ethnographic Approach*, Berghahn Books, 1999, p. 19, works on a 'puzzle, provided by a specific religious phenomenon' as a way of elaborating different interpretive frameworks, and in so doing, offers models for understanding mechanisms at work in a number of modern societies.

4. J. M. Keynes, *Essays in Biography*, Macmillan, 1933, p. 170, on Alfred Marshall.

5. R. H. Preston, *Confusions in Christian Social Ethics: Problems for Geneva and Rome*, SCM Press, 1994, p. 148.

6. D. Forrester, *Truthful Action: Explorations in Practical Theology*, T & T Clark, 2000, p. 116.

7. This procedure is followed by D. Winch, *Riches and Poverty: An Intellectual History of Political Economy in Britain, 1750–1834*, Cambridge University Press, 1996.

8. Keynes, p. 262.

9. M. Taylor, *Poverty and Christianity*, SCM Press, 2000, p. 5.

Chapter 1 Unresolved Dilemmas: Challenging Global Change

10. Keynes quoted in H. E. Daly and J. B. Cobb, *For the Common Good*, Merlin Press, 1990, p. 1.

11. See N. Kamergrauzis, *The Persistence of Christian Realism: A Study of the Social Ethics of Ronald H. Preston*, Acta Universitatis Upsaliensis, 2001, pp. 197–8; R. Schreiter, *The New Catholicity: Theology Between the Global and the Local*, Orbis, 1997.

12. Schreiter, p. ix.

13. In F. Wheen, *Karl Marx*, Fourth Estate, 1999, p. 121.

14. S. Sassen, *Globalization and its Discontents*, The New Press, 1998, p. xxi.

15. *Official Report of the Lambeth Conference 1998*, Morehouse, 1999, p. 120.

16. D. Landes, *The Unbound Prometheus: Technological Change and Industrial Development in Western Europe from 1750 to the Present*, Cambridge University Press, 1969, p. 247, quoting Phelps-Brown.

17. see P. Heslam, *Globalization: Unravelling the New Capitalism*, Grove Books, 2002.

18. G. DeMartino, *Global Economy, Global Justice: Theoretical Objections and Policy Alternatives to Neoliberalism*, Routledge, 2000, p. 2.

19. Heslam, p. 13.

20. Z. Bauman, *Globalization: The Human Consequences*, Polity Press, 1998, p. 71, quoting J. Kavanagh.

21. B. Barber, *Jihad Versus McWorld*, Times Books, 1995.

22. P. Kennedy, *Preparing for the Twenty-First Century*, HarperCollins, 1993, pp. 48–9.

23. Bauman, p. 55; Kennedy, p. 25.

24. Landes, p. 122; C. Marrs, 'Globalization: A Short Introduction', in *Political Theology*, vol. 41, November, 2002, pp. 91–116.

25. Marrs, p. 99; Daly and Cobb, p. 215.

26. DeMartino, p. 17.

27. D. Landes, *The Wealth and Poverty of Nations*, Little, Brown and Company, 1998, p. 363.

28. Landes, 1969, p.6.

29. Landes, 1998, p. 517.

30. Landes, 1969, p. 513.

31. Schreiter, p. 11.

32. S. Sassen, *Losing Control*, Columbian University Press, 1996, in C. Grenholm and G. Helgessen, eds., *Studies in Ethics and Economics 7*, Uppsala University Press, 2000, p. 71.

33. Heslam, p. 3.

34. Landes, 1998, p. 49.

35. Landes, 1969, p. 276.

36. Landes, 1969, p. 442.

37. Landes, 1998, p. 284.

38. Landes, 1969, p. 514.

39. P. Jay, *Road to Riches or the Wealth of Man*, Weidenfeld and Nicolson, 2000, p. 319.

40. Daly and Cobb, p. 199.

41. A. Ure, *The Philosophy of Manufacturers (1835)*, in Daly and Cobb, p. 307.

42. Landes, 1969, p. 323.

43. Kennedy, p. 91.

44. Kennedy, p. 70, quoting *Technology, Public Policy, and the Changing Structure of American Agriculture*, US Congress Report, 1986.

45. Kennedy, p. 73.

46. Bauman, p. 8.

47. M. Castells, *The Rise of the Network Society*, Blackwell, 2000.

48. Schreiter, p. 11.

49. W. Brueggeman, *The Land-Place as Gift, Promise and Challenge in Biblical Faith*, SPCK, 1977.

50. A. Davey, *Urban Christianity and Global Order: Theological Resources for an Urban Future*, SPCK, 2001, pp. 36–7; M. Castells, *The End of the Millennium*, Blackwell, 2000.

51. Landes, 1969, p. 555.

52. T. Malthus, *An Essay on the Principle of Population as it Affects the Future Improvement of Society*, edition with Introduction by A. Flew, Penguin, 1970, p. 71.

53. Kennedy, 1993, pp. 45, 36, 46.

54. G. Paterson, 'HIV/AIDS', in C. Reed, ed., *Development Matters: Christian Perspectives on Globalization*, Church House Publishing, 2001, p. 46.

55. Sassen, 1998, p. xxi.

56. Kennedy, 1993, p. 46, quoting *New York Times*, 12 August 1990, p.16.

57. Davey, p. 7.

58. Davey, p. 21.

59. L. Green, *The Impact of the Global: An Urban Theology*, New City Specials 13, 2001, pp. 18–19.

60. Kennedy, 1993, pp. 26–7.

61. Davey on Sassen.

62. M. Castells, *The End of the Millennium*, p. 95.

63. I. Young, *Justice and the Politics of Difference*, Princeton University Press, 1990, p. 241.

64. L. Boff, *Cry of the Earth, Cry of the Poor*, Orbis, 1997.

65. Jay, p. 324.

66. Kennedy, 1993, p. 98, referring to the Worldwatch Institute.

67. Kennedy, p. 100, quoting Gabriel Garćia Márquez.

68. Boff, p. 3.

69. Boff, p. 13.

Chapter 2 Death or Mutation: Changing Christianity

70. Brown, p. 1.

71. G. Davie, *Religion in Modern Europe: A Memory Mutates*, Oxford

University Press, 2000, p. 1; see also G. Davie, *Europe: The Exceptional Case: Parameters of Faith in the Modern World*, Darton, Longman and Todd, 2002.

72. Davie, 2000, p. 26, quoting Berger.

73. Brown, p. 1.

74. C. Brown, *Religion and Society in Scotland Since 1707*, Edinburgh University Press, 1997, p. 174.

75. G. Davie, *Religion in Britain since 1945: Believing Without Belonging*, Blackwell, 1994, p. 107.

76. Gill, p. 93.

77. H. McLeod, *Religion and the People of Western Europe 1789–1989*, Oxford University Press, 1997, p. 139.

78. Davie, 2000, p. 113.

79. McLeod, p. 141.

80. Davie, 2000, p. 24 on S. Bruce.

81. Davie, 2000, p. 25.

82. M. Percy, *A Knowledge of Angles: How Spiritual are the English?*, 15 Eric Symes Abbott Memorial Lecture, 2000, p. 14; B. Wilson, *Religion in Sociological Perspective*, Oxford University Press, 1982, p. 149.

83. Brown, 2001, p. 19, quoting W. Cowper, p. 27; E. R. Wickham, *Church and People in an Industrial City*, Lutterworth, 1957, p. 14; Brown, 2001, p. 27, quoting A. Winnington-Ingram.

84. Winch, p. 199, on Burke; S. Bruce, *From Cathedrals to Cults: Religion in the Modern World*, Oxford University Press, 1996, pp. 46–7.

85. S. J. D. Green, *Religion in the Age of Decline: Organisation and Experience in Industrial Yorkshire 1870–1920*, Cambridge University Press, 1996, p. 385.

86. Brown, 2001, p. 9.

87. Green, p. 380.

88. McLeod, p. 100, quoting the American economist Patten in 1912.

89. G. Ward, *Cities of God*, Routledge, 2000, p. 28.

90. McLeod, pp. 27–8.

91. Green, p. 111.

92. A. Hastings, *A History of English Christianity 1920–1990*, SCM Press, 1991, p. 445.

93. Schreiter, p. 91.

94. Davie, 2000, p. 112.

95. Davie, 2000, p. 141.

Chapter 3 Marginalization: Why Some are Rich and More are Poor.

96. Marrs, pp. 112–13.

97. D. Hicks, *Inequality and Christian Ethics*, Cambridge University Press, 2000, p. 45.

98. Landes, 1998, p. xx.

99. Malthus to Ricardo, 26 January 1817, in Landes, 1998, Frontispiece.

100. R. H. Tawney, *Religion and the Rise of Capitalism*, Murray, 1926, p. 268.

101. W. Temple, *Christianity and Social Order*, SPCK, 1977, p. 37.

102. Marrs, p. 103.

103. D. Forrester, *On Human Worth: A Christian Vindication of Equality*, SCM Press, 2001, pp. 2–3. For accounts of 'the normality of suffering' see M. Taylor, *Poverty and Christianity*, SCM Press, 2000, Chapter 1.

104. A. Sen, *Development as Freedom*, Oxford University Press, 2001, p. xi.

105. Forrester, 2001, p. 254; R. H. Tawney, 'Poverty as an Industrial Problem', in J. Atherton, *The Scandal of Poverty*, Mowbray, 1983, p. 48.

106. J-F. Lyotard, 'Just Gaming', University of Minnesota Press, pp. 71–2, in I. Young, *Justice and the Politics of Difference*, Princeton University Press, 1990, p. 4.

107. Young, 1990, p. 5.

108. A. Sen, *Poverty and Famines: An Essay on Entitlement and Deprivation*, Oxford University Press, 1981, p. 156.

109. Hicks, p. xvii.

110. P. Townsend, *Poverty in the United Kingdom: A Survey of Household Resources and Standards of Living*, Penguin, 1979, p. 31.

111. D. Wedderburn, ed., *Poverty, Inequality and Class Structure*, Cambridge University Press, 1974, p. 4.

112. Adam Smith, *An Inquiry into the Nature and Causes of the Wealth of Nations*, 1776, pp. 351–2; K. Marx, *Das Kapital*, vol. 1, p. 150, in Sen, 1981, p. 17.

113. P. Sheldrake, *Spaces for the Sacred: Place, Memory, Identity*, SCM Press, 2000, p. 166.

114. Taylor, p. 91; B. Harrison, *Making the Connections: Essays on Feminist Social Ethics*, Beacon Press, 1985, in Taylor, pp. 115–16.

115. R. F. Thiemann, *Constructing a Public Theology: The Church in a Pluralistic Culture*, Westminster-John Knox Press, 1991, pp. 105–6.

116. Daly and Cobb, p. 49.

117. Hicks, p. 23, quoting E. Anderson, 'What is the Point of Equality?', *Ethics 109*, January 1999.

118. Sen, 1999, p. 72, quoting J. Rawls, *A Theory of Justice*, Oxford University Press, 1971, pp. 60–5.

119. Sen, 1999, p. 74.

120. Sen, in Reed, p. 57; Sen, 1999, p. xi.

121. *Studies in Ethics and Economics 3*, Uppsala University Press, 1998, p. 22.

122. Sen, 1999, p. 92.

123. A. Sen, *Inequality Reexamined*, Harvard University Press, 1992, p. 114.

124. Sen, 1992, p. 82.

125. T. Jenkins, *Religion in English Everyday Life: An Ethnographic Approach*, Berghahn Books, 1999, p. 159.

126. *Studies in Ethics and Economics 2*, Uppsala University Press, 1998, p. 81.

127. Hicks, p. 23, referring to E. Anderson, *Ethics 109*, January 1999.

128. A. Shanks, *Civil Society, Civil Religion*, Blackwell, 1995, p. 177.

129. I. Young, *Inclusion and Democracy*, Oxford University Press 2000, pp. 31–2.

130. A-C. Jarl, *Women and Economic Justice*, Uppsala University Press, 2000, p. 25, referring to R. Ruether, 'Women and Culture', in CONSCIENCE, vol. xvi, no. 4, Winter, p. 13.

131. P. Sundman, *Human Rights Justification and Christian Ethics*, Uppsala University Press, 1996, p. 94. I am greatly in the debt of Ann-Cathrin Jarl and Per Sundman for their work on feminist economics and human rights respectively.

132. Jarl, pp. 145–6, referring to K. Lebacqz, *Justice in an Unjust World: Foundations for a Christian Approach to Justice*, Augsburg Publishing House, 1987.

133. Jarl, p. 148.

134. G. Collste, 'Political Philosophy for the Global Era: Is there a Need for Revision?', in C-H. Grenholm, ed., *Studies in Ethics and Economics 7, Efficiency, Justice and Stability: Ethical Perspectives in Economic Analysis and Practice*, Uppsala University Press, 2000, p. 83.

135. L. Boff and C. Boff, *Introducing Liberation Theology*, Burns and Oates, 2000, pp. 2–3.

136. Kennedy, p. 11.

137. Hicks, p. 147.

138. Forrester, 2001, p. 246, quoting R. Wilkinson, *Unhealthy Societies: The Afflictions of Inequality*, Routledge, 1996, p. 3.

139. Davey, p. 24, quoting A. Giddens, *Beyond Left and Right*, Polity Press, 1994, p. 148.

140. E. Hobsbawm, *Age of Extremes: The Short Twentieth Century 1914–1991*, Michael Joseph, 1994, p. 309; D. Sassoon, *One Hundred Years of Socialism: The West European Left in the Twentieth Century*, Fontana, 1997, p. 764.

141. Bauman, pp. 22, 127.

142. DeMartino, p. 156.

143. S. Sassen, *Globalization and its Discontents*, The New Press, 1998, p. xxxiv.

144. Bauman, p. 103, quoting P. Bourdieu.

145. Winch, pp. 1, 5.

146. Landes, 1998, p. xvii, referring to P. Samuelson, 'Illogic of Neo-Marxian Doctrine of Unequal Exchange', in D. Belsley *et al.*, eds., *Inflation, Trade and Taxes*, Ohio State University Press, 1976, pp.96–107; Landes, 1998, p. xx.

147. Landes, 1969, p. 335.

148. Kennedy, 1993, p. 341.

149. K. Ziegler, 'Corruption', in Reed, p. 72.

150. Reed, p. 73.

151. Landes, 1998, p. 507, quoting *New York Times*, 17 March 1996.

152. Sen, 1999, p. 52.

153. Sen, 1999, p. 154.

154. J. K. Galbraith, *The Culture of Contentment*, Houghton Mifflin, 1992; D. Gosling, 'the Environment', in Reed, p. 55.

155. Boff, p. 66.

156. P. Berryman, *Religion in the Megacity: Catholic and Protestant Portraits from Latin America*, Orbis, 1996, p.1.

157. Daly and Cobb, p. 93.

158. Wheen, p. 201, quoting Marx, 1856.

159. Bauman, p. 72.

160. J. Nelson, 'Feminism, Objectivity and Economics', in C-H. Grenholm, ed., *Studies in Ethics and Economics 3*, Uppsala University Press, 1998, p. 11.

161. Taylor, p. 29, quoting Eleazar Fernandez, *Toward a Theology of Struggle*, Orbis, 1994, p. 36.

162. Young, 1990, p. 41.

163. Winch, p. 5.

164. R. H. Tawney, *Commonplace Book*, Cambridge University Press, 1972, p. 45; C. Wright Mills, *The Sociological Imagination*, Penguin, 1970, p. 15.

165. A. Sen, *Inequality Reexamined*, Oxford University Press, 1995, pp. 122, 123.

166. DeMartino, p.120.

167. Young, 1990, p. 60, quoting W. Du Bois, *The Souls of Black Folk*, New American Library, 1903, p. 45.

168. Young, 1990, p. 214.

169. DeMartino, p. 82.

170. Young, 1990, p. 20.

171. Young, 1990, p. 71, quoting M. Smith and D. Judd, 'American Cities: The Production of Ideology', in *Cities in Transformation*, M. Smith, ed., Sage, 1988, p. 184.

172. Hicks, p. 62, quoting J. Speth in *New Perspectives Quarterly*, Fall 1996, pp. 32–3.

173. Landes, 1998, p. 523.

174. Young, 2000, p. 165, referring to S. Vera, K. Scholzman and H. Brady, *Voice and Equality: Civic Voluntarism in American Politics*, Harvard University Press, 1995.

175. Keynes, p. 306–7; Wheen, p. 107, quoting Marx, *Misère de La Philsophie*, 1847.

Chapter 4 The Great Double Whammy: A Case Study of Marginalization And Religion

176. J. Major, *The Autobiography*, HarperCollins, 1999, p. 294.

177. P. Ackroyd, *The Times*, 15 August 2000; E. Duffy, *The Voices of Morebath: Reformation and Rebellion in an English Village*, Yale University Press, 2001.

178. T. Jenkins, *Religion in English Everyday Life: An Ethnographic Approach*, Berghahn Books, 1999.

179. G. Gutiérrez, *The Power of the Poor in History*, Orbis, 1983, p. 203.

180. Schreiter, p. 60, quoting M. Budde, *The Two Churches: Catholicism and Capitalism in the World-System*, Duke University Press, 1992.

181. E. Hobsbawm, *Industry and Empire*, Penguin, 1969, p. 11.

182. See, for example, J. N. Morris, *Religion and Urban Change: Croydon, 1840–1914*, Royal Historical Society, 1992.

183. G. Ward, p. 39, quoting P. Hall, *Cities of Tomorrow*, 1996, p. 364; Hall, *Cities*, p. 99.

184. Davie, 2000, pp. 80–1.

Chapter 5 Performative Christianity: Demarginalizing Theology and Church: Reflections On Religious Theory And Organization

185. A. MacIntyre, *After Virtue*, University of Notre Dame Press, 1981, p. 207; R. Thiemann, p. 136; M. Castells, *The Power of Identity*, Blackwell, 1997, p. 360.

186. Jarl, p. 26, quoting A. Jaggar, *Feminist Politics and Human Nature*, Rowman and Littlefield, 1983, pp. 54–60.

187. Landes, 1998, p. 278, referring to K. Polanyi, *The Tacit Dimension*, Routledge and Kegan Paul, 1967, and K. Arrow, 'The Economic Implications of Learning by Doing', in *Review of Economic Studies*, vol. 9, June, 1962.

188. Forrester, 2000, p. 31; P. Ballard and J. Pritchard, *Practical Theology in Action: Christian Thinking in the Service of Church and Society*, SPCK, 1996; J. Holland and P. Herriot, *Social Analysis: Linking Faith and Justice*, Orbis, 1983.

189. C. Gore, *Christ and Society*, Allen and Unwin, 1928, p. 14.

190. E. Graham, 'Towards a Practical Theology of Embodiment', in P. Ballard and P. Couture, eds., *Globalization and Difference: Practical Theology in a World Context*, Cardiff Academic Press, 1999, pp. 82–3.

191. Kamergrauzis, p. 247, quoting R. Niebuhr, 'Why is Barth Silent on Hungary?', in *The Christian Century*, 23 January 1957.

192. Boff, p. 11.

193. T. Schubeck, 'Liberation Theology and Economics', quoting A. Fontaine, in J. Dean and A. Waterman, eds., *Religion and Economics: Normative Social Theory*, Kluwer Academic Publishers, 1999, p. 72.

194. P. Moll, 'Liberating Liberation Theology: Towards Independence from Dependency Theory', *Journal of Theology for Southern Africa*, March 1992, Mills Letho Ltd, Cape Town.

195. S. Shakespeare, 'The New Romantics: A Critique of Radical Orthodoxy', *Theology*, May–June 2000, vol. CIII, no. 813, p. 174.

196. L. Sandercock, *Towards Cosmopolis – Planning for Multicultural Cities*, J. Wiley and Sons, 1998, p. 205; Davey, p. 50.

197. Young, 2000, p. 56.

198. Young, 2000, p. 63.

199. Young, 2000, pp. 74, 75.

200. Jarl, p. 136, using Harrison.

201. Taylor, pp. 5–6.

202. Forrester, 2000, p. 28.

203. A. Hammar, *Globalisering – ett problem för Kyrkan?* Tro and Tanke Svenska Kyrkan, 2000, p. 149; see also D. Tracy, *Plurality and Ambiguity: Hermeneutics, Religion, Hope*, SCM Press, 1987, pp. ix–x.

204. Schreiter, p. 40, referring to F. Matsuoka, 'A Reflection on "Teaching Theology from an Intercultural Perspective" ', in *Theological Education 36, no. 1*, 1989, pp. 35–42.

205. Young, 1990, p. 186.

206. E. Graham, *Transforming Practice: Pastoral Theology in an Age of Uncertainty*, Mowbrays, 1996, p. 7.

207. K. Marx, *Theses on Feuerbach*, 1845, in Wheen, pp. 54–5.

208. Boff, p. xi.

209. Hicks, p. 157.

210. Sen, 1999, p. 286.

211. Hicks, p. 144, referring to S. Pope, 'Proper and Improper Partiality and the Preferential Option for the Poor', *Theological Studies 54/2*, 1993, pp. 256–62.

212. Forrester, 2001, pp. 161–2.

213. Forrester, 2001, p. 99.

214. Hicks, p. 138; E. Graham, 'Good News for the Socially Excluded? Political Theology and the Politics of New Labour', *Political Theology 2*, May 2000, pp. 49–50.

215. Hicks, p. 237, referring to Theda Skocpol, *Targeting within Universalism*, Discussion Paper Series H-90-2, Center for Health and Human Resources Policy, John F. Kennedy School of Government, Harvard University, 1990.

216. Gill, p. 239.

217. *Overcoming Human Poverty: United Nations Development Programme, Poverty Report 2000*, UNDP 2000, p. 82.

218. Young, 1990, pp. 158, 199.

219. Forrester, 2000, p. 127. My meeting with the Archbishop of Sweden, 15 November, 2001.

220. P. Selby, 'The Silent Word Still Speaks', in Reed, ed., p. 100, quoting F. Watson, *Text, Church and Word*, T & T Clark, 1994, p. 152.

221. Thiemann, 1991, p. 21.

222. D. Forrester, *Christian Justice and Public Policy*, Cambridge University Press 1997, p. 31.

223. R. Thiemann, *Religion in Public Life: A Dilemma for Democracy*, Georgetown University Press, 1996, pp. 135–41.

224. Gill, p. 137.

225. Young, 2000, p. 147.

226. Hicks, p. 105, quoting from the Puebla *Final Document*, para. 1228, in J. Eagleson and P. Scharper, eds., *Puebla and Beyond*, Orbis, 1979.

227. Hicks, p. 111, quoting from *Economic Justice for All*, United States Catholic Conference, 1986, para. 347, citing the Synod of Bishops, *Justice in the World*, para. 40, in D. O'Brien and T. Shannon, eds., *Catholic Social Thought: The Documentary Heritage*, Orbis, 1992.

228. Thiemann, 1996, p. 139.

229. D. Long, *Divine Economy: Theology and the Market*, Routledge 2000, p. 27, referring to M. Stackhouse, *Creeds, Society and Human Rights*, Eerdmans, 1984.

230. Forrester, 2000, p. 119f.; D. McCann, *New Experiments in Democracy*, Sheed and Ward, 1987.

231. MacIntyre, pp. 6–21.

232. Young, 1990, pp. 236, 231.

233. J. Rawls, *Political Liberalism*, Columbia University Press, 1993.

234. Young, 2000, p. 9.

235. D. Koh, *A Christian Social Ethics for Singapore with Reference to the Works of Ronald H. Preston*, Durham PhD (unpublished); Kamergrauzis, p. 120, notes a kind of middle axioms in *Towards the Common Good: Statement on the Future of the Welfare Society by the Bishops of the Evangelical Lutheran Church of Finland*; C. Villa-Vincencio, *A Theology of Reconstruction: Nation-Building and Human Rights*, Cambridge University Press, 1992, pp. 9–10, 13, 280–2.

236. Gill.

237. Forrester, 2000, p. 91.

238. WCC 5th World Conference on Faith and Order, 1994, in Forrester, 2000, p. 188.

239. E. Graham, 'The Ecclesiology of Unemployment and the Future of Work', in M. Brown and P. Sedgwick, eds., *Putting Theology to Work: A Theological Symposium on Unemployment and the Future of Work*, CCBI and the William Temple Foundation, 1998, p. 46.

240. D. Fergusson, *Community, Liberalism and Christian Ethics*, Cambridge University Press, 1998, pp. 172–3.

241. A. Mawson, 'Community Regeneration', in M. Northcott, ed., *Urban Theology: A Reader*, Casell, 1998, p. 48.

242. J. Tiller, 'The Associational Church and its Communal Mission', in Northcott, p. 276.

243. Davey, pp. 115–17.

244. U. Beck, *Risk Society: Towards a New Modernity*, Sage Publications, 1992, p. 135; U. Beck, A. Giddens and S. Lash, *Reflexive Modernization: Politics, Tradition and Aesthetics in the Modern Social Order*, Polity Press, 1994.

245. M. Northcott, pp. 11f., 43f., 233f.

246. Taylor, p. 100.

247. Green, pp. 23–4.

248. Jarl, p. 83.

249. Young, 1990, p. 85.

250. Young, p. 244.

251. R. Garner, PhD thesis, Manchester, 2002, unpublished.

252. Gill, pp. 31–2, 103, 149, 175, 176, 117, 110, 217–18, 225.

253. K. Cronin, *Rights and Christian Ethics*, Cambridge University Press, 1992, p. 233.

254. Gill, p. 198.

255. Jenkins, p. 178.

256. H. Küng, *A Global Ethic for Global Politics and Economics*, SCM Press, 1997, p.92, referring to S. Huntington, *The Clash of Civilizations and the Remaking of World Order*, Simon and Schuster, 1997.

257. Schreiter, p. 30f.

258. W. Tyndale, 'the World Faiths Development Dialogue,' in Reed, ed., p. 113.

259. Boff, p. 114.

Chapter 6 Engaging Marginalization by Reconnecting Economics, Ethics and Religion: Reflections for a Reformulated Tradition of Christian Political Economy

260. Jarl, p. 136.
261. Jarl, p. 17.

262. A. Waterman, *Revolution, Economics and Religion: Christian Political Economy, 1798–1833*, Cambridge University Press, 1991, p. 206.

263. L. Udehn, 'The Political Philosophies of Economics and Sociology', in *Studies in Ethics and Economics 5*, Uppsala University Press, 1999, p. 15, quoting J. Keynes, 1936, p. 383.

264. Landes, 1998, Frontispiece.

265. M. Meeks, *God the Economist: The Doctrine of God and Political Economy*, Fortress Press, 1989; Long.

266. Davey, p. 107.

267. Long, p. 235.

268. Long, p. 260.

269. Long, p. 270.

270. Shakespeare, p. 172.

271. R. H. Preston, review of D. Jenkins, *Market Whys and Wherefores*, Cassells, 2000, in Theology, vol. CIII, no. 814, July/August, 2000. The quotation is from a privately circulated longer draft.

272. Young, 1990, p. 234.

273. A. Yuengert, 'Uses of Economics in Papal Encyclicals', in J. Dean and A. Waterman, eds., *Religion and Economics: Normative Social Theory*, Kluwer Academic Publishers, 1999, p. 37.

274. Atherton, 2000, Chapter 1.

275. A. Waterman, 'Social Thinking in Established Protestant Churches', in Dean and Waterman, eds., pp. 53–4.

276. Boff, p. 132.

277. Long, p. 79, quoting R. Williams.

278. A. Sen, *On Ethics and Economics*, Blackwell, 1999 edition, p. 89.

279. Winch, p. 6, quoting E. Thompson.

280. Winch, p. 42.

281. Winch, p. 402.

282. Winch, p. 6.

283. Waterman, in Dean and Waterman, eds., p. 58.

284. Winch, p. 295, quoting Malthus.

285. Winch, pp. 289–90.

286. Daly and Cobb, p. 32.

287. Winch, p. 87, from *Wealth of Nations*, I, VIII. 36.

288. Winch, p. 23.

289. Winch, p. 287, quoting Whewell, 1822.

290. Keynes, p. 165, quoting from Marshall's *Principles of Economics*, 1890.

291. Keynes, p. 120.

292. I. Steedman, 'On Doing the Impossible', in Dean and Waterman, eds., p. 171.

293. Sen, 1999, p. ix.

294. Jarl, p. 197.

295. Daly and Cobb, p. 30.

296. Daly and Cobb, p. 30.

297. Jarl, p. 42.

298. D. Munby, *Christianity and Economic Problems*, Macmillan, 1956, pp. 44–5.

299. L. Robbins, *An Essay on The Nature and Significance of Economic Science*, Macmillan, 1935, p. 148.

300. Sen, *On Ethics and Economics*, pp. 2–7.

301. F. McChesney, 'Economics and Technology', in Dean and Waterman, p. 154.

302. M. Friedman, *Essays in Positive Economics*, University of Chicago Press, 1953, p. 7, in *Studies in Ethics and Economics 8*, Uppsala University Press, 2001, pp. 11–12.

303. G. Collste, 'Value Assumptions in Economic Theory', in *Studies in Ethics and Economics 2*, Uppsala University Press, 1998, p. 12.

304. Daly and Cobb, pp. 19, 8.

305. I. Steedman, *From Exploitation to Altruism*, Polity Press, 1989, p. 194: J. S. Mill, 'Unsettled Questions', 1844.

306. M. Parkin, *Economics*, Addison-Wesley Publishing Company, 1990, p. 19, in Malin Löfstedt, 'Tracing the Picture of Human Behaviour in Economics', *Studies in Ethics and Economics 7*, Uppsala University Press, 2000, p. 172.

307. M. Löfstedt, p. 182, referring to K. Rothschild, 'Homo Oeconomicus – Homo Sociologicus', in *Ethics and Economic Theory*, University of Cambridge Press, 1993, pp. 30–1.

308. Collste, p. 12, *Studies in Economics and Ethics 2*.

309. Stephen Leacock, *Hellements of Hickonomics*, Dodd, Mead and Co., 1936, p. 75, in Sen, 1987, p. 21. Reproduced by kind permission of Blackwell Publishing.

310. Sen, 1999, p. 272; A. Smith, *The Theory of Moral Sentiments*, D. Raphael and A. MacFie, eds., Clarendon Press, 1976, p. 189.

311. G. Helgesson, 'Ethical Preconditions in Economic Theory – A First Inventory', in *Studies in Ethics and Economics 3*, p. 66; see also Sen, *On Ethics and Economics*, pp. 41–45, 47f.

312. G. Stigler, 'Smith's Travel on the Ship of State', in A. Skinner and T. Wilson, eds., *Essays on Adam Smith*, Clarendon Press, 1975, in Sen, 1999, p. 271.

313. W. Temple, *Christianity and Social Order*, SPCK, 1976, p. 65.

314. G. Collste, p. 13, *Studies in Ethics and Economics 2*, referring to J. Butler, *'Fifteen Sermons Preached at Rolls Chapel'*, Oxford, 1726.

315. Sen, *Ethics and Economics*, 1987, p. 18.

316. R. Granqvist, 'Efficiency for Rational Fools?,' in *Studies in Ethics and Economics 7*, Uppsala University Press, 2000, pp. 15–16.

317. Gill, p. 26.

318. Jarl, p. 72, quoting S. Harding in *Feminist Economics*, 1995, vol. 1, no. 1, p. 18.

319. M. Löfstedt, *Studies in Ethics and Economics 3*, p. 98.

320. Daly and Cobb, p. 164.

321. Jarl, p. 74, referring to N. Folbre, *Who Pays for the Kids: Gender and the Structure of Constraint*, Routledge, 1994, p. 20.

322. C-H. Grenholm, 'Ethical Reflection in Economic Theory and Practice', *Studies in Ethics and Economics 1*, p. 28.

323. M. Löfstedt, *Studies in Ethics and Economics 3*, p. 89, referring to Sen, *Ethics and Economics*, pp. 40–5.

324. A. Yuengert, 'Uses of Economics in Papal Encyclicals', in Dean and Waterman, eds., p. 44.

325. DeMartino, p. 119.

326. Sen, *Ethics and Economics*, p. 32.

327. Hicks, p. 239.

328. I. Linden, 'Globalization and the Church: An Overview', in Reed, ed., p. 10.

329. Sen, 1999, p. 259.

330. Boff, p. 66.

331. J. Broome, 'Ethics out of Economics', in *Studies in Ethics and Economics 3*, p. 26.

332. Collste, *Studies in Ethics and Economics 2*, p. 14.

333. A. Sen, *Poverty and Famines*, 1981.

334. Collste, *Studies in Ethics and Economics 2*, p. 15.

335. *UN Human Development Report, 2000*, UNDP, Oxford University Press, 2000, p. 70.

336. Boff, p. 112.

337. Young, 2000, p. 221.

338. Young, 2000, p. 237.

339. *UNHDR 2000*, p. 126.

340. Hicks, pp. 214, 216; UNHDR, 1995.

341. *UNHDR 2000*, p. 141.

342. Schreiter, p. 111.

343. *UNHDR 2000*, p. 143.

344. Hicks.

345. Hicks, p. 212.

346. Hicks, p. 227.

347. Daly and Cobb, p. 76.

348. See Anders Melin, *Judgements in Equilibrium? An Ethical Analysis of Environmental Impact Assessment*, Linköping University, 2001.

349. Daly and Cobb, pp. 439, 454.

350. DeMartino, pp. 217, 219.

351. *Overcoming Human Poverty: UNHDP Poverty Report 2000*, pp. 47–8.

352. C. Reed 'General Synod and International Development', in Reed, ed., p. 23.

353. See S. Buckley, *Teaching on Usury in Judaism, Christianity and Islam*, Edwin Mellen Press, 2000; R. H. Preston, *Religion and the Ambiguities of Capitalism*, SCM Press, 1991, Appendix 1, 'Usury and a Christian Ethic of Finance'; R. Wilson, *Economics, Ethics and Religion: Jewish, Christian and Muslim Economic Thought*, Macmillan, 1997.

354. See also Ex. 2.25; Lev. 25.35–7; Ex. 22.28; Lev. 25.35–7.

355. Buckley, pp. 32, 79.

356. Buckley, p. 172, quoting E. Roll, *A History of Economic Thought*, Faber and Faber, 1938, p. 53.

357. Jay, p. 89.

358. Buckley, p. 245.

359. Buckley, p. 267.

360. Buckley, p. 308, quoting 'International Association of Islamic Banks'.

361. Buckley, pp. 287, 335–6, quoting E. Gellner, *Postmodernism, Reason and Religion*, Routledge, 1992, p. 22.

362. Reed, in Reed, ed., p. 29.

363. Young, 2000, pp. 274–5.

364. See P. Berger, *The Heretical Imperative: Contemporary Possibilities of Religious Affirmation*, Collins, 1980.

365. Long, p. 111.

366. J. K. Galbraith, *A Short History of Financial Euphoria*, Penguin, 1993.

367. T. Malthus, *Essay on the Principle of Population*, p. 287, in Winch, p. 257.

368. Daly and Cobb, pp. 256–8.

369. D. Munby, *Christianity and Economic Problems*, Macmillan, 1956, p. 275, critique of V. A. Demant, *Religion and the Decline of Capitalism*, Faber and Faber and Scribners, 1952.

370. Moll, p. 27, quoting G. Gutíerrez, *A Theology of Liberation*, SCM Press, 1971, 1988, p. 51.

371. R. H. Preston review of D. Jenkins, *Market Whys amd Human Wherefores: Thinking Again about Markets, Politics and People*, Cassells, 2000, in Theology, vol. CIII, no. 814, July/August, 2000, pp. 300–1.

372. D. Long, *Divine Economy*.

373. Bauman, p. 5.

374. J. Boswell, *Community and the Economy: The Theory of Public Cooperation*, Routledge, 1990, p. 163.

375. Long, p. 269.

376. A. MacIntyre, 'Epistemological Crises, Dramatic Narrative and the Philosophy of Science', in S. Hauerwas, ed., *Why Narrative? Readings in Natural Theology*, Eerdmans, 1989, p. 143; Kamergrauzis, p. 221.

377. MacIntyre, p. 140, in Kamergrauzis, p. 222.

378. Kamergrauzis, p. 235.

379. Beverley Harrison, 'Making the Connections: Essays in Feminist Social Ethics', C. S. Robb, ed., Beacon Press, 1985.

380. Atherton, 2000, p. 143, referring to J. Stout, *Ethics after Babel*, Clarke, 1988; J. Gray, *False Dawn*, Granta, 1998.

381. Boff, pp. xii, 24.

SELECT
BIBLIOGRAPHY

Alkire, S., *Valuing Freedoms: Sen's Capability Approach and Poverty Reduction*, Oxford University Press, 2002.

Atherton, J., *The Scandal of Poverty: Priorities for the Emerging Church*, Mowbray, 1983.

——*Faith in the Nation: A Christian Vision for Britain*, SPCK, 1988.

——*Christianity and the Market: Christian Social Thought for our Times*, SPCK, 1992.

——*Public Theology for Changing Times*, SPCK, 2000.

Bauman, Z., *Globalization: The Human Consequences*, Polity Press, 1998.

Ballard, P., and Pritchard, J., *Practical Theology in Action: Christian Thinking in the Service of Church and Society*, SPCK, 1996.

Berger, P., *The Heretical Imperative: Contemporary Possibilities of Religious Affirmation*, Collins, 1980.

Berryman, P., *Religion in the Megacity: Catholic and Protestant Portraits from Latin America*, Orbis, 1996.

Boff, L., *Cry of the Earth, Cry of the Poor*, Orbis, 1997.

Boff, L. and Boff, C., *Introducing Liberation Theology*, Burns and Oates, 2000.

Boswell, J., *Community and the Economy: The Theory of Public Cooperation*, Routledge, 1990.

Brown, C., *The Death of Christian Britain: Understanding Secularisation 1800–2000*, Routledge, 2001.

Bruce, S., *From Cathedrals to Cults: Religion in the Modern World*, Oxford University Press, 1996.

Brueggeman, W., *The Land-Place as Gift, Promise and Challenge in Biblical Faith*, SPCK, 1977.

Buckley, S., *Teaching on Usury in Judaism, Christianity and Islam*, Edwin Mellen Press, 2000.

Brunner, E., *The Divine Imperative*, Lutterworth, 1936.

Castells, M., *The Power of Identity*, Blackwell, 1997.

——*The Rise of the Network Society*, Blackwell, 2000.

—— *The End of Millennium*, Blackwell, 2000.

Chalmers, T., *The Christian and Civic Economy of Large Towns*, vol. i, 1821: vol. ii, 1823; vol. iii, 1826, Chalmers and Collins.

Cronin, K., *Rights and Christian Ethics*, Cambridge University Press, 1992.

Daly, H. and Cobb, J., *For the Common Good: Redirecting the Economy Towards Community, the Environment and a Sustainable Future*, Merlin Press, 1990.

Davey, A., *Urban Christianity and Global Order: Theological Resources for an Urban Future*, SPCK, 2001.

Davie, G., *Religion in Britain Since 1945: Believing Without Belonging*, Blackwell, 1994.

—— *Religion in Modern Europe: A Memory Mutates*, Oxford University Press, 2000.

—— *Europe: The Exceptional Case: Parameters of Faith in the Modern World*, Darton, Longman and Todd, 2002.

Dean, J. and Waterman, A., eds., *Religion and Economics: Normative Social Theory*, Kluwer Academic Publishers, 1999.

DeMartino, G., *Global Economy, Global Justice: Theoretical Objections and Policy Alternatives to Neoliberalism*, Routledge, 2000.

Demant, V., *Religion and the Decline of Capitalism*, Faber and Faber, 1952.

Duffy, E., *The Voices of Morebath: Reformation and Rebellion in an English Village*, Yale University Press, 2001.

Faith in the City: A Call for Action by Church and Nation, Church House Publishing, 1985.

Fergusson, D., *Community, Liberalism and Christian Ethics*, Cambridge University Press, 1998.

Forrester, D., *Christian Justice and Public Policy*, Cambridge University Press, 1997.

—— *Truthful Action: Explorations in Practical Theology*, T&T Clark, 2000.

—— *On Human Worth: A Christian Vindication of Equality*, SCM Press, 2001.

Friedman, M., *Essays in Positive Economics*, University of Chicago Press, 1953.

Galbraith, J., *The Culture of Contentment*, Houghton Mifflin, 1992.

—— *A Short History of Financial Euphoria*, Penguin, 1993.

Gill, R., *Churchgoing and Christian Ethics*, Cambridge University Press, 1999.

Graham, E., *Transforming Practice: Pastoral Theology in an Age of Uncertainty*, Mowbrays, 1996.

—— 'The Ecclesiology of Unemployment and the Future of Work', in M. Brown and P. Sedgwick, eds., *Putting Theology to Work: A Theological Symposium on Unemployment and the Future of Work*, CCBI and the William Temple Foundation, 1996.

Graham, E., 'Towards a Practical Theology of Embodiment', in P. Ballard and P. Couture, eds., *Globalisation and Difference: Practical Theology in a World Context*, Cardiff Academic Press, 1999.

—— 'Good News for the Socially Excluded? Political Theology and the Politics of New Labour', *Political Theology* 2, May 2000, Sheffield Academic Press.

Green, L., *The Impact of the Global: An Urban Theology*, New City Specials 13, 2001.

Green, S., *Religion in the Age of Decline: Organisation and Experience in Industrial Yorkshire 1870–1920*, Cambridge University Press, 1996.

Grenholm, C-H., ed., *Studies in Ethics and Economics 1: Etik och ekonomi*, Uppsala University Press, 1998.

—— *Studies in Ethics and Economics 2: Value Assumptions in Economic Theory*, Uppsala University Press, 1998.

—— *Studies in Ethics and Economics 3: Ethics, Economics and Feminism*, Uppsala University Press, 1998.

—— *Studies in Ethics and Economics 4: Objectivitetsproblemet i ekonomisk vetenskap*, Uppsala University Press, 1998.

—— *Studies in Ethics and Economics 5: Värderingari ekonomisk teori och forskning*, Uppsala University Press, 1999.

—— *Studies in Ethics and Economics 6: Ideology in Science and Economics*, Uppsala University Press, 1999.

—— *Studies in Ethics and Economics 7: Efficiency, Justice and Stability: Ethical Perspectives in Economic Analysis and Practice*, Uppsala University Press, 2000.

—— *Studies in Ethics and Economics 8: Efficiency, Welfare and Altruism. Moral Assumptions in Economic Theory and Practice*, Uppsala University Press, 2001.

Gutiérrez, G., *The Power of the Poor in History*, Orbis, 1983.

—— *A Theology of Liberation*, SCM Press, 1971, 1988.

Hammar, A., *Globalisering ett problem för Kyrkan?* Tro and Tanke Svenska Kyrkan, 2000.

Harrison, B., *Making the Connections: Essays in Feminist Social Ethics*, Beacon Press, 1985.

Hastings, A., *A History of English Christianity 1920–1990*, SCM Press, 1991.

Heslam, P., *Globalization: Unravelling the New Capitalism*, Grove Books, 2002.

Hicks, D., *Inequality and Christian Ethics*, Cambridge University Press, 2000.

Hills, J., Le Grand, J., Piachaud, D., *Understanding Social Exclusion*, Oxford University Press, 2002.

Hobsbawm, E., *Industry and Empire*, Penguin, 1969.

—— *Age of Extremes: The Short Twentieth Century 1914–1991*, Michael Joseph, 1994.

Holland, J., and Herriot, P., *Social Analysis: Linking Faith and Justice*, Orbis, 1983.

Hollenbach, D., *The Common Good and Christian Ethics*, Cambridge University Press, 2002.

Human Development Report 2000, UNDP, Oxford University Press, 2000.

Jarl, A-C., *Women and Economic Justice*, Uppsala University Press, 2000.

Jay, P., *Road to Riches or the Wealth of Man*, Weidenfeld and Nicholson, 2000.

Jenkins, T., *Religion in English Everyday Life: An Ethnographic Approach*, Berghahn Books, 1999.

Kamergrauzis, N., *The Persistence of Christian Realism: A Study of the Social Ethics of Ronald H. Preston*, Acta Universitatis, Upsaliensis, 2001.

Kennedy, P., *Preparing for the Twenty-First Century*, HarperCollins, 1993.

Keynes, J. M., *Essays in Biography*, Macmillan, 1933.

Küng, H., *A Global Ethic for Global Politics and Economics*, SCM Press, 1997.

Landes, D., *The Unbound Prometheus: Technological Change and Industrial Development in Western Europe from 1750 to the Present*, Cambridge University Press, 1969.

—— *The Wealth and Poverty of Nations*, Little, Brown and Company, 1998.

Lebacqz, K., *Justice in an Unjust World: Foundations for a Christian Approach to Justice*, Augsburg Publishing House, 1987.

Long, D., *Divine Economy: Theology and the Market*, Routledge, 2000.

MacIntyre, A., *After Virtue*, University of Notre Dame Press, 1981.

Major, J., *The Autobiography*, HarperCollins, 1999.

Malthus, T., *An Essay on the Principle of Population as it Affects the Future Improvement of Society*, edited with Introduction by A. Flew, Penguin, 1970.

McLeod, H., *Religion and the People of Western Europe 1789–1989*, Oxford University Press, 1997 edn.

Meekes, M., *God the Economist: The Doctrine of God and Political Economy*, Fortress Press, 1989.

Melin, A., *Judgements in Equilibrium? An Ethical Analysis of Environmental Impact Assessment*, Linköping University, 2001.

Mills, C. Wright, *The Sociological Imagination*, Penguin, 1970.

Moll, P., 'Liberating Theology: Towards Independence from Dependency Theory', *Journal of Theology for Southern Africa*, March 1992, Mills Letho Ltd., Cape Town.

Morris, J., *Religion and Urban Change: Croydon 1840–1914*, Royal Historical Society, 1992.

Munby, D., *Christianity and Economic Problems*, Macmillan, 1956.

Northcott, M., ed., *Urban Theology: A Reader*, Cassell, 1998.

Overcoming Human Poverty: United Nations Development Programme, Poverty Report 2000, UNDP, Oxford University Press, 2000.

Percy, M., *A Knowledge of Angles: How Spiritual are the English?*, 15 Eric Symes Abbot Memorial Lecture, 2000.

Preston, R., *Religion and the Ambiguities of Capitalism*, SCM Press, 1991.

—— *Confusions in Christian Social Ethics: Problems for Geneva and Rome*, SCM Press, 1994.

Rawls, J., *A Theory of Justice*, Oxford University Press, 1971.

—— *Political Liberalism*, Columbia University Press, 1993.

—— *The Law of Peoples*, Harvard University Press, 1999.

Reed, C., ed., *Development Matters: Christian Perspectives on Globalization*, Church House Publishing, 2001.

Robbins, L., *An Essay on the Nature and Significance of Economic Science*, Macmillan, 1935.

Roll, E., *A History of Economic Thought*, Faber and Faber, 1938.

Sassen, S., *Globalization and its Discontents*, The New Press, 1998.

Sassoon, D., *One Hundred Years of Socialism: The West European Left in the Twentieth Century*, Fontana, 1997.

Schreiter, R., *The New Catholicity: Theology Between the Global and the Local*, Orbis, 1997.

Sen, A., *Poverty and Famines: An Essay on Entitlement and Deprivation*, Oxford University Press, 1981.

—— *Inequality Reexamined*, Harvard University Press, 1992.

—— *On Ethics and Economics*, Blackwell, 1999 edn.

—— *Development as Freedom*, Oxford University Press, 2001.

Shakespeare, S., 'The New Romantics: A Critique of Radical Orthodoxy', *Theology*, May–June 2000, vol. CIII, no. 813.

Shanks, A., *Civil Society, Civil Religion*, Blackwell, 1995.

Sheldrake, P., *Spaces for the Sacred: Place, Memory, Identity*, SCM Press, 2000.

Smith, A., *An Inquiry into the Nature and Causes of the Wealth of Nations*, Penguin, 1970 edn.

Steedman, I., *From Exploitation to Altruism*, Polity Press, 1989.

Sundman, P., *Human Rights Justification and Christian Ethics*, Uppsala University Press, 1996.

Tawney, R. H., *Commonplace Book*, Cambridge University Press, 1972.

Taylor, M., *Poverty and Christianity*, SCM Press, 2000.

Temple, W., *Christianity and Social Order*, SPCK, 1976 edn.

Thiemann, R. F., *Constructing a Public Theology: The Church in a Pluralistic Culture*, Westminster-Knox Press, 1991.

—— *Religion in Public Life: A Dilemma For Democracy*, Georgetown University Press, 1996.

Townsend, P., *Poverty in the United Kingdom: A Survey of Household Resources and Standards of Living*, Penguin, 1979.

Tracy, D., *Plurality and Ambiguity: Hermeneutics, Religion, Hope*, SCM Press, 1987.

Villa-Vicencio, C., *A Theology of Reconstruction: Nation-building and Human Rights*, Cambridge University Press, 1992.

Ward, G., *Cities of God*, Routledge, 2000.

Waterman, A., *Revolution, Economics and Religion: Christian Political Economy, 1798–1833*, Cambridge University Press, 1991.

Weber, M., *The Protestant Ethic and the Spirit of Capitalism*, Allen and Unwin, 1930.

Wedderburn, D., ed., *Poverty, Inequality and Class Structure*, Cambridge University Press, 1974.

Wheen, F., *Karl Marx*, Fourth Estate, 1999.

Wickham, E. R., *Church and People in an Industrial City*, Lutterworth, 1957.

Wilson, R., *Economics, Ethics and Religion: Jewish, Christian and Muslim Economic Thought*, Macmillan, 1997.

Winch, D., *Riches and Poverty: An Intellectual History of Political Economy in Britain, 1750–1834*, Cambridge University Press, 1996.

Young, I., *Justice and the Politics of Difference*, Princeton University Press, 1990.

—— *Inclusion and Democracy*, Oxford University Press, 2000.

INDEX

Ackroyd, P. 95, 187n
altruism 107, 123, 125, 130, 131,
    137, 154, 168, 169
Anderson, E. 64, 68, 184n, 185n
anti-globalization 11, 81, 127, 147,
    172
Aquinas, T. 110
Argentina 77
Aristotle 110, 170
Atherton, J. 184n, 191n, 195n
Arrow, K. 110, 156, 187n
atonement, age of 115

Bagehot, W. 147
Baker, C. xii, 133
Ballard, P. 110, 187n, 188n
Bangladesh 28, 66, 77
Banner, M. 107
baptism 33, 34, 100, 144
Barber, B. 181n
basic human needs 67–9, 71, 72,
    128
Bauman, Z. 78, 87, 181n, 182n,
    185nn, 194n
Belgium 77
Bentham, J. 147
Berger, P. 183n, 194n
Berkeley, G. 145
Berryman, P. 186n
Beveridge, W. 58, 79
biotechnology 20
Blatcherism 36
Boff, L. 27, 30, 74, 85, 112, 141,
    146, 160, 179, 182nn, 185n,
    186n, 188n 190n, 191n, 193nn,
    195n

Boswell, J. 194n
Brazil 32, 77
Britain xii, 1, 23, 24, 31, 32, 35, 39,
    46, 48, 49, 54, 67, 75, 77, 78, 81,
    83, 84, 88, 94, 107, 125, 130,
    133, 147, 165, 174, 175
Broome, J. 193n
Brown, C. 31, 33, 180n, 182n,
    183nn
Brown, M. 190n
Bruce, S. 39, 183nn
Brueggemann, W. 22, 43, 182n
Brundtland Report 85, 158, 165
Brunner, E. 55
Büber, M. 116
Buckley, S. 194nn
Burke, E. 39
Burkina Faso 76
Butler, J. 154, 192n
Butskellism 36

Caird, E. 58, 59
Canada 76, 164
capability 61, 70, 71, 76, 80, 89, 91,
    115, 120, 127, 142, 157, 159,
    160, 161, 163, 168
    functioning 66, 69, 80, 82, 98,
        100, 126, 162, 163, 166, 178
    human 64–73, 162
capital 21–2, 157
capitalism 48, 86, 87, 93, 105, 135,
    175, 176, 177
    global 14, 25
    informational 22
    neoliberal 14, 16
    new 16

Cariyle, T. 147
Castells, M. 21, 22, 108, 132, 133, 132, 182nn, 187n
CEDAW 71
Chalmers, T. 48
China 14, 28, 60, 73, 75
Christ 3, 9, 62, 63, 69, 73, 109, 110, 112, 116, 123, 144, 145, 168, 179
  body of 118, 120, 130, 160
Christian Aid 133, 134
Christian political economy xii, 6, 48, 49, 53, 79, 92, 106, 124, 142, 143, 145, 146–79
Christian social ethics xii, 5, 32, 108, 109, 114, 126, 128, 129, 131, 146, 174, 176
christendom 129, 131, 144
  group 175
Church
  as more effective 132–8, 142
  associational 22, 35, 41, 43, 44, 45, 95, 132
  decline 1, 5, 25, 94, 112, 135, 136, 138, 144
  disestablished 122
  ecumenical 130, 138–41
  empowering bottom-up 134–5
  local xiii, 1, 22, 94, 97
  marginalized 4 , 6, 11, 43, 45, 54, 55, 94, 95, 96, 98–102, 109, 113, 114, 117, 118, 120, 121, 122, 123, 129, 132, 177
  multilayered 132–4
  networking 133
  Pentecostal 32, 133
  Roman Catholic 35, 127, 139
  of Scotland 31, 122
  urban xiii, 2, 94, 97, 129
churchgoing 33, 34, 35, 44, 46, 47, 48, 69, 94, 96, 98, 123, 125, 130, 131, 136, 137, 154
  in and for community 135–8
Church Action on Poverty 133
Church Urban Fund 45, 97
cities 9, 21, 25–7, 35, 38, 39, 41, 42, 48, 61, 62, 133
civil religion 46, 47
civil society 1, 6, 161

class 36, 39, 43, 61, 89, 90, 94
  working 38, 41, 43, 78
Cobb, J. and Daly, H. 63, 45, 151, 155, 163, 165, 181nn, 184n, 186n, 191n, 192nn, 193nn, 194n
Coleridge, S. 147, 148, 176
Collste, G. xi, 72–3, 151, 153, 185n, 192n, 193nn
Columbia 77
common good 107, 124, 125, 126, 127–9, 139, 141, 153
common religion 34, 46, 47, 96, 98
communications 15, 80, 81, 132
comparative advantage 13
competition 112, 144, 159, 174
computers 14, 19, 22, 42
Condorcet, M. 174
Cone, J. 173
confirmation 34, 45, 100
Copleston, E. 145
corruption 15, 82, 83, 84, 123
Costa Rica 77
Cowper, W. 183
crime 26, 66, 78, 101, 136
Cronin, K. 137, 190n
Crosland, A. 81

Davey, A. 97, 182nn, 185n, 188n, 190n, 191n
Davie, G. 32, 108, 182n, 183nn, 187n
Demant, V. 86, 175, 176, 194n
DeMartino, G. 181n, 185n, 186n, 193nn
democracy 24, 61, 84, 85, 146, 159, 172
  inclusive 85, 91–2, 95, 116, 118, 121, 128, 160, 161
  majoritarian 85, 91, 121, 160
dependency theory 110, 176
deprivation, relative 58, 60, 61
Dickens, C. 114
difference 5, 9, 17, 67, 69, 107, 116, 120, 121, 127, 128, 139, 178
  principle 73, 90, 119, 160
differentiated plurality 117
distribution 154, 156, 157, 158
division of labour 15, 79, 81, 89, 90

DNA 19
double whammy xiii, 6, 93, 94,
    102, 118, 120, 121, 132, 135,
    138, 142, 144, 177
Duffy, E. 95, 187n

economic development 16
economic growth 15, 16, 17, 18, 19,
    23, 24, 29, 30, 80–3, 84, 85, 86,
    88, 91, 92, 93, 112, 117, 151,
    158, 160, 162, 165
  pro-environment 158, 160
  pro-poor 90, 91, 121, 158, 160
economic man 151, 152–6, 162
economics
  engineering 143, 150, 151, 152,
    178
  ethical 143, 150, 151, 152, 156,
    157, 158, 161, 178
  neoclassical 63, 86, 87, 147, 149,
    150, 151, 152, 154, 155, 156,
    157, 159, 161, 169, 172, 177,
    178
  religious 6, 106, 140, 146,
    166–72, 173, 174, 177
  welfare 157
economy
  command 12
  global 1, 9, 10, 11, 12, 13, 14, 15,
    16, 17, 21, 22, 26, 27, 35, 37, 48,
    53, 54, 56, 58, 63, 70, 72, 77, 87,
    89, 123, 124, 151, 153, 157, 159,
    172
  market 12, 24, 156, 158, 175, 176,
    177
  political 3, 7, 30, 48, 53, 59, 106,
    118, 143, 144, 145, 148, 149,
    161, 172, 175, 178
ecosystem 10, 27, 28, 29, 30, 86,
    159, 178
education 18, 23, 24, 36, 48, 60, 64,
    65, 67, 68, 70, 75, 76, 77, 80–82,
    83, 84, 89, 91, 93, 98, 157, 158,
    162, 164
efficiency 12, 151, 152, 154, 159
  and equity 156–8
Egypt 28
electoral roll 100, 101

empowerment 6, 70, 85, 90, 91,
    107, 113, 118, 121, 132, 134,
    135, 140, 160, 167
Enlightenment 24, 37, 68
environment 1, 2, 3, 9, 14, 19, 20,
    21, 22, 23, 25, 27–30, 54, 56, 57,
    60, 65, 69, 70, 81, 83, 84, 87, 94,
    108, 112, 118, 119, 137, 141,
    147, 151, 155, 156, 160, 161,
    162, 165, 168, 173, 177, 178
  sustainable 11, 57, 85, 158
equality 59, 60, 66, 68, 121
  of capabilities 69
  of functioning 66
  of primary goods 67
Ethiopia 24, 60, 140
Eucharist 45, 137, 144
European Union 17

faith as connections 178–9
Faith in the City 42, 45, 54, 97,
    127
Fernandez, E. 186n
Fergusson, D. 132, 190n
finance 11, 13, 15, 80, 166
finitude 19, 20, 23, 29, 174
Folbre, N. 193n
foreign direct investment 14
foreign exchanges 14
Forrester, D. 55, 57, 59, 110, 120,
    122, 123, 124, 131, 180n,
    184nn, 185n, 187n, 188nn,
    189n, 190n
France 43, 47
Fraser, Bishop 46
freedom 6, 65, 66, 70, 82, 85, 90,
    110, 126, 149, 154, 162
  political 57, 85
Friedman, M. 149, 151, 192n
Fukuyama, F. 16
fundamentalism 12, 32, 107, 137,
    172

game theory 155
Galbraith, J. 78, 81, 85, 173, 186n,
    194n
Garner, R. xii, 190n
Gaskell, E. 114

Gaza strip 25
Gender-related Development
    Index 163, 164
genesis factor 17–22
genetic engineering 19, 20
George, H. 174, 175
Gewirth, A. 73
Ghana 82
ghetto 78, 112
Giddens, A. 133, 185n, 190n
Gill, R. 44, 47, 125, 131, 132, 135,
    136, 137, 138, 154, 168, 180n,
    183n, 189nn, 190nn, 193n
Gini coefficient 165
Global warming 27, 28
Globalization xi, 9, 11, 12, 14, 17,
    25, 26, 53, 63, 71, 72, 78, 80, 87,
    95, 105, 130, 138, 139, 142, 170,
    176
Godwin, W. 23, 175, 176
Gore, C. 107, 110, 187n
Gosling, D. 186n
governance 15, 16, 17, 30, 64, 80,
    82, 83–5, 86, 92, 152
  democratic 5, 69, 160, 161, 164
  and economics 159–61
  global 83, 161
grand narratives 36, 37, 127
Graham, E. xii, 110, 117, 131,
    188nn, 190n
Grameen Bank 171
Granqvist, R. 192n
Gray, J. 195n
Green, L. 190n
Green, S. 40, 183nn
Grenholm, C.-H. xi, 185n, 186n,
    193n
Gross National Product 13, 23, 24,
    58, 76, 82, 163
Guinea 76
Guild Socialism 175, 176
Gutiérrez, G. 96, 175, 187n, 194n

Habermas, J. 86, 114
Halifax 40, 41, 45
Hall, P. 99, 187n
Hammar, A. 116, 188n
Harlem 66, 77

Harrison, B. 62, 114, 184n, 188n,
    195n
Hastings, A. 45, 183n
Hauerwas, S. 107, 131, 194n
Headlam, S. 174, 176
health 36, 48, 60, 64, 65, 66, 67, 68,
    75, 76, 77, 80, 82, 83, 84, 91, 98,
    140, 157, 158, 162, 164
Helgesson, G. 192n
heresies 146, 172, 173, 177
Heslam, P. 181nn
heteroclitical tradition xii, 6, 16,
    146, 173–8
Hicks, D. 59, 119, 121, 146, 163,
    164, 165, 183n, 184nn, 185n,
    186n, 188nn, 189nn, 193nn
HIV/Aids 24
Hobsbawm, E. 97, 185n, 187n
Holland, J. 110, 187n
Hong Kong 15, 77
Howard, E. 99
Hull 135–6, 138
human development 56, 69, 70,
    71, 76, 81, 84, 91, 95, 125, 134,
    137, 158, 163, 168
  flourishing 4, 5, 11, 59, 67, 68
  fulfilment 3, 4, 65, 67, 68, 69, 76,
    81, 82, 84, 110, 127, 132
  needs 5, 123, 156
  rights 5, 24, 64, 65, 68, 69, 70, 71,
    72, 84, 85, 91, 123, 125, 137,
    154, 160, 164
  well-being 57, 64, 65, 66, 67, 83,
    100, 142
Human Development Index 66,
    76, 80, 98, 111, 117, 163, 164,
    165
  Inequality Adjusted 59, 118,
    146, 163, 165
Huntington, S. 139, 190n

incarnation 116
inclusive church 41, 118, 120, 137
  society 60, 64, 105, 118, 120, 159
inclusivity 5, 6, 17, 30, 60, 62, 68,
    69, 119, 121, 122, 128, 139
  bias for 6, 96, 107, 108, 117–22,
    124, 130, 160, 161, 167, 172, 178

inclusivity (*cont.*)
income 64, 65, 66, 67, 68, 76, 77,
82, 84, 91, 98, 158, 162, 165
Index of Sustainable Economic
Welfare 165
India 13, 28, 70, 73, 75, 77, 84, 134
Indices of Multiple Deprivation
97, 98
individual reflexivity 134
Indonesia 14
industrial revolution 17, 18, 22,
40, 75
inequality 6, 12, 13, 26, 27, 53, 59,
60, 61, 66, 72, 73, 74, 76, 77, 78,
79, 81, 89, 90, 91, 98, 102, 117,
135, 151, 156, 157, 158, 163,
164, 165, 166
information technologies 21, 35,
133, 166
interaction 4, 9, 18, 29, 30, 67, 80,
106, 109, 111, 115, 116, 117,
118, 124, 132, 137, 148, 167,
177, 178
interdisciplinary xi, 2, 5, 29, 32, 55,
56, 106, 108, 111, 112, 114, 122,
143, 144, 145, 146, 152, 169,
172, 177
interest (usury) 168, 169, 170, 171,
176
interfaith 5, 106, 113, 114, 129, 130,
131, 138, 139–41, 167, 172, 178
intergenerational 29 ,70, 58, 165
IMF 12, 56, 83, 84, 161, 168, 169
interstitial zone 116
Ireland 77, 164
Islam 32, 35, 47, 68, 74, 139, 166,
167, 169, 170, 171
Islamic Development Bank 171
Israel 25

Jaggar, A. 109, 187n
Jamaica 76
Japan 15, 20, 77, 154, 160
Jarl, A.-C. 72, 142, 151, 185nn,
187n, 188n, 190nn, 192nn,
193nn
Jay, P. 181m, 182n, 194n
Jenkins, D. xiii, 130, 175, 191n, 194n

Jenkins, T. 95, 131, 136, 138, 180n,
184n, 187n, 190n
Job 68
Johnson, S. 31, 79, 88
Jubilee 2000 166, 167–9
Judaism 68, 166, 167, 169
justice 62, 64, 71–3, 74, 90, 111,
121, 127, 131, 140, 150, 153,
154, 158
distributive 65, 72, 73, 90, 119,
172
efficiency and equity 156–8
social 90
theory 56, 59, 73, 115

Kamergrauzis, N. xii, 180n, 188n,
189n, 194n, 195nn
Keynes, J. M. 3, 10, 92, 143, 149,
180nn, 187n, 191nn
Kuznets, S. 18
Kenya 24
Keighley 40, 45
Kerala 84
Kingswood 95, 138
Kingsley, C. 114
Küng, H. 139, 141, 190n
Kennedy, P. 181nn, 182nn, 185n,
186n
Koh, D. 189n

labour 20, 21, 57
Lambeth Conference 11, 118
land 20–2, 25, 86, 157, 175, 176
Landes, D. 181nn, 182nn, 184nn,
186nn, 187nn, 191n
Leacock, S. 153, 192n
Least Developed Countries 75
Lebacqz, K. 72, 185n
Leech, K. 99
liberalism 25
liberation theology 2, 3, 27, 74, 86,
96, 109, 110, 111, 112, 113, 115,
117, 129, 135, 143, 144, 160,
175, 176
libertarian 64, 65, 72
Limerzel 35, 37
Linköping xi, 72, 143
Linden, I. 193n

Lipsey, R. 150
Local Strategic Partnerships 97
Löfstedt, M. 192n, 193n
London 43
Long, D. 144, 176, 189n, 191nn, 194nn
Lowe, S. xiii
Lyotard, J.-F. 184n

MacIntyre, A. 67, 108, 127, 177, 187n, 194n, 195n
Major, J. 94, 187n
Major Douglas Social Credit scheme 175, 176
Malaysia 77
Malthus, T. 22, 23, 29, 53, 59, 60, 143, 144, 145, 147, 148, 149, 174, 176, 182n, 184n, 191n, 194n
Manchester xii, xiii, 1, 19, 38, 43, 54, 94, 95, 96, 98, 99, 113, 121, 130, 135, 136, 149
  Cathedral xiii
  Diocese of xiii, 31, 34, 40, 94, 97, 98, 99, 100, 101, 118, 140
Mandeville, B. 79
manufacturing 12, 13, 79, 88
margins 62, 63, 64, 157
marginal utility 63
marginalization, definitions of 75–73
  explanations 79–92
  wild facts of 73–78
  see also Church, marginalized
market, 15, 16, 81, 82, 86, 87, 91, 144, 153, 156, 159
  free 42, 115, 156, 159
Marrs, C. 181n, 183n, 184n
Marshall, A. 3, 5, 54, 149, 150, 191n
Marx, K. 11, 56, 62, 87, 92, 109, 110, 112, 117, 175, 184n, 186n, 187n, 188n
Matsuoka, F. 116, 188n
Maurice, F. D. 112, 174, 176
Mawson, M. 133, 134, 190n
McCann, D. 127, 141, 189n
McLeod, H. 35, 43, 183nn

measurement 6, 36, 48, 49, 60, 66, 67, 69, 80, 97, 98, 107, 111, 118, 151, 161, 162, 163, 166, 177,178
Medellin 119
Meekes, M. 143, 191n
Melin, A. 193n
mercantilism 159
Methodists 34, 35, 96, 133
Micah 63
microcredit 171, 176
middle axioms 12, 128, 129, 162
Milbank, J. 107, 131
Mill, J. S. 53, 152, 156, 192n
Mills, C. W. 88, 100, 186n
modernization xii, 16, 28, 37, 39, 40, 44, 48, 56, 74, 80, 86–7, 94, 138, 144, 148, 176
Moll, P. 112, 176, 188n, 194n
Morebath 97, 187n
Morris, J. 187n
Morris, W. 147
Munby, D. 150, 175, 176, 192n, 194n
Munuswamy 57, 59, 65
Muslim interest-free banking 166, 169–72
mutating religion 46–9

narrative 92, 95, 114, 118, 123, 130, 160, 177, 179
natural law 127
Nelson, J. 87, 186n
neoliberal 64, 77, 151, 159, 175, 176
neo-orthodoxy 107, 135
Neuhaus, R. 127
Newcomen, T. 18
New Age religion 46, 47, 134
Noel, C. 175
Northcott, M. 190nn
Norway 13, 76, 164
Nozick, R. 64, 68

overlapping consensuses 4, 92, 128, 141, 145, 155, 160
Owen, R. 174
ozone layer 27, 28

Pareto Optimality principle 157

Parker, B. 99
Parkin, M. 192n
Parsons, C. 18
Paterson, G. 182n
Partnership Officer 97, 140
peace 84, 131, 139, 160
Peacock, A. xiii
Percy, M. 183n
performative theology 106, 109,
    110, 111, 117, 146, 161, 167
perichoresis 179
Peru 77
Philippines 133
pick-and-mix religion 46, 47, 134
Pickstock, C. 107
Poland 164
Polanyi, K. 110, 187n
politics 3, 4, 6, 30, 84, 86, 87, 125,
    149, 159, 172, 176, 178
Pope, S. 188n
population 1, 9, 12, 14, 15, 16, 20,
    22–7, 28, 35, 40, 48, 54, 58, 60,
    61, 74, 75, 79, 81, 82, 83, 123,
    175
poverty 14, 15, 26, 30, 53, 54, 57,
    58, 59, 60, 61, 65, 66, 74, 76, 78,
    79, 80, 82, 84, 85, 88, 91, 110,
    118, 119, 140, 141, 142, 143,
    149, 172, 175
    absolute 6, 74
Porvoo Agreement 139
post-industrial 4, 36, 47, 109, 123,
    130, 133, 135, 155
post-modern 4, 26, 36, 47, 67, 71,
    108, 109, 123, 130, 133, 155,
    170
praxis 6, 29, 56, 59, 95, 106, 107,
    108–17, 118, 124, 161, 167
Preston, R. H. xii, 56, 86, 150, 175,
    176, 180n, 191n, 194nn
primary goods 65, 66, 67
privatization 12, 36
production 9, 11, 12, 13, 14, 15, 16,
    18, 20, 21, 23, 36, 75, 80, 81,
    152, 156, 157, 158, 165, 174
productivity 17, 19, 20, 24, 66, 81,
    82, 89, 157, 158
protestant work ethic 15, 80

Puebla 119, 189n

radical injustice 77, 88, 89
radical orthodoxy 109, 110, 112,
    131, 135, 143, 147, 167, 176,
    177
Rauschenbusch, W. 107
Rawls, J. 56, 65, 68, 72, 73, 90, 119,
    125, 160, 189n
Rayman, P. 162
Reckitt, M. 175
reconciliation 116
Reed, C. 182n, 186nn, 189n, 190n,
    193n, 194nn
regeneration xiii, 1, 97, 107, 130,
    133, 135, 136
research and development 9, 18
rhetoric 113, 114
Ricardo, D. 13, 53, 143, 151, 184n
rich 5, 10, 13, 53, 54, 58, 59, 60, 73,
    78, 79, 84, 87, 88, 89, 90, 96, 100
    127, 134
    religiously 48
Robbins, L. 150, 151, 192n
robotics 19, 20
Roll, E. 194n
romanticism 38, 144, 147, 174, 176
Rothschild, K. 192n
Rousseau, J. 79
Ruether, R. 71, 173, 185n
Ruskin, J. 147

Samuelson, P. 79, 186n
Sandercock, L. 113, 188n
Sassen, S. 11, 17, 25, 26, 181nn,
    185n
Sassoon, D. 185n
Saudi Arabia 164
Savery, T. 18
scarcity 23, 29, 79, 144, 150, 151,
    152,
Schreiter, R. 140, 180n 181n, 182n,
    183n, 187n, 188n, 190n, 193n
Schubeck, T. 188n
Schumpeter, J. 86
Scotus, D. 110
secularization theory 1, 32, 34,
    37–49, 94

Sedgwick, P. 190n
Selby, P. 189n
self-determination 69, 91, 161, 172
self-development 69, 91, 172
self-interest 153, 154, 155, 169
Sen, A. xii, 56, 57, 58, 59, 61, 65, 69,
   70, 85, 89, 118, 119, 127, 144,
   147, 150, 151, 154, 157, 158,
   159, 160, 163, 184nn, 185nn,
   186nn, 191n, 192nn, 193nn
Shakespeare, S. 112, 188n, 191n
Shanks, A. 185n
Sheffield 38, 39
Short, C. 171
Sierra Leone 76
sin 19, 63, 120, 174
Singapore 77
Single Tax 174
Smith, A. 3, 48, 53, 59, 62, 83, 89,
   143, 147, 148, 153, 154, 159,
   184n, 192n
sociology of religion 1, 31, 37
solidarity 63, 109, 111, 113
   differentiated 107, 121, 128, 129,
   141, 160, 161, 172, 178
Somalia 82
South Africa 24, 129, 149
South Korea 14, 76, 82
Southey, R. 174
Sri Lanka 77
Stackhouse, M. 127, 128, 141, 189n
Steedman, I. 149, 191n, 192n
Stigler, G. 154, 192n
Stout, J. 195n
structural injustice 86, 88–90, 92
Sub Saharan Africa 12, 13, 14, 22,
   24, 75, 76, 84, 164, 168
Sumner, J. 145
Sunday Schools 33, 34, 40, 44, 45
Sundman, P. 185n
Sweden xii, 10, 56, 77, 122, 143,
   160, 165
Switzerland 13

Taiwan 77
Tanzania 140
Tawney, R. H. 55, 58, 79, 88,
   184nn, 186n

Taylor, M. 62, 134, 140, 180n,
   184nn, 186, 188n, 190n
technology 1, 9, 11, 13, 15, 17, 18,
   19, 20, 21, 22, 23, 26, 27, 37,
   44, 80, 81, 82, 87, 93, 95, 123,
   158
Temple, W. 55, 58, 79, 116, 154,
   192n
Thailand 77
Thatcher, M. 150, 159
theism 125
theological realism xii
theology, public 108, 122–9, 178
Thiemann, R. 108, 125, 128, 140,
   184n, 187n, 189nn
Thompson, E. 147, 191n
Tiller, J. 133, 190n
toleration 123, 126
Toynbee, A. 147
Tracy, D. 116, 188n
trade 11, 13, 14, 15, 21, 90
   free 13, 90
Trade Related Intellectual
   Property Rights 13
training 18, 82, 93
transnational corporations 13, 14,
   20, 21, 54
Tucker, J. 145
Tyndale, W. 190n

underclass 27, 77, 78
unemployment 14
United Nations Declaration of
   Human Rights 70
Development Programme 12,
   60, 65, 75, 90, 118, 159, 160,
   162, 171
Human Development Reports
   56, 57, 58, 59, 65, 66, 67, 68, 70,
   74, 76, 80, 91, 157, 158, 163,
   164, 189n, 193nn, 194n
universalism 71, 90, 113, 120, 160
Uppsala xi, xii, xiii, 143
urbanization 25–7, 28
urban-industrial processes 1, 32,
   37, 38, 39, 46, 74, 75, 86, 94,
   105, 174, 175, 176
Ure, A. 19, 181n

USA 2, 20, 28, 32, 42, 76, 77, 78, 138, 164, 165, 174
utilitarianism 64, 65, 72, 73, 119, 123, 147
utility 63, 64, 86, 119, 149, 151, 153, 159
utopian 23, 173, 174

vicious cycle 82
Vietnam 76
Villa-Vicencio, C. 162, 189n
virtuous cycle 81–2, 83
voluntarism 1, 42, 97, 107, 115, 116, 123, 130, 131, 136, 137, 138, 154, 157, 168

Walras, A. 149, 150, 151
war 23, 25, 84, 88, 139
Ward, G. 42, 97, 107, 183n, 187n
Waterman, A. 188n, 191nn, 192n
Watson, R. 144
Weber, M. 15, 93
Wedderburn, D. 61, 184n
welfare state 36, 83, 116
Whately, R. 145, 150
Wheen, F. 181n, 186n, 187n
Whewell, W. 149, 191n
Wickham, E. 38, 183n
wild facts 10, 14, 28, 31, 33, 34, 53, 56, 58, 73, 74, 76
Wilberforce, W. 168
Wilkinson, R. 185n

William Temple Foundation xiii, 130
Williams, R. 147, 191n
Wilson, B. 38
Wilson, R. 194n
Winch, D. 180n, 183n, 186nn, 191nn
Wolfensohn, J. 53, 57
women xii, 24, 33, 34, 41, 43, 57, 58, 70, 71, 77, 82, 83, 85, 87, 98, 110, 119, 121, 134, 157, 160, 163, 164, 172
World Bank 12, 53, 56, 57, 83, 84, 134, 140, 159, 161, 168, 169
World Council of Churches 118, 131
World Faiths Development Dialogue 140
World Trade Organisation 12, 17, 56, 161
Wordsworth, W. 148, 174
worship 130, 131, 137
Wythenshawe 99

Yuengert, A. 191n, 193n
Young, I. 56, 69, 72, 90, 113, 114, 128, 132, 135, 145, 160, 172, 182n, 184nn, 185n, 186nn, 187n, 188n, 189n, 190nn, 191n, 193nn, 194n

Zambia 168
Ziegler, K. 186n